We Hold These "Truths"

We Hold These "Truths"

☆

How to Spot the Myths That Are Holding America Back

Casey Burgat

AUTHORS
EQUITY

Authors Equity
1123 Broadway, Suite 1008
New York, New York 10010

Edited by Grace Rubenstein
Cover design by Chris Sergio
Book design by Scribe Inc.

Most Authors Equity books are available at a discount when purchased in quantity for sales promotions or corporate use. Special editions, which include personalized covers, excerpts, and corporate imprints, can be created when purchased in large quantities. For more information, please email info@authorsequity.com.

Library of Congress Control Number: 2024947639
Print ISBN 9798893310184
Ebook ISBN 9798893310245

Printed in the United States of America
First printing

www.authorsequity.com

To Chuck and Huck.
Because we don't talk about it. We be about it.

Contents

Introduction

Dr. Casey Burgat

I recently got back from Uzbekistan. I bet you didn't see that coming.

While tough for most to locate on a map, Uzbekistan has thousands of years of cultural and religious heritage to brag about. Many of its cities sit directly along the famous Silk Road, and at various points, it was viewed as the economic and intellectual powerhouse of the Muslim world. It also has a long and tortured history of being overtaken by dictators, including Genghis Khan in the early 13th century and the Soviets in the early 20th century. Though the Uzbeks declared independence in 1991, the country has struggled to maintain a transparent, stable democracy ever since.

I was asked to help.

I traveled there as part of a small, bipartisan American delegation sponsored by the House of Representatives. Our mission was to meet with senior Uzbek leaders—presidential advisors, members of parliament, Supreme Court justices—and offer expertise and advice to aid their government's transition from a former Soviet satellite to a steady, representative democracy.

Beyond the translators, security personnel, and administrative staff, our team was made up of a warm, chatty former Republican congressman from Illinois; a semi-paranoid national security expert with years of CIA and State Department service; and me, a former Capitol Hill staffer turned think tanker turned professor who spends his waking hours trying to make American politics work just a little bit better.

Throughout the week on the ground, a team of security officials, interpreters, and local officials shepherded us from one military-patrolled, decorative government hall to the next. As soon as one meeting ended, we'd be cattle called right back into our secure vehicle and whisked directly to the next reception line. In the few minutes in the van between meetings, we'd receive a quick rundown of who we were about to meet next. And always, always, we'd hear yet another reminder to assume that every electronic device around us was bugged and that any journalist in the room was more likely to have Jason Bourne skills than any real media training.

Some Uzbek government officials clearly wanted us there; others very much did not. Some conversations were fruitful; others felt like a contest over who could chew up the most time without actually saying anything. From our earliest conversations, it became clear that there was a generational divide between the Uzbek leaders. The younger leaders yearned for democracy to take root and flourish. The older ones, however, wanted our plane to depart back West as quickly as humanly possible so they didn't have to spend another minute hearing from the Americanskis. They were simply from a different era. They preferred to turn back the clock to the pro-Russia alliances they grew up with and curtly shut down anyone who dared suggest alternative ways of thinking. In fact, our handlers told us Americans in no uncertain terms to not explicitly mention Russia—which at the time had recently invaded Ukraine—because it would immediately shut down the dialogue. A few meetings got so tense because of this internal division I was afraid someone on our side of the table would purposefully break their glass water bottle over their own head just so they'd have an excuse to extricate themselves from the awkwardness.

The most memorable interaction, though—one that has messed up my REM cycle ever since—didn't come from an Uzbek senator, the solicitor general, or the deputy ambassador. No, it came from a small, soft-spoken, kind-eyed Uzbek driver who had a firmer grip on the English language than I did. Let's call him Pavel because I'm not allowed to relay his real name. Pavel's task was to silently drive us around those parts of Tashkent, Uzbekistan's capital, that the government authorized us to see. At one point, I shimmied close to the front seat to pepper him with questions out of earshot of our handlers.

As he drove, I did my best to ask Pavel open-ended questions about what life was really like for the Uzbek people. His answers started off short and rehearsed. His eyes spent more time on the rearview mirror than the scooter-invaded streets in front of him. It was clear he had been coached on what to say and, more importantly, what not to say.

I asked what he thought about the government's attempts to transition from Soviet-style communism to a more open, pro-Western, pro-blue-jeans-and-Quarter-Pounders-with-cheese government.

He smiled. I couldn't tell if he was collecting his thoughts or thinking, "Shut the hell up, Americanski, before we both get in trouble." I asked again.

"You see that apartment building? And that one? And that one?" His nail-bitten finger pointed at the endless line of utilitarian, perfectly rectangular buildings painted in a wide variety of colors that were all beige. The fancy ones had railings cemented to the outside walls for decor, but there were barely any fancy ones. Their purpose was clear: House as many people as possible as efficiently as possible. No frills. Just boxes. It was the Soviet way.

I assumed he was deflecting, looking for literally anything to change the conversation before he said something he shouldn't.

"Those are called Stalinkis," he said. As in Stalin, the ruthless former Soviet dictator. "Those buildings are the best example I can give for how likely we are to truly become a strong democracy or make any really meaningful changes in Uzbekistan. Ninety percent of people in the capital live in Stalinkis. Every generation, mine included, grew up in them, and we all promised we'd be the last ones. Everyone hates them. Every leader promises to get rid of them. And yet there they stand."

Then he landed the plane for me.

"The same is true for our government. Every generation says they will bring about change. Democracy. But we can't ever make any progress because we're still having the same fights our parents did, our grandparents, even. We can't move on, even from Stalinkis even though everyone hates them. How can we have any real change when all we do is argue about the same things over and over and over?"

Before I could respond, we pulled up to yet another set of frozen iron gates and a cadre of assault-rifle-laden security guards. I sat through the next meeting barely paying attention. I smiled and nodded, pretending to listen intently to the simultaneous translation in my ear.

All I could think about was how Pavel, who wasn't even supposed to talk to me in the first place, finally cracked a riddle that had been plaguing me for months (years, if I'm being honest). I finally had the answer I'd been looking everywhere for. I just never thought to look in Uzbekistan.

Let me back up. I'm a political scientist. I have a PhD in American government and a couple of master's degrees, and through my years as a staffer on Capitol Hill, in think tanks around DC, and in my current role as a graduate professor at George Washington University, I have carved out a solid reputation for understanding American politics. I literally wrote the textbook on how Congress *really* works (or more often than not, how it doesn't work).

More specifically, I study, research, and write about political reforms, or the changes we can make to our system of government to ensure it's the freest, fairest, and stablest version of itself it can be. That's why I was invited to Uzbekistan, Iraq about a year before that, and Guatemala more recently. It was my charge to explain the good, the bad, and the ugly of the US political system to hopeful, nascent democracies. I was there to offer their leaders any warnings, insights, and lessons gleaned from America's nearly 250 years of experimenting with democracy.

Back in the United States, I work regularly with members of Congress (from both sides of the aisle), journalists, lobbyists, nonprofits, and advocacy associations. Anyone with a question on how politics really plays out often comes to me. I'm their guy because they know they're going to get an honest, understandable assessment of what is often a dishonest, undecipherable business.

Let's just say it's an interesting, if not flammable, time to be a political scientist, particularly one whose job it is to recommend cures to the ailing body politic. Everyone, and I mean everyone, is more than willing to voice their disdain for politics—and usually one party or politician—before our hands even break from our first handshake.

Often, I admit, I answer the "What do you do for a living?" question with a simple "professor," hoping against hope they don't ask the inevitable follow-up, "What subject?" Once they learn I'm in politics, they want me to confirm everything they've ever thought on the subject or else face their passive-aggressive version of "Wow, I don't know how you do it."

The across-the-board frustration with politics, ironically, is one of the very few things upon which most people, from granola-crunching liberal to pistol-packing conservative, agree. Hating nearly everything about politics is a rare bipartisan issue. Ask 1,000 US citizens—Black, white, farmer, city dweller, rich, poor, voter, and abstainer—if they're satisfied with our current state of government, and only a depressingly tiny minority will respond with a thumbs-up. Americans across the political spectrum lambaste the sleaziness, inaction, and tit-for-tat practices of politics.

I don't blame them.

And yet my whole goal, inside and outside the classroom, is to get more people to *understand* politics rather than run away from it. To get involved rather than angry on the sidelines. To lean in rather than lean out. That's how we make it work.

But if you've been paying even passive attention, you know full well we're nowhere near this personal utopia of mine. Our democratic breakdowns are tearing our social and political fabrics like the hamstring of a 45-year-old has-been sprinting to first base in his beer league softball game. The dysfunction leads to disgust and detachment—which only exacerbates the dysfunction, which perpetuates the detachment. We are caught in a countrywide doom loop that's only accelerating.

My job is to help us break this trend. I've had some successes, but not nearly enough. More recently, I've felt like I'm just bashing my head against the wall, and the only dent I'm making is in my own skull.

In one sense, this struggle to get anyone to change their mind and behavior is understandable. No one likes to be told what they're doing or thinking is wrong—me included. This reluctance is especially true in politics. In fact, researchers have repeatedly shown that those who care the most about politics, who follow it the closest, are actually the least willing to hear new ideas or alter their stances.

And here's where we return to my kind, fingernail-munching, Uzbek friend Pavel, who inadvertently cracked my personal riddle with his Stalinkis metaphor.

"How can we have any real change when all we do is argue about the same things over and over and over?"

In my middle-of-the-night ruminations since our car ride, I have added to Pavel's question a critical, needling question of my own: *And, even worse, what if we're arguing about the wrong things to begin with?*

Right now, in our country, we can't achieve genuine political change because we're having the wrong conversations. We're fighting about the wrong things. Just like our parents did, and our grandparents before them. We can't move on.

Our apartment buildings—the things we can't ever seem to get past—are the many pervasive, often well-intentioned myths in

American politics. These are not myths about which politicians secretly want to take away your granny's Medicare or why one party wants to spend billions subsidizing organic kale. The dark assumptions we make about those whose views differ from ours are also harmful, but those are more the symptom than the disease. The myths I'm talking about, the ones that trap us in the past like Soviet apartment blocks, are about the *nature of our political system itself.*

Think of the widely accepted notions that bipartisanship is dead or that the Founders got everything exactly right when setting up our government in 1787. These kinds of ideas are so popular that they have come to be accepted as fact. But they are not. And our commitment to them is causing us—and our democracy—harm.

These common misunderstandings involve all facets of our democracy—our institutions, our leaders, the media, Congress, the president, and yes, even ourselves. They fuel our anger, cloud our judgment, and quash our ability to see and pursue the possible (and notice how I didn't say the perfect).

The most damaging consequence of these myths' pervasiveness is that they've convinced far too many of us that there are simple fixes to our politics—and that the people with the power to implement these obvious solutions are just ignoring them for their own power-hungry reasons. We chalk up our problems to ineptitude and immorality, and we check out. It's easy that way. But it's wrong. And it's dangerous.

Here's the reality. Everyone who says they're disgusted with American politics—politicians especially—points to a silver-bullet antidote to make the pain go away. Right now, as a country, we're like a fast-food addict who thinks he's one fad diet away from looking like the Rock. We tell ourselves and one another that just one new election law, one campaign finance reform, or one good court decision would solve the sickness.

But what no one will say out loud is this: It ain't true.

We have reduced our varied and impossibly intertwined political problems down to a few convenient scapegoats, like gerrymandered districts, money in politics, or feckless, self-serving politicians. These are (huge!) problems, but they are far from the entire story. And the oversimplified solutions we seek for them ignore two fundamental truths in politics: Nothing—no issue, politician, or solution—exists in isolation, and nothing comes without trade-offs.

Nothing.

The very present danger is that fixating on supposedly simple cures prevents us from seeing the real picture. Which, in turn, only perpetuates the cycle.

What's worse, our monomaniacal focus on our pet political problems allows us—invites us, even—to be hoodwinked by the horde of talking heads, politicians, pillow tycoons, or outright snake-oil salesmen tossing out simple fixes like Mardi Gras beads on Bourbon Street. After all, convincing voters that someone else is to blame for all the bad in the world is one of the most tried-and-true ways to win elections. "Give me the power," political candidates say, "and I'll fix everything so fast it will make your head spin." We fall for it every time.

As a result, we've convinced ourselves that we could easily cure all our ills, if only our damned leaders would grow some vertebrae. My students talk like this. My half-interested friends talk like this. Hell, even our elected leaders talk like this. And I'd bet the $1.12 in my Venmo account that you've said or thought something similar.

This quicksand is killing us. We've all seen the signs. Spinning in our same old political debates actually makes it *harder* to do the many things we must do to have a functioning, representative government. Our hunger for simple solutions simply crushes any chance of implementing reforms that will achieve positive, lasting results.

The tough-to-swallow truth about our politics is that there are no quick fixes to our big problems. And we have big problems. Many. But there is no savior candidate with the cure-all political platform coming to rescue us—and expecting one is actually perpetuating our dysfunction. The sooner we accept this, the sooner we can have the necessary and honest conversations on what to do about it. And the sooner we, the people, can return from our cliff edge of futility and *engage* in solutions. Because there *are* things we can do, lots of them. And because our country needs us.

That's where this book comes in. To have any shot at detoxifying our politics and reversing our dangerous political trends—and we are careening toward democratic breakdown faster than a Kardashian finds a camera—we must change the conversations themselves. We must stop pouring our attention, our energy, our dollars, and yes, even our anger into the mythical fixes that have distracted us for decades. We're only growing increasingly cynical and disillusioned, and the cycle is proving more and more difficult to break. It's long past time to take our vision back.

To begin the climb out of this rut we find ourselves in, we first need to collectively concentrate on what is *actually* wrong with our politics. As anyone who has ever spent a minute in therapy can attest, getting out of a doom loop requires starting at the uncomfortable beginning, challenging the assumptions that we have too long left unquestioned. That is, well before any ideological debates about specific policies or politicians that inescapably lead to shouting matches—before we even approach what to do about immigration, education, military spending, taxes, abortion, climate change, or any other of the thousand huge policy challenges we face—we have to burst the myths about how politics work and fall short and how we, the people, are contributing to the problems we hate.

That's the fundamental purpose of this book: to finally get past the myths that keep us stuck in our Stalinkis. We do this to free ourselves to act on what actually matters. It won't be easy by any means, but as the great philosopher Tom Hanks taught us in *A League of Their Own,* "The hard is what makes it great."

What you'll find in this book is a myth-busting tour of our favorite untrue truisms. The chapter titles should look familiar; they are the beliefs you hear over and over again from friends, social media memes, and maybe inside your own head. Each chapter breaks down one such myth and equips you with the knowledge to finally lay it to rest.

To help, I enlisted some of the brightest, most respected, most effective people in politics. The chapter authors include academic experts widely viewed as the best in their fields and political practitioners—those who have literally done the jobs, including former members of Congress and one of the most influential lobbyists in DC. This dream team mix of academic and professional perspectives gives you the best of both kinds of wisdom, from the scientific to the practical: book smarts and street smarts within a single book.

You'll also find that I took pains—mostly logistical, but sadly a few physical—to recruit contributors from across the ideological spectrum, ranging from former President Trump's White House director of strategic communications to progressive Pennsylvania Sen. John Fetterman's former chief of staff. Let this bipartisan mix of contributors be your signal that this book is not just liberal or conservative propaganda and that the myths debunked here aren't, on their face, political in nature. One party may believe some of the myths more strongly than the other at this particular moment. But they are, at their core, false distractions that harm us all.

Are we here to change your mind about specific policies or convince you that all elected leaders are saints? No. (Spoiler alert: They aren't.) In fact, in talking about this book idea to friends, colleagues, and even potential publishers, one of the first questions I was asked was why in the hell I thought we could get people to change their minds about politics. It's a fair question. And the genuine answer is I'm not positive I can. I just know we must.

Our goal is to help you extricate yourself from a problem that you didn't know you were a part of. You'll learn how to exit the echo chamber and advance the solutions you might be unwittingly making it harder for us to achieve. Your first essential tool for this mission will be myth-spotting—the ability to call a myth a myth (or perhaps an even choicer phrase) when you see it bandied about, which will be often. Each chapter spells out the telltale signs of its particular myth. Thus equipped, you can steadily shift from myth-spotting to myth-busting to effective action, to start building something better and stronger than Stalinki democracy.

This book will also equip you to deploy a critical stealth maneuver that I'll sum up in one word: pause. Instead of reacting to anything political—a politician, a policy, a campaign—instantaneously, with emotion leading the charge, you'll be better positioned to take a beat. To consider. To listen before adding volume to the same old argument. Simply by taking a momentary pause—literally just a second or more—libraries full of research show that a different part of our brain kicks in: away from the defensive and reactionary and toward the purposeful and rational, even empathetic. That single moment empowers us to act for a far more lasting impact. For the sake of both our sanity and our shared future, the pause is vital.

At the very least, it's our hope that after reading, no politician will ever again catch you under the same "I alone can fix it" spell, because you'll be equipped to see politics for what it has always been: a messy, imperfect, critical pursuit of a better future. And that will make you a more effective, more thoughtful, and certainly less dupable participant in our collective effort at self-government.

After reading *We Hold These "Truths,"* we believe that what once was maddening and hopeless will feel clear and, yes, even fixable. You'll know the real solutions we need and the role you play in bringing them about. That's a win for this book, a win for you, and most importantly, a win for our democracy at a time when we need all the wins we can get.

Let's get to work.

We Hold These "Truths"

"The Founders, in Their Infinite Wisdom, . . ."

Dr. Lindsay M. Chervinsky

On September 17, 1787, 42 men filed into the first-floor chamber of the Pennsylvania State House, known today as Philadelphia's Independence Hall. The clerks closed the windows and locked the shutters against nosy ears and prying eyes. They lit candles and Argand oil lamps to offset the lack of daylight. The men took their seats, clumped by state around tables arranged in half circles facing the front of the room. George Washington took his place before them in a large wooden chair with a rising sun carved in the back. He called the attendees to order. The final session of the Constitutional Convention had begun.

The delegates had spent the previous four months in this room, debating each clause and carefully crafting language for the young nation's new charter. They worked six days per week in the stifling chamber. Now, they had one final task before they could finally return home—voting on the draft Constitution.

Before the delegates cast their votes, Benjamin Franklin cleared his throat. At 81, Franklin was the oldest member present and a widely revered statesman, diplomat, scientist, and politician. He had not spoken often over the past four months, but when he offered his ideas, they carried weight. Franklin's health had faltered recently, his voice shook, and he struggled to stand. He handed his written comments to James Wilson, a fellow Pennsylvania delegate, to read on his behalf.

"I confess that I do not entirely approve of this Constitution at present," Franklin wrote. "I am not sure I shall never approve it: For having lived long, I have experienced many Instances of being oblig'd, by better Information or fuller Consideration, to change Opinions even on important Subjects, which I once thought right, but found to be otherwise. It is therefore that the older I grow the more apt I am to doubt my own Judgment and to pay more Respect to the Judgment of others." With this humility, he continued, "I agree to this Constitution, with all its Faults" because "I doubt too whether any other Convention we can obtain, may be able to make a better Constitution."[1]

The draft Constitution was passable, not perfect.

George Washington, one of Franklin's most esteemed colleagues and the assumed first president under the new charter, agreed. In a letter to a colleague, Washington confessed his disappointment that the proposed government did not include all the elements he had sought. "I wish the Constitution which is offered had been made more perfect, but I sincerely believe it is the best that could be obtained at this time," he wrote. Washington expressed hope that future generations would amend the document as needed to address future challenges.[2]

None of the delegates in the room—weary, sweaty, and grouchy as they were—would have called the draft Constitution perfect. In fact, they explicitly admitted it wasn't. Yet 38 of the 42 delegates present on voting day signed it. In their estimation, a set of compromises, grounded in sound principles and with plenty of opportunity for future revision, was an acceptable starting point—and the only achievable one.

When Americans reference that same document today, however, we often exercise none of that balance. In our modern imagination, the Constitution is not a rubric but an edict, written by oracles with unified ideas and indisputable intentions, etched in stone.

Congressional debates, Supreme Court decisions, and even Broadway musicals abound with appeals to the Founding Fathers. Politicians, justices, and everyday citizens defend their position by claiming it adheres faithfully to the Founders' intentions—a mic-drop moment that spells the end of whatever discussion is at hand. In the words of one sitting member of Congress, to even suggest the Constitution is lacking in any respect "spits in the face of every single one of our founders."[3] Over the two and a half centuries since that steamy summer in Philadelphia, we have refashioned the Founders into infallible gods and their intentions into a singular, unshakable vision.

These claims reveal a shocking historical illiteracy. The truth is that the Founders agreed on very little. In fact, one of the only things they *did* agree on was that for the Constitution to be adopted, it would have to be a hodgepodge of compromise, and they explicitly created it as such. They had to do this to secure the delegates' approval and win state ratification—in short, for the Constitution to exist at all. They did not expect their version of the nation's design to be the final word. And they couldn't let the perfect be the enemy of the good.

This distinction matters big-time. The Constitution's mythical perfection is not a matter of mere debate; it shapes actual policy. This skewed view of history corrodes lawmaking, campaigns, court decisions, and public debates. It stops new ideas, healthy discussions, and promising policies before they've begun. Perhaps worst of all, the Constitution's prophetic status inhibits our own thinking as citizens, calcifies our conclusions, and stymies needed innovation and collaboration.

What's more, many aspects of our modern political life are often thought to have been handed down from on high to the Founding Fathers, when, in reality, they're not even in the original script. Political parties, the separation of church and state, executive orders, and even the number of Supreme Court justices—none of these appear in the original Constitution. It's as if the Founders left us an ingenious introduction to a book with lots of blank pages for us to fill in. Yet we tiptoe around these gaps like we're afraid to offend the ghost of Ben Franklin.

From Jefferson to Madison to Franklin to Washington, the Founders were undeniably men of vision and leadership: the best read and among the most courageous of their time. Their Constitution, while not perfect, remains a cornerstone of democratic ideals, providing a flexible framework that has guided the nation through centuries of change. But despite their obvious and many talents, we ascribe to the Founders infinite wisdom they themselves didn't even pretend to possess. And too often, we cherry-pick their words, ideas, and intentions to advance and defend our own political ends. In short, considering the Founders immovable and their work unquestionable keeps us stuck where we are.

The Founders themselves would be shocked to find that their creations have been so imperfectly remembered, celebrated, and deployed by future generations. They had a bigger vision for us. In their view, American democracy was meant to be an ongoing project, a never-ending pursuit of a "more perfect union." They could not possibly anticipate all the problems that would arise once their model was put into practice—or agree on how to solve them—and they knew it. They expected their plan to keep developing long after the ink dried in 1787. And they trusted future generations to be not only the Constitution's protectors but also its codesigners.

"I am not an advocate for frequent changes in laws and constitutions, but laws and institutions must go hand in hand with the progress of the human mind," wrote Thomas Jefferson. "As that becomes more developed, more enlightened, as new discoveries are made, new truths discovered and manners and opinions change, with the change of circumstances, institutions must advance also to keep pace with the times. We might as well require a man to wear still the coat which fitted him when a boy as civilized society to remain ever under the regimen of their barbarous ancestors."[4]

If we see the Constitution as a living, breathing document, we serve our country so much better. The way forward starts with a clear view of the Constitution and its crafters and with the understanding that they intentionally left room for us to grow. And that understanding begins in that steamy room in Philadelphia in the summer of 1787.

Inside the Constitutional Convention

By the end of that summer, the delegates were hot, tired, and eager to return home. But they also understood that their work was just beginning; the Constitution would continue to develop in practice long after the ink dried on the final draft. Many of the document's phrases were left vague and the silences immense. These choices were no accident; the drafters left room for improvement because they knew they could not fail. Not again.

"It appears to me that the political concerns of this Country are, in a manner, suspended by a thread," Washington wrote that summer. If the delegates failed to craft a constitution and win public support, "anarchy would soon [ensue]—the seeds being . . . sown in every soil."[5]

He wasn't wrong. The nation was unraveling. The context around the Constitution is required to understand its design. This revered document was not, in fact, the original blueprint of our nation's government. It was a second chance when nations rarely get second chances.

The Articles of Confederation was the first attempt at a US government, created and approved by the Continental Congress and many of the same brains who ultimately drafted the Constitution. Their first experiment with self-government had devolved into a hot mess. Congress under the Articles of Confederation did not have the power to raise funds through taxation and was broke. It had no money to pay off its wartime debts, raise and supply an army, or send diplomats abroad. The states bickered with one another over economic, military, and foreign policy, and the federal government was far too weak to mediate. Even worse, Congress had no way to fix its problems because any amendments to the document required unanimous consent of the states. Unsurprisingly, unanimity was just as difficult to achieve in the 1780s as it is today.

By 1787, many Americans concluded that the young nation needed a new governing structure if it was to survive beyond its first decade. Twelve of the 13 states sent delegates to Philadelphia—Rhode Island refused to participate—under the pretext that they only meant to tweak the Articles of Confederation, not scrap the whole thing. Why the cloak-and-dagger routine? The conveners knew that if they openly pitched another major overhaul, they'd stir up enough panic and opposition to scuttle the whole endeavor.

Over four months, the delegates crafted a powerful federal government with a single executive, a two-chamber Congress empowered to levy taxes and declare war, and a theoretical federal judiciary that would have the power to check the state courts. The resulting Constitution is one of the shortest in the world: only 4,543 words before any amendments. The delegates left much about how the new government was supposed to organize and operate unwritten. On purpose.

Their stinginess with words was for practical as well as philosophical reasons. They learned from their earlier mistakes that governing officials needed room to move as the realities of governing set in. But mostly, they just needed to get the damn thing passed. If they had tried to argue and agree on every single detail, they'd still be there today. The delegates kicked important cans down the road to us because trying to decide everything all at once would have undone the entire deal. Everything beyond the essential—and the agreeable—they left for future generations to solve. It was the Founding Father version of shoving the issue in a closet to deal with later.

Delegates acknowledged that they had swept many problems under the proverbial rug. Features of our modern government that we often assume were set forth in the Constitution but were actually sorted out later include the creation of the judicial branch, the development of executive departments, and the foundation of a capital city.

They also purposefully left ambiguities in the language that quickly became apparent after its passage and continue to create critical ramifications today. These are handy bits to remember the next time you're tempted to think of the Constitution as a complete instruction manual. Take the following all-too-familiar ones as prime examples.

"HIGH CRIMES AND MISDEMEANORS"

Article II and Article III empower Congress to impeach the president, federal judges, and officers for "treason, bribery, and high crimes and misdemeanors." Yet the delegates were frustratingly silent on exactly what offenses constituted a high crime or misdemeanor. Should these breaches be limited to illegal acts—does crime actually require a crime? Or are there immoral acts that qualify? Jaywalking is a crime, but surely Congress would not remove a president or judge for a petty offense. On the other hand, if a president revealed state secrets to another nation and harmed national security, they might not have technically committed treason, which requires a declaration of war. They might not have broken the law but betrayed their oath of office.

This ambiguity has shaped impeachment efforts ever since. Did President Clinton's lying about his affair meet the constitutional threshold, or was it just a poor private decision that should be considered separate from his presidential role?

More recently, Republicans used the vagueness of the phrase "high crimes and misdemeanors" as an explicit defense in the first impeachment of President Donald Trump. After a whistleblower revealed that President Trump threatened to withhold foreign aid from Ukraine unless they investigated his political opponent, the Democratic-led House of Representatives charged that Trump committed grave abuses of power that clearly warranted impeachment.

Republicans disagreed. They argued that while Trump's behavior wasn't exactly presidential, he didn't commit an impeachable offense. Neither Clinton's nor Trump's impeachment resolved the underlying question.

So what did the Founders really mean? Because they knew they could never offer a clear and exhaustive list of clearly impeachable offenses, they expected future generations to define those phrases for our own times. They gave us the tool but relied on us to decide when and how to use it. And as a result, President Gerald Ford had it exactly right when he argued high crimes and misdemeanors are "whatever a majority of the House of Representatives considers them to be at a moment in history."[6]

"NECESSARY AND PROPER"

Article I, Section 8 authorizes Congress "to make all Laws which shall be necessary and proper for carrying into Execution the foregoing Powers, and all other Powers vested by this Constitution in the Government of the United States." What does necessary and proper mean? Necessary for what? Proper to whom? Depends on who you ask about what and when.

The "necessary and proper" clause has been stretched so far to ensure a law's constitutionality it is often referred to as the "elastic" clause or even the "sweeping" clause. All the way back in 1792, Secretary of the Treasury Alexander Hamilton used this phrase to justify the formation of the First Bank of the United States. Since then, Congress has deployed these amorphous powers to justify legislation on everything from infrastructure to gun control to defense spending and everything in between.

On the flip side, history is littered with constitutional challenges to federal laws on the basis that they weren't sufficiently "necessary and proper." In 2012, the clause was used as the primary reason to strike down the individual mandate within the Affordable Care Act (Obamacare). The court threw out the mandate on a razor-thin vote of 5–4, all hinging on how nine justices interpreted what the Founders meant by those three words over 200 years prior.[7] Was that what the Founders intended? Who knows. That is the problem with trying to understand the Constitution through the Founders' intent.

"ADVICE AND CONSENT"

Article II grants the president the power, with the "advice and consent" of the Senate, to make treaties and appointments, including ambassadors and Supreme Court justices. Article II also mentions executive secretaries but does not specify how many or which departments. In the summer of 1789, when Congress created the executive departments, they empowered the Senate to confirm senior-level presidential appointees as well. But what does advice and consent mean? Is there a threshold required for the Senate to officially consent? Is the president obligated to seek advice for every appointment? How is the Senate supposed to communicate its advice?

On these questions and many others, it was up to George Washington and the first Congress to create the precedents lacking in the Constitution.

Congress gave Washington and many of his successors enormous deference over their appointments. Only in the last few decades have cabinet and Supreme Court appointments become partisan battlegrounds. Hardly what the Founders intended or demonstrated with their own actions.

Constitutional Compromises

At each step on the Constitution's path to passage, the model had to morph to meet a diverse array of demands. Any one of these compromises could stand as evidence of the document's practicality rather than perfection.

One of the biggest hurdles it had to clear was the first: approval by the delegates in Philadelphia. As the debates extended into the July humidity, they hit several critical impasses. And the delegates increasingly understood that they had to make compromises to push it through.

The major fault lines lay between large and small states and the North and the South. Representation was a central conflict. Delegates from smaller states worried that if representation was based on population, they would be effectively squeezed out in the new federal government. Bigger states wanted their bigger populations to afford them more lawmakers in Congress.

The delegates tackled this thorny issue in a roundabout way. First, they crafted a compromise on the bicameral legislature. To appease smaller states, each state would receive equal representation in the upper house (two senators each). To appease bigger states, representation in the lower house (the House of Representatives) would be based on population. No one was completely satisfied with this plan, but it was the only arrangement that kept big states like Virginia and small states like Delaware from stomping out of the room, climbing into their carriages, and beginning the long journey home.

Next, however, came the big question of how the population would be counted. And this debate led to a seemingly intractable conflict over slavery.

In 1787, slavery existed in all 13 states, but it looked quite different across the country. Relatively few enslaved laborers lived and worked in New England, though many New Englanders did business that supported or benefited from enslaved labor, including the rum, sugar, timber, and fish trades. Slavery was more prevalent in the mid-Atlantic, but abolition sentiment was growing. In the Deep South, however, states' entire economies depended on enslaved plantation labor. And unsurprisingly, many of the delegates from slave-heavy states were not keen to hand power to those who might threaten the economic system that provided them extraordinary wealth.

Thus, Southern states pushed to count their populations (and congressmen) based on total residents, including enslaved men and women and poor whites without the vote. Northern states balked.

"Upon what principle is it that the slaves shall be computed in the representation?" Gouverneur Morris, a delegate from New York, wondered aloud in a speech to fellow delegates. "Are they men?" he asked. "Then make them Citizens and let them vote." When delegates from the South booed and hollered, Morris replied, "Are they property? Why then is no other property included? The Houses in this City (Philada.) are worth more than all the wretched slaves which cover the rice swamps of South Carolina."[8] There was no good answer to Morris's questions, either in 1787 or today.

Reluctantly, the delegates settled on a compromise called the three-fifths clause, in which five enslaved or indentured persons would count as three for determining a state's population. This construction was patently absurd, and many Framers viewed it that way. But for the Constitution and the nation it would preserve, compromise was not just congenial; it was existential.

And it became so again at the very end of the convention, when the slavery debate reignited. As the delegates discussed granting the federal government power to control the slave trade, John Rutledge of South Carolina issued a fierce ultimatum: Unless regulation of the slave trade was left to the states, the southernmost states "shall not be parties to the union." No state control of slavery, no nation. The other delegates from South Carolina and Georgia backed his threat.[9]

More recently, historians have argued that the Southern delegates were bluffing. They are probably right. But the other delegates at the convention *believed* the threats to leave were serious. Hamilton wrote that without a compromise, "no union could possibly have been formed."[10] It was that simple: Compromise and have at least a shot at a durable democracy, or let the squabbles topple the entire endeavor. They chose the former.

To resolve the matter, the delegates added one of their trademark vague clauses. This one blocked any federal law restricting migration or "Importation" of "such Persons" whom the states "shall think proper to admit" before 1808. This meant the Southern states could import enslaved laborers without limitation until that date. After 1808, Congress could limit the slave trade, but it didn't have to.

In other words, on the most difficult issue of their time—slavery—the Founders punted. Which is a helpful thing to remember when you catch a pundit pinning their argument on the idea that the Constitution was a perfect plan for all time.

Amending from Day One

Even after the Constitution cleared the convention, its fate was hardly certain. The document still had to be ratified by the states. During that process, a document that was already a mishmash of dealmaking and good-enough measures had to adapt again.

Far from being accepted as a work of divine brilliance, the document alarmed and outraged various factions within different states. Did the Framers then put their collective foot down and insist that their Constitution could not be improved in any way? No—they worked to strengthen it.

From the very beginning, Americans demanded amendments to protect individual liberties, insisting on what they called a Bill of Rights.

Anti-Federalists, or those who opposed the Constitution, were particularly worried about its absence of a Bill of Rights. They feared the government would evolve into autocracy or monarchy without such protections. Four years earlier, they had won a war to declare independence from such a monarchy, so these concerns remained fresh in their minds.

Federalist majorities, or those who supported the Constitution, secured quick ratification in states like Delaware, Pennsylvania, New Jersey, and Massachusetts. Yet Anti-Federalist factions there argued vehemently for amendments to protect specific rights, including freedom of speech, worship, and congregation. Patrick Henry argued that without a Bill of Rights, "the rights of conscience, trial by jury, liberty of the press, all your immunities and franchises, all pretensions to human rights and privileges, are rendered insecure."[11]

Washington tried to assuage these concerns by pointing out that the Constitution could be amended with the approval of two-thirds of Congress and three-quarters of the states. The Framers had intentionally inserted this clause to provide a road map for successive generations. "As a constitutional door is op[e]ned for amendment hereafter," Washington wrote, "the adoption of it under present circumstances of the Union is in my opinion desirable."[12] Henry and many of his fellow Anti-Federalists were unconvinced.

It took nine months to secure approval from nine states, as required in the Constitution. But in June 1788, New Hampshire became the ninth to ratify it, and the document went into effect. And still, the debate was not over. Nor was it meant to be.

In states like Massachusetts, New York, and South Carolina, the conventions ratified the Constitution but officially recommended amendments. Madison, campaigning for a seat in the first House of Representatives, quickly deduced that most residents of Orange, Virginia, supported the Constitution but wanted a Bill of Rights. He publicly promised to support amendments once the new federal government commenced.

Just one year after Madison had traveled to Philadelphia and played a critical role in drafting the Constitution, he was campaigning on a platform to fix it. It was a remarkably frank acknowledgment that the Framers were doing the best they could to create a new government from scratch and were likely to make mistakes, despite their best intentions.

In April 1789, Madison arrived in Philadelphia—where the first Congress met—to take his seat in the very first House of Representatives. Within two months, he launched a discussion of a Bill of Rights. "It will be a desirable thing to extinguish from the bosom of every member of the community any apprehensions, that there are those among his countrymen who wish to deprive them of the liberty for which they valiantly fought and honorably bled," he wrote.[13]

Madison had gathered amendments from the dozens and dozens of proposed revisions submitted by the states' ratification conventions and offered a list of suggested amendments to begin the conversation. The House then created a committee, including one member from each state, to draft a report. On July 28, the committee delivered its recommendations, which were printed in newspapers across the country.[14]

The House ultimately recommended 17 amendments. The Senate approved 12 from the House list, which were then sent to the states for ratification in August 1789. In December, Virginia became the final state to ratify 10 of the amendments, now known as the Bill of Rights. It's worth noting that what we now recognize as the First Amendment—widely considered the bedrock of all amendments—was actually number three on the original list presented to the states in 1789. The key point: Just months after the First Federal Congress took office, it had already amended the Constitution many times over.

The Bill of Rights, which we think of today as an inalienable, inseparable part of the Constitution itself, was just that—an amendment. An effort made after the Constitution was written to improve it. Which is, in principle at least, what the Framers expected we would still be doing today.

Sometimes we have. Subsequent generations continued this constitutional evolution. They prohibited citizens from suing states in the 11th Amendment, improved the electoral system in the 12th Amendment, gave Congress the right to levy income taxes in the 16th Amendment, provided for the direct election of senators (previously elected by their state legislatures) in the 17th Amendment, and prohibited the sale, manufacturing, and transportation of liquor in the 18th Amendment, then changed their mind in the 21st Amendment.

Perhaps most important, the 13th, 14th, 15th, and 19th Amendments updated the Constitution to modern ethical standards by granting full citizenship to women and people of color. Imagine if we'd considered the Constitution too precious to update who counted as a citizen.

Real-Life Adaptation

Thus ratified and amended, the Constitution faced its next test: reality. A challenge that it continues to confront today.

Many of the Framers themselves assumed offices in the new federal government, and they quickly discovered that the Constitution's flexibility was less like a useful tool and more like a map with many of the major roads left unlabeled.

The Framers had agreed on a general outline of the executive branch but had not tackled the details of the presidency, including what the president would be called. (Vice President John Adams suggested "His Highness, the President of the United States, and Protector of the Rights of the Same," a title that lawmakers thankfully dismissed.) Nor were they particularly eager to hash out the powers and limitations of that office with Washington in the room. Everyone present knew that if the Constitution was ratified, Washington would become the first president. They trusted him to flesh out the intricacies of the presidency and establish wise precedents for his successors. But it was also awkward to discuss potential misconduct and how to prevent it in Washington's presence.

Accordingly, Washington was left to determine how presidents should dress, speak, socialize, and interact with other branches of government. And he proved quite willing to innovate, within the law, when the pressures of governing demanded different solutions.

Here the ambiguity of "advice and consent" crops up again. The Framers granted the president authority over foreign policy, but they fully expected the Senate to play a sizable role, too.

In August 1789, Washington planned his first visit to seek "advice and consent" from the Senate with these expectations in mind. Because it was an important "first," Washington carefully managed every detail of his visit. He met with a committee ahead of time to coordinate where he would sit, where Vice President John Adams (as president of the Senate) would sit, how the president would be announced, and more. Weeks before his arrival, Washington sent all relevant existing treaties and papers for the Senate to study. On the day of his appointment, Washington handed his prepared remarks and questions to John Adams, who read them aloud.

Washington fully expected that the questions would prompt the senators to debate the issues and offer their advice and ultimate consent. He had used similar strategies when he met with his officers for advice as commander in chief of the Continental Army. Vigorous discussion permitted Washington to observe the weaknesses and strengths of each position and empowered him to make the best decision possible.

Yet in the Senate chambers, Washington's questions were met with silence. Some senators shuffled their papers; others twiddled their thumbs. Most avoided eye contact. Finally, Sen. William Maclay from

Pennsylvania stood up and suggested this issue was new to the Senate and the senators needed more time to deliberate. He suggested they refer Washington's questions to committee and requested the president return the following week.

Washington stood up and yelled, "THIS DEFEATS EVERY PURPOSE OF MY BEING HERE!" He eventually regained control of his temper and agreed to return for the Senate's recommendation, but on the way out of the building, he reportedly said that he would never again call on the Senate for advice. He kept his word. And in the nearly 240 years since, no president has ever returned to the Senate for formal advice on foreign policy.

Where, then, was the president supposed to find timely advice? The Senate was too slow and infuriatingly uncooperative to serve as an effective council of foreign affairs. Washington would have to find advisors elsewhere and turned to individual meetings with his department secretaries to discuss matters pertaining to their portfolio. He also sought advice separately from Supreme Court justices and select congressmen. But this process proved too ad hoc in moments of crisis.

So Washington improvised again. In November 1791, he convened the secretaries of state, treasury, and war and the attorney general for advice on matters that encompassed multiple departments. The cabinet was born.

Over the next six years, Washington convened almost 100 cabinet meetings. He met with his cabinet when he faced an unprecedented situation, sought consensus among the secretaries, or needed advice. The secretaries provided invaluable support when Washington faced domestic insurrection, threats of foreign war, and challenging constitutional questions.

The cabinet—a feature of the modern presidency we assume always existed—is one of Washington's most influential and enduring inventions. Every president since the first has met with a cabinet, and their secretaries are involved with the most important legislative and diplomatic initiatives. If the Founders had gotten it all right, the cabinet would be written into the Constitution. Or there would be no need for a cabinet at all.

Another innovation of Washington's that peppers the front pages today is executive privilege. Early in his presidency, Washington willingly complied with congressional requests for executive documents. But in 1796, Democratic-Republicans in the House requested all executive documents pertaining to the negotiations surrounding the Jay Treaty—which had resolved lingering tensions between Great Britain and the United States and established a new trade relationship between them. The treaty was already inked; the Senate had ratified it, and Washington had signed it. But Democratic-Republicans hated specific terms that they felt unfairly targeted Southerners. They hoped the documents would embarrass the administration and scuttle the treaty.

Washington replied to the request with uncharacteristic bombast and snark. He reminded Congress that he had repeatedly complied with previous requests. But this time was different. Diplomacy required secrecy, he argued, and foreign partners should feel safe that their negotiations would remain private. Accordingly, for the first time in American history, Washington asserted executive privilege.

Then, he seized the opportunity to deliver a history lesson. He reminded the representatives that he had served as president of the Constitutional Convention when the delegates distributed foreign policy authority between the president and the Senate—not the House. And he called out the House for trying to overstep its constitutional bounds.

The House backed down and accepted the treaty without revision—which effectively codified executive privilege, a power that commanders in chief have loved to put into use and extend ever since. Dwight Eisenhower, for example, invoked privilege to withhold meeting notes to protect executive branch personnel and army officers from Joseph McCarthy's smear accusations. Nixon attempted to stall and squash the Watergate investigation by claiming the tapes that caught him executing the cover-up should be protected by executive privilege.

More recently, the Trump administration invoked executive privilege to prevent officials from cooperating with congressional investigations of the January 6 attack on the US Capitol. Congress, which narrowly dodged the mob that breached the Capitol doors and windows, issued subpoenas for documents and witnesses to investigate Trump's state of mind and his response—or lack thereof—to his supporters overwhelming Capitol police. In response, Trump made an unprecedented move, even for presidents: He claimed executive privilege across the board. He asserted that Congress had no right to access any private communications that involved him or *anyone* within his administration. Trump went so far as to literally sue the director of the National Archives, the nonpartisan agency that keeps all presidential records, to prevent the agency from turning over documents to Congress.

The irony is that Washington created a new presidential power not articulated in the Constitution while grounding this authority on his own personal experience with the Constitutional Convention—a bit of living proof that the Constitution was always intended to be a starting point, even by those who crafted it.

Today: Living the Myth

If the Framers and their contemporaries clearly saw the Constitution as a work in progress, how did we come to treat it as a sacred relic too precious to amend?

This form of patriotic worship took root in the wake of the Civil War, as both the North and the South searched for anything to bring them back together. The history of the nation's founding was a shared cultural touchstone that both sides could and did celebrate.

During this time, a cult of the Founding Fathers emerged. Scores of biographies were published glorifying and mythologizing the first generation of Americans. Thousands of tourists flocked to historic sites like Mount Vernon (Washington's home), the White House, and Peacefield (home of President Adams) to pay respects and find a memento whenever possible. Presidents regularly replaced the carpets and draperies in public reception rooms because visitors would snip a corner from the fabric to take home as a souvenir.

With every successive anniversary or celebration—1876, 1926, 1976—the cult of the Founders grew stronger. The longer the nation survived, the more powerful the attachment citizens felt for the founding documents. But with more powerful attachment and with each passing generation, we see the documents with decreasing clarity.

And doing so holds us back from the pursuit of the more perfect union that the Founders' genius, bravery, and foresight gave us a chance to achieve.

In 1819, with the nation wracked by the question of whether to permit slavery in the Western territories, John Adams wrote to Thomas Jefferson, "The Missouri question I hope will follow the other waves under the Ship and do no harm—I know it is high treason to express a doubt of the perpetual duration of our vast American Empire, and our free Institution." But Adams continued, saying he sometimes had nightmares about dangerous characters that "might rend this mighty Fabric in twain—or perhaps into a leash, and a few more choice Spirits of the same stamp, might produce as many Nations in North america as there are in Europe."[15]

Adams feared that debates over slavery and other divisive issues could tear apart the young United States. He worried that if these contentious issues weren't handled carefully, they could potentially split the country into several separate nations. In public, Adams was cautious about doubting the permanence of the American republic, but privately, he feared that powerful disagreements might eventually break up the nation.

Today, Americans—conservative and liberal—have deep angst about political polarization, misinformation, election integrity, political violence, inequality, gerrymandering, and corruption. We may not yet have the solutions to these complex problems, but we know we must combat them all.

To have any hope of overcoming these obstacles, we should emulate the Founders' innovation rather than blindly adhere to their words that were written for a specific time, a specific generation. Next time you hear someone say, "The Founders intended . . . ," take a beat. The Founders unanimously agreed on two, and only two, things: We should not have a king, and George Washington should be the first president. Everything else required compromise and adaptation.

The Founders provided us with useful examples of flexibility and realism. More than their words, their humility is the true source of their genius. They understood that no battle plan survives first contact with the enemy and fully expected future generations to tackle the challenges facing the nation with similar vigor and creativity. They approached the Constitution with this attitude and fully expected us to do so as well.

We have proven them wrong.

"I Vote the Issues, Not the Party"

Dr. Lilliana Mason

In the months leading up to the 2024 presidential election, news outlets across the United States sent armies of rookie reporters out into the streets, parks, and senior centers to find answers to a burning political question: Which issues are most important to American voters? The responses were resounding.

"People want to stop seeing the debt ceiling climb and climb," a construction estimator in Texas told *The New York Times*.[1]

"I feel like if Trump just shut his mouth . . . and just did the policy and his work, I would, I would say, 'Yes, please come back,'" a woman named Virginia told MSNBC.[2]

"I look at what he did with NAFTA," a union member in Michigan told NBC News.[3]

"I'm a smart guy. No left-wing or right-wing media has any effect on the way that I think about things," an Oklahoma lawyer told *The New York Times*.[4]

A businesswoman from Georgia told NPR, "I am not a party voter. I vote for a candidate based on fiscal policies and also based on some social policies as well."[5]

Voters everywhere professed their dedication to certain policies and the candidates who promised to pursue them. Then the talking heads on cable news amplified and analyzed these statements until they (and we) could barely breathe. These were the voters' choices—clear and rational—explained.

Except for one inconvenient fact: Voters don't actually make their choices that way. They only think they do.

To see what I mean, let's take a little trip to Sweden.

During the final stretch of the 2010 general election in Sweden, researchers at Lund University played a trick on their fellow citizens.[6] They recruited 162 volunteers of all ages from nearby cities and asked them to fill out a questionnaire about their voting intentions and views on political issues. The issues were ones on which Sweden's left- and right-wing political coalitions had taken opposite sides. They asked about the extent to which respondents agreed or disagreed with statements like "Gasoline taxes should be increased" or "Healthcare benefits should be time limited."

After volunteers answered the policy questions, researchers asked them to explain and justify their positions. During this conversation, the participants tallied up how many of their positions matched those of the right-wing versus left-wing coalition. At the end, researchers asked them again who they planned to vote for—making the exercise a sort of candidate-policy-candidate sandwich.

Except that for some volunteers, the conversation wasn't so straightforward. The researchers secretly made a duplicate copy of their answer sheets but changed a number of their answers. They then used sleight of hand to switch the original answer sheet with the doctored one. After this trick, they asked the respondents to explain and justify their positions (now the opposite of what they had written). So if the respondent had originally answered that a tax should be raised, the researchers asked why they believed it should be lowered. If the subjects noticed that their written answers looked incorrect, they were allowed to change them. Then, just like with the other volunteers, they tallied up their positions and indicated who they planned to vote for—closing the sandwich.

Surely the volunteers would have spotted the trick, yes?

Not so much. For those with the bogus answer sheet, 47 percent—nearly half of respondents!—did not correct any of their answers. The rest of them corrected only one to four of their answers, though on average seven had been changed. These participants were able to explain to a researcher why they held beliefs that were the opposite of what they had indicated. Consciously or not, they came up with reasons to defend the new opinion.

How did this new view affect their intended votes? For almost all these participants, it looked for all the world like their chosen candidates (as indicated beforehand) didn't match their preferred policies (as tallied on the doctored surveys). If they had preferred the left-wing candidate at first, their changed answers made it look like they agreed more with the right-wing coalition (and vice versa).

So did they stick with their original policy ideals and candidates, or did they treat these "new" attitudes as something that they had been thinking all along and choose new candidates to match?

Among this group, fully 10 percent of participants changed their vote choice from strongly right wing to strongly left wing (or vice versa)—moving to the opposite end of the political spectrum due only to a trick of the experimenters. Another 19 percent changed enough to shift from preferring one side to being uncertain. That is nearly a third of the participants who took their "revised" answers seriously enough to reevaluate their vote choice on the spot. (And thankfully, at the end of the experiment, the researchers explained the trick to participants and revealed their original answers.)

The moral of the story: Voters' opinions on the *issues* can be easy to change.

This isn't only true of the Swedes. It's comforting—inspiring, even—to think that come Election Day, millions of dedicated voters weigh the country's most pressing problems and cast their well-considered votes for the candidates they believe are best equipped to solve them. It's also comfortable, and entirely natural, for each of us to believe that we reason our way to our votes in that fashion. If you had asked me the reasons behind my votes 20 years ago, I would have said the same thing.

But the truth is that most people, in every country and system of government, can be persuaded to change their policy preferences. In fact, most of the research on this phenomenon comes from the United States. We Americans are relatively easy to influence and quite vulnerable to the prevailing messages we receive from political leaders. We constantly hear (and say) that we vote for the candidate with the best platform regardless of the D or R next to their name. But unfortunately, deep down, we're guided by different influences.

The myth of rational voting holds that democracy is a process by which voters evaluate information objectively, apply those evaluations to the political choices in front of them, and choose the candidate who best matches their preferences or maximizes their material well-being. In this view, sometimes called the "folk theory" of democracy, people prefer that the government enact a particular policy, and they choose their party based on that preference.[7]

In reality, a huge set of political psychology research has found that the relationship between policy beliefs and vote choices flows both ways—meaning that sometimes the candidates we've chosen determine the policies we prefer. And "flow" is the right word here. We often feel that our beliefs about the best approach to government are central and unchanging. But study after study shows that people change their policy preferences all the time. Often, they don't even realize they've done it.

These revelations make for some exciting dinner-table conversation (try telling your Uncle Edwin at the July Fourth picnic that his pet political views were fed to him by his favorite Libertarian candidates). But their real implications are orders of magnitude bigger.

That's because the truth is not just that our beliefs are flexible. It's that our beliefs can be manipulated. And they are manipulated, regularly, by the leaders we support, among others. In fact, believing that we're immune to this persuasive power makes us easier targets for politicians who know how to take advantage of our overconfidence—and makes it harder for us to hold our elected leaders accountable.

A central responsibility of voters is to electorally punish leaders who break their promises and perform poorly. When we cede our decision-making to leaders and influencers, even unknowingly, are we really doing our jobs as citizens of a democracy? And who is doing our job in our place?

Luckily, this near-universal human tendency does not have to rule us. If we understand how the process in our minds works, we can counteract it. If we know the tools of manipulation, we can spot and deflect attempts to influence us. If we see how our minds really work—instead of how we wish they would work—we can begin to reclaim our own power as voters and elect leaders who might actually try to make our lives better.

The Influencers

As much as we hate to admit it, our policy preferences can be manipulated in a number of ways. In the Swedish case, people were convinced to change their policy preference because they were tricked into thinking they already held that belief. In more common cases, political leaders convince their supporters to change their minds on a particular issue, or they reverse course themselves, and supporters follow.

In the United States, for example, Republican support for free trade—a core tenet of conservatism for generations—declined between 2008 and 2016. This was driven by a combination of factors that included declining working-class quality of life, increasing anti-trade rhetoric from far-right politicians, and finally Donald Trump's distinctly anti-trade 2016 campaign.

But even more interesting is what happened next: Between 2016 and 2020, this trend reversed course entirely. Interviewing the same people at different points in time, political scientist Diana Mutz found 42 percent of Republicans opposed free trade in 2016, but only 7 percent of those exact same Republicans did in 2020. A change of this magnitude, over this short a time, "is striking and virtually unheard of," she writes.[8]

How did this happen? Mutz analyzed the factors. In general, the more pro-Trump Republicans were the most likely to change and favor trade. Trump had changed these minds in part by changing what trade meant for his biggest fans. Mutz writes, "The version of trade that Republicans believed they were getting from Trump was completely different from how they thought of trade before. Instead of being taken advantage of by international trade, trade became an opportunity to dominate other countries in an international arena. . . . What was viewed previously by Republicans as a zero-sum game that we were losing, was replaced in their minds as a means to dominance. . . . Trump promised not only to fight trade wars; he also claimed that 'winning' trade wars would be easy."[9]

This is a key tool in the influence kit. The easiest way for others to manipulate our opinions is to change how the issues are framed. We can even reframe our own beliefs ourselves. In this case, Trump reframed trade to make it sound good (winning) instead of bad (losing). In the Swedish case, voters rationalized their wrong answers to make them fit into their own personal narratives in a way that made sense to them. We don't simply blindly change our opinions according to our leaders' positions—we are convinced to hold different opinions by expert framing and a personal need to make sense to ourselves.

Most Americans don't want to believe that we are so easily manipulated—even American political scientists. Decades of political science operated on the assumption that voters make decisions to maximize their material well-being, that they prioritize "pocketbook issues" rooted in how financially secure they feel.[10] Political pollsters and pundits today assume the same thing. But psychologists have designed tests to illuminate what people are really thinking—even if they don't know it themselves. And it's critical to understand what they've found, to see how our policy preferences can change without our knowledge, with relatively simple tricks used on purpose by our political leaders.

PARTY OVER POLICY

One thing about politics that many of us know for sure is that our political party is "us" and the other party is "them." And we are capable of remarkable mental gymnastics to make sure we're on the right side. A landmark study in 2003 showed how.

That year, psychologist Geoffrey Cohen conducted a series of simple experiments to understand whether regular people were more influenced by policy details or party loyalty.[11] He gave liberal and conservative college students information about one of two different welfare policies.

One policy was "generous." A family with one child would receive almost $800 per month, and every additional child added $200 per month. The family would receive full medical insurance, $2,000 in food stamps, subsidies for housing and childcare, job training, and two years of tuition at a community college. The benefits would last eight years, after which the heads of the family were guaranteed a job. If the family had another child, the benefits would begin again. These benefits were far more generous than any offered in the United States at the time.

The other policy was "stringent." This one offered only $250 per month, with $50 added per additional child. It provided only partial health-care coverage and ended after one and a half years with no chance for renewal. None of the food, housing, childcare, job support, or educational benefits were included. These benefits were far more stringent than any offered in the United States at the time.

The researchers also told some of these students that the policy they read about was overwhelmingly endorsed by either Democrats or Republicans. Other students received no party information. When Democrats favored the policy, students read quotes from a Democrat saying the policy would "lighten the financial burden of the poor" and a Republican saying the program was "too costly." When Republicans favored a policy, students read quotes from a Republican saying the program "provides sufficient coverage . . . without undermining a basic work ethic and sense of personal responsibility," while a Democrat called the program "only a band-aid effort."[12] Importantly, the researchers randomly assigned the policies to the parties.

Researchers then asked students to rate their support for the policy they read about and the extent to which they believed their own opinion was influenced by four factors: "The specific details of the proposal," "[Their] own personal philosophy of the role of government in social issues," "What the typical Democrat or Republican believes," and "[Their] own background/experience with people on welfare."[13]

When the students received no information about which party supported which policy, the liberal students who saw the generous policy rated it higher than the liberal students who saw the stringent policy, and conservative students who saw the stringent policy rated it higher than conservatives who saw the generous policy—as one would expect. However, when they read about which party preferred their policy, their views changed. Regardless of the policy details, liberal students liked the policy that Democrats supported, and conservative students liked the policy that Republicans supported.

How did these students explain their choices? All of them asserted that their attitude was based on the "details of the proposal" and their own "philosophy of government." They also told the researchers that "what the typical Democrat or Republican believes" was the *least influential factor* in determining whether they approved or disapproved of the policy.[14] In other words, they believed they had chosen their preferred policy independently and rationally, free from any partisan sway.

Alas, not even close.

The data, of course, showed that party position was the *most influential factor* in determining whether the students liked or disliked the policy. They simply had no idea that they had been influenced by that.

This result already seemed to smash the claim that our political evaluations are rational and unbiased. But then, the study continued.

In the next phase, Cohen had conservative students read not just one welfare policy but both policies side by side and tweaked the information about which party supported which.[15] The results were unchanged. Even when they could directly compare the two wildly divergent policies, students preferred the policy that they believed their party favored.

The final stage of this study is perhaps the most remarkable. The researchers asked liberal students to evaluate a job training program in either its generous or its stringent form—and to write an editorial about it to inform public policy. When given no party information, 76 percent of the students wrote an editorial supporting the generous policy. When told that Democrats opposed the generous policy, 71 percent of students wrote an editorial opposing it. Based on party cues, the students were able to construct and write an entire narrative opposing the policy they would have otherwise supported—even while knowing that their argument could shape future policymaking.

How did the students themselves explain this? After the experiments, researchers asked them what factors had contributed to their policy decision and the other students' decisions. And it turned out that they believed their opinions had formed differently from other people's opinions.

The results here have bad news for those of us who think we could never fall victim to such tricks. Most of the participants ascribed their own beliefs to relevant facts and real-world experience. But they ascribed the beliefs of their political allies, and even more so those of their adversaries, to group influence. In other words, they thought everyone else was vulnerable to party influence, but they were uniquely immune.

Surely these students must have been politically uninformed or simplistic thinkers? It would be comforting to think so. Yet study after study shows that the opposite is true. The people who are *most* susceptible to party influence are those who are the most politically knowledgeable and the best at solving complicated logic puzzles.[16] The take-home message: If you're smart and politically aware, you're even more likely than others to make up your mind this way.

The divisive political moment we live in only makes this worse. A 2013 study found that "political polarization intensifies the impact of party endorsements on opinions, decreases the impact of substantive information and, perhaps ironically, stimulates greater confidence in those—less substantively grounded—opinions."[17] In other words, the more different the parties appear to be, the more we believe what our parties tell us. When politics gets contentious, we put party loyalty over truth. Almost all of us. Including me. And probably you.

We believe that we are rational and independent thinkers, even though we know that others are not. Mathematically, we can't all be correct.

LEADERSHIP TRUMPS IDEOLOGY

Parties aren't the only heavyweights that can tip our political opinions. This power also lies with individual leaders, especially charismatic ones.

Several years ago, political scientists Michael Barber and Jeremy Pope devised a way to disentangle the influence of partisanship on preferences for liberal or conservative policies.[18] Their experiment was like the Cohen study, but it took advantage of the fact that Donald Trump took both the liberal and the conservative sides of many issues during his 2016 presidential campaign.

In their example, Trump said in November 2015 "that he supported a policy in which any and all illegal immigrants would have to exit the country in order to be eligible for any type of legal status or citizenship." The following August, media outlets reported that he favored "a plan that would allow certain people who were in the United States illegally to remain in the country and be eligible for legal status."[19]

Trump took similarly contradictory positions on a number of issues. The researchers chose 10 of these, including the minimum wage, universal health care, climate change, and abortion. For all these issues, Barber and Pope randomly assigned participants to read either Trump's liberal position or his conservative position.

Republicans who read the liberal Trump position became about 15 percentage points more liberal on that issue than the control group (who got no information about Trump's position). For some issues, like immigration and climate change, the liberal Trump message moved people nearly 20 percentage points more liberal. On the flip side, those who read the conservative Trump position became about 10 percentage points more conservative. All in all, the Republicans who read the liberal Trump position had opinions that made them look more like Independents than typical Republicans.

"Hypocrisy" is a favorite battle cry between political factions. But it's worth remembering when that word leaves our lips that what we call hypocrisy often springs from a hardwired human condition—and we are all human. Evangelical Republicans denounced marital infidelity by Bill Clinton but had no problem with it in Donald Trump. Democrats hated the idea of national digital surveillance under George W. Bush but grew more comfortable with it under Obama. A majority of Joe Biden and Donald Trump supporters rejected the idea of a "strong leader who doesn't have to bother with Congress and elections" but also believed their favorite candidate should be able to take unilateral action without constitutional authority in multiple scenarios.[20] Should the loser acknowledge the winner of an election? Voters' answers depend on who wins. Should Congress have oversight over the executive branch? That depends on who's in the White House and which party is investigating.

Call it hypocrisy or call it vulnerability. The fact is that consistency among leaders connects with consistency among constituents. When leaders are consistent, repeating the same position frequently, supporters are most likely to stay committed to those opinions. But if leaders change their position, partisans tend to follow along.

THE HARD TRUTH

It might seem like the subjects in these experiments—and voters at large—just aren't thinking. But the truth is that they are thinking, just not in the objective, fact-based way we usually believe. They're thinking with a part of their brains that often takes precedence over rational thought. And it's not a bad part.

What takes the driver's seat in these kinds of decisions is the part of us that connects us not to facts but to one another. We all have an immediate, deeply rooted desire to be good members of our groups. This stems from a primal need to avoid being banished. We can't survive alone. Humans are built to live among other humans—and to be accepted by them.

To be accepted, we must follow the norms and values of the group. If we discover that we disagree with the group, we would rather change our own positions than leave. This can be to fit in, or it can be because we trust our group to make better decisions than we might as individuals.

In Cohen's experiment, subjects didn't blindly change their preferences without thinking. They changed the way they evaluated the policies to match the norms of their party. And to do this, they created a whole new explanation for their new views. This is called "motivated reasoning," and we do it all the time. Sometimes we're motivated to look for things that we want to be true, like a new study that says a nightly glass of wine is actually healthy for you (so then, four glasses provide four times the benefits, right? It's just math). Other times, we'll spend extra energy looking for flaws in the study or problems with the news outlet that reported what we don't want to be true.

The other type of motivated reasoning is the one we do to stick with our people. Your child's soccer team lost? You can likely identify multiple examples of unfair play from the other team and blown calls by the ref. Also, that other coach is wearing ugly shoes and practices too much (they're just kids!). Our motivations drive us to trust and privilege our groups, and our opinions fall into line.

This instinct exists for good reason. But if left unchecked, it can lead us to bad outcomes: not only embarrassing behavior at a soccer match but, on a larger scale, profound divisions between fellow citizens, political gridlock, and even human disaster. A fascinating field of psychology shows us why.

Us and Them

Before World War II, a young Polish man named Henri Tajfel wanted to study chemistry. In 1930s Poland, a university education was out of reach for Jewish students. Instead, Tajfel went to France to study at the Sorbonne from 1937 to 1939. He was an inattentive chemistry student, preferring to explore French culture and language, and by 1939, he could speak French fluently. This would likely save his life.

Tajfel joined the French Army when World War II started and was captured by Nazi forces in 1940. He spent the rest of the war in prison camps, where he pretended to be French rather than Polish. He believed, with good evidence, that the only reason he was allowed to live was that the Nazi guards believed him to be a French Jew, not a Polish Jew. Tajfel thought often of the fact that keeping his nationality secret allowed him to stay alive.

When he was freed in 1945, Tajfel learned that his entire family in Poland had been killed. He decided to devote his career to studying group identity, the roots of intergroup animosity, and how our identities can so powerfully motivate us to love, hate, and even eradicate other people. His work would ultimately become the foundation of our modern understanding of group identity.

THE SIMPLEST POSSIBLE GROUP

Tajfel began by trying to find an identity so weak that it inspired no prejudice at all. From there, he planned to add small differences to identify the precise point at which an identity creates a bias. He started with meaningless group identities that he randomly assigned to research subjects.[21] In one experiment, he told subjects they were "overestimators" or "underestimators." In another, he said they were the types of people who preferred the paintings of Klee over the paintings of Kandinsky. In further experiments, he tried giving people a number or a letter to represent their group. In one case, he frankly told them they had been randomly assigned to meaningless groups.

All these experiments failed, in a sense—and that failure contained their shocking revelation.

Tajfel found that none of these identities worked as a "baseline" because they all produced bias. Even meaningless categories inspired favoritism for fellow members of the randomly assigned group and prejudice against those in randomly assigned other groups. Every time, subjects who were asked to allocate money to others chose to give more to people in their brand-new group and less to those outside it. They were also willing to sacrifice the total amount of money their group received (receiving less overall) as long as people in the other group got less still.

These findings—which have been confirmed again and again by many studies since—have powerful implications for both our human relationships and our political thinking. They demonstrate that even the weakest, most unimportant identity can inspire competition, prejudice, and a willingness to sacrifice the well-being of "in-group" members for a sense of superiority over the "out-group." What Tajfel discovered is that people don't need deeply rational or even logical disagreements to discriminate against others. We do that automatically. It's in our DNA.

POLITICAL MEGA-IDENTITIES

If a meaningless identity can inspire prejudice, imagine what a real identity can do. We are all born into identity groups—racial, religious, geographic, ideological, cultural. Most of us also choose to join or remain in these or other groups, as parents, athletes, manual laborers, car dealership owners, professors, folks who are interested in political myths . . .

In my own research, I have found that even these innocuous identities can inspire powerful competition between groups and often generate prejudice against people who are "not us."[22] This has especially potent implications for our political thinking, considering that over the last few decades, a lot of our most powerful social identities have become associated with our political parties. Back in the 1950s, the parties organized our politics but not our social divisions. We mingled with a mix of Democrats and Republicans at church functions and community gatherings. Racial and religious identities were not strongly associated with party affiliations (except for Catholics being generally more favorable to Democrats).

The civil rights acts of the 1960s began to change that. The laws ended Jim Crow segregation and the widespread disenfranchisement of Black Americans—and simultaneously sparked a party realignment that set up race as a dividing line between Democrats and Republicans. Many conservative white Southern Democrats, enraged by that legislation, pulled away from the Democratic Party. Over the span of a generation, these white voters became Republicans, while Black Americans moved toward the Democratic Party that had championed their rights.

Religious identity, too, became a more important party divide as the religious right emerged as a political force. Before this, Evangelical Christians had intentionally stayed out of politics, a secular space. But in the 1970s and 1980s, fundamentalist Christian leaders began to champion the use of political power to spread their faith. By 2000, every item on the Christian Coalition's agenda had been added to the Republican Party platform.[23]

Then these murmurs of division gained a megaphone. In the early 2000s, partisan cable news and social media emerged, making it easier to communicate broadly who counts as "us" or "them." Access to a diverse array of informational sources made it easier to consume a bespoke news and entertainment diet. Democrats and Republicans—already divided by race and religion—began to watch different television shows, shop at different grocery stores, and move into politically aligned neighborhoods.

Being a Democrat or a Republican never used to tell us much about someone's race, religion, geography, or culture. Now it tells us a lot. We have one political party representing the interests of traditionally high-status demographic groups (white, Christian, male) and another representing the interests of everyone else. (Not every single Republican or Democrat fits that mold, of course. But on the whole, that is how the party priorities align.) Politics have become a battle over group status and social power dynamics. This merging takes the power of one identity, magnifies it many times, and then gives us a chance to vote about which groups we like best.

As a result, policy differences between Democrats and Republicans have deepened, but not as much as their hatred for each other has grown. To the extent that this battle is about policy, it is about policy relevant to that divide. The policy debates that make Americans most angry at one another are over racial justice and gender roles. Recent surveys show that the Republicans who hate Democrats the most are those who believe racial inequality is due to cultural deficiencies among Black Americans and that women have more rights than men and should stop complaining. The Democrats who hate Republicans the most are those who believe that racial inequality is rooted in structural racism and that women have yet to achieve social and political equality with men.[24]

These tensions fester in the context of incredibly fast social change. As a quick review, legal segregation prevailed in the American South until 1965, women needed their husbands' permission to get a credit card until 1974, and same-sex marriage was banned in the majority of US states until 2015. This stunning progress feels slow in a human lifetime but is remarkably fast from a historical perspective. My own mother graduated from college and got her first job in an America that didn't trust her to manage a bank account. My father attended segregated schools in Virginia. It's not a coincidence that the parties have become divided by identity at the same time minority rights have accelerated—or that our most passionate political debates, from book bans to abortion to school prayer, are directly connected to the change.

We voters have enacted this partisan realignment ourselves by large-scale self-sorting along social lines. Over the past few decades, for example, many white Democrats have grown more racially progressive, yet others with more conservative views of race and gender have left the party to become Republicans.

But we've also been inspired to do this by increasingly clear messaging about who is "us" and who is "them." Politicians and political parties juice their own fame by drawing our attention to social debates—and can push us to passionately hold positions that we might not have thought about even a few years ago. Meanwhile, political media stars like Tucker Carlson have repeated the threat that "they" want to control "you."[25]

Tajfel would not be surprised by how this identity stacking poisons our perception of one another. In my 2022 book with Nathan Kalmoe, we found that a significant number of Democrats and Republicans in 2020 were willing to call their partisan opponents "evil" (40 to 70 percent depending on the year) or "subhuman" (20 to 40 percent depending on the year). The best predictor of holding those attitudes was having opposite positions on racial resentment. In other words, it was the most racially resentful Republicans and the least racially resentful Democrats who were the most likely to vilify and dehumanize their partisan opponents (though the effect is stronger for Republicans).

These types of social divides tend to lead to violence in other countries. For example, one study from 2011 found that in countries where political divides map onto racial, ethnic, or religious divides, the chance of descending into civil war is 12 times higher than in countries where the political divide is unconnected to race or religion.[26]

Yet far short of warfare, and far more within each voter's control, this rift plays out in our everyday political tensions. For all of us who want to reclaim our decision-making, it's crucial to know that identity-based parties take our natural susceptibility to group influence and supercharge it. When a political divide is existential, it's difficult to admit that the other side might have a point about welfare policy. Shrewd political leaders know that and use it to their advantage.

Opportunistic Leaders

It should be no surprise that divisive conditions make it easier for leaders to use their influence for self-serving purposes. If they want us to focus on a particular issue, they can frame it with an argument that plays on our identities. If they want to distract us from a matter that they totally botched, they can play on our divisions to point us elsewhere. The one-two punch of rhetoric and identity knocks us out. Unfortunately, it is very difficult to recognize when this is happening. We don't want to believe we're vulnerable. But we are, and we need to know how.

RHETORIC

We trust what our favored leaders tell us for some very good reasons. First, we elected them to represent us; it's their job to do the work, figure things out, and then tell us what's going on. We're too busy to do their job for them. Second, they're supposed to be the experts. We expect them to use their judgment wisely and tell us their reasoning. A representative system of government is at least partially based on our trust. It is also based on our skepticism, and that is where leaders' rhetoric can interfere.

Let's try an example. Bernie Sanders (senator from Vermont) has a famously loyal following. He is generally known for speaking frankly and fighting against economic inequality. Sanders has repeatedly attacked Republicans (and Hillary Clinton) for selling themselves out to wealthy donors. He implies that political candidates who accept campaign donations from very wealthy people are corrupt. In a 2016 debate with Clinton, he argued, "You know, there is a reason why these people are putting huge amounts of money into our political system. And in my view, it is undermining American democracy and it is allowing Congress to represent wealthy campaign contributors and not the working families of this country."[27]

A vast amount of political science research (and Steve Israel's campaign finance chapter in this book) explains that most elected representatives don't trade votes for cash. The repeated assertion that they do undermines faith in the vast majority of legislators' work. But Sanders's version of the story is unquestioningly accepted by much of the Left. This is partly because people feel loyal to Sanders, partly because the story "feels" true, and partly because it appeals to the interests of middle-class Democrats who feel disempowered. Sanders's personal appeal, plus his powerful rhetoric, guts our usual skepticism.

All people are equally vulnerable to these influences, but not all political leaders take advantage of them in equally cynical ways. And some leaders stretch this manipulative rhetoric from insinuations into outright falsehoods. Why? Because stretching the truth works—on many levels.

We all want (and need) lies to be disqualifiers in American politics, but the reality is that politicians face very minimal punishment for being less than truthful. Leaders, political parties, and the media understand that we're all susceptible to believing what we want to be true and are far less likely to critically examine any statements that tell us we're right. They know if they make statements that confirm our instincts—about immigrants, climate change, guns, terrorists, anything—they prime us to believe whatever comes out of their mouths no matter what a fact-checker says.

The more craven leaders go further to prey on one of the most broadly shared sentiments in American politics: that all politicians lie. Understanding that this view cannot and will not be altered, some politicians are just fine flooding the zone with particularly aggressive falsehoods so that no one knows for certain what is true. "The goal is not always to sell a lie," explains a recent report from the nonpartisan organization Protect Democracy, "but instead to undermine the notion that anything in particular is true."[28] If everything is questionable, we're all more likely to cherry-pick what we want to believe are facts.

In this way, the development of "alternative facts" shouldn't be all that surprising.

As a voter, it's also worth watching what leaders lie about. One study reviewed false statements by different presidents in their first hundred days. Biden lied about the minimum wage ("If we kept [it] indexed to inflation, people would be making $20 an hour right now") and immigration enforcement ("We're sending back the vast majority of the families that are coming"). Trump, on the other hand, lied both much more often and about subjects with a potent emotional charge—for example, murder rates in the United States ("Here in Philadelphia murder has been steady—I mean—just terribly increasing") and refugees committing terrorist attacks in Sweden ("We've got to keep our country safe. Look at what's happening last night in Sweden. Sweden, who would believe this? Sweden. They took in large numbers. They're having problems like they never thought possible").[29]

Those conditions—low certainty, high emotion—lend charismatic leaders more power.

Before you blame Trump supporters for buying what he's selling, remember that anyone can be influenced by a charismatic leader. And once you have been, it can be hard to go back. We're all motivated to believe that we're smart, important, and good—and our brains naturally tend to choose reasoning that keeps us feeling this way. A manipulative leader takes advantage of this by counting on the fact that we hate to admit we've been tricked.

IDENTITY

At a political science conference in 2017, I presented research demonstrating that some opinions on controversial issues like abortion or gun control were rooted in identities rather than detailed policy knowledge. A few minutes into my presentation, an older white man in the audience stood up and started yelling at me: "What am I supposed to be?? You keep talking about identity being everywhere. You're a woman—you have an identity! What am I supposed to be? A hundred different things??" This man then followed me to the rest of my presentations at that conference and to many subsequent conferences all over the country, and he hounded me at every one. My answers never satisfied him. He needed me to explain how all this identity stuff was supposed to work for him—a white man, who supposedly had no identities at all.

This spectacle was a small snapshot of how one particular sort of rhetoric—the sort centered on identity—can overwhelm our rational thinking.

First, let's clear up a little term that has become a taboo phrase in America: "identity politics." In common parlance, this refers to politics focused on the grievances of marginalized groups. Leaders and pundits on the right often dismiss arguments about the influence of racism, sexism, or homophobia as identity politics. But the fact is that every person, left or right, possesses identities. And participating in politics in defense of one's social groups is as old as democracy. Even during less polarized times, political campaigns referred to courting the "Catholic vote," the "Black vote," or the "soccer mom vote." These are all identities. If you want to build political support, appealing to the common interests of particular groups is simply an effective way to do it.

How does this play out in America today? Right-wing pundits are right that today's Democratic Party appeals to groups who have been mistreated and attempts to offer more representation, power, and solutions to their problems. In a 2023 speech, Vice President Kamala Harris urged, "Let us continue to work to secure our most foundational freedoms: the freedom to vote, the freedom of women to make decisions about their own bodies, and the freedom to live free from hate and violence."[30]

But identity is also a frequent tool in Republican politics. Instead of appealing to the concerns of marginalized groups, today's Republican Party appeals to the grievances of traditionally dominant groups.

Being white, male, or Christian is also a powerful identity—contrary to the beliefs of my conference buddy. When Trump characterizes Mexicans as "rapists," tells congresswomen of color to "go back" to their countries, bans Muslims from entering the United States, or calls Democratic women "nasty," "angry," "ditzy," or "crazy"—even his seemingly innocuous claims that "We're saying 'Merry Christmas' again in this country"—these are appeals to a particular identity. And that is not an accident.

Studies have shown that Trump's language appeals primarily to voters with strong white, male, and Christian identities, as well as those worried about feeling out of place in an increasingly culturally diverse America.[31] In my own work with Julie Wronski and John Kane, we found that Trump's language—unlike that of Mitch McConnell, Paul Ryan, or the Republican Party in general—was a lightning rod, drawing new people into the Republican Party who had previously remained mostly outside either party and were united in their dislike for marginalized groups. This pattern has, in turn, influenced the Republican Party as a whole, deepening and calcifying the identity-based partisan divides that were already forming. All of which hardens our perspectives and narrows the range of candidates and ideas we're likely to support.

This matters to all of us, whatever our party, because it illustrates the vision-clouding power of identity. When our leaders emphasize identities, status threats, and intergroup animosity, our brains often get stuck there. Thus prodded into our primal reactions, we judge politicians more on how they make us feel than on their actual effectiveness at improving the material conditions of our lives. We believe them too much. We let them off easy. Trump is not the first politician in American history or even in contemporary Western democracies to employ this strategy.[32] Nor will he be the last.

The lesson here is that when leaders constantly tap into a well of anger, fear, and defensiveness, it is worth considering their motives.

When a leader, left or right, tells you how they will protect you from your "enemies" instead of how they will help you—that is a red flag. The good news is that finding the red flags is an important step to resisting manipulation.

Overcoming the Myth

This is where we, the voters, have an important role to play. Understanding our vulnerabilities is only the first step to becoming more effective members of our democracy. There are also practical approaches—backed by political, psychological, or sociological science—that can help us exit the influence chamber and exercise more genuine choice within the psychological reality of democracy. It starts with spotting the mythmakers in action.

IDENTIFY THE INFLUENCE CAMPAIGNS

One clever technique comes from a team of psychologists at Cambridge University who decided to use biology as a model for inoculating us against misinformation.[33] With a biological vaccine, a doctor introduces a small, harmless version of a virus into the bloodstream so that a person's immune system can quickly spot and kill the real virus when it arrives. In that vein, these psychologists developed an online game in which they taught players how to create their own misinformation (getbadnews.com). By acquiring the tools used to make misinformation more attractive, persuasive, and yes, viral, people learned to recognize when others were using those tools against them.

In the case of identity-based thinking, a similar approach could be effective. If we know how leaders can leverage identity to change our minds on policy and harden us against our political opponents, and how that might even feel affirming to us, it becomes easier to recognize these attempts as they occur. The next time you listen to a politician—or any political commentator—pay attention to how they're framing the issues. Are they using rhetoric about social identities (women, poor people, immigrants) to amp up their arguments? Is today's issue really about Republicans' selfish aims to enrich big corporations or Democrats' feckless wish to hand out more welfare to the unemployed? Or is there actually a reasonable debate about government spending and social welfare hiding underneath it? Listen for words like "poison" or "evil"—tried-and-true adjectives to light your fear-fire. Spot arguments that cast all opponents as extremists ("socialists" or "fascists") or malign their motivations ("They are coming to hurt . . ."). All these tactics appeal to your identities to rile up your innate "us versus them" instinct. Don't let them.

IDENTIFY WHEN YOU'RE VULNERABLE

Particular factors—such as stage of life, personal environment, and emotional stability—make us more susceptible to messages about our identities, and these factors can change over time. If you know those factors too, you're better equipped to intercept attempts to influence you.

1. **Uncertainty:** When people feel uncertain about their own identity—whether that is their status in their community, their family structure, their political place—they are more attracted to authoritarian leaders and extremist movements.[34] If you have recently lost a job, gotten divorced, or lost a loved one, these more extreme political influences provide a sense of certainty that can feel comforting. In this state, it is especially important to pay attention to any attraction to charismatic leaders. One way to

reduce this vulnerability is to build healthy certainty by joining groups—especially those with members who don't share your primary identities—and engaging in regular activity with them.[35]

2. **Anger:** Different emotional states allow us to think about things in different ways. Anger, for example, makes it harder to cognitively process new information.[36] When we feel angry, we rely more on what we already know and are less inclined to learn and change our minds. Leaders can pull this lever by inducing anger through threats to our social groups or families, highlighting obstacles to our goals, identifying scapegoats we can blame for our frustration, or even playing angry music in a campaign ad.[37] A politician who can make and keep us angry can also keep us in a state where we can't learn. Knowing this, you can notice your emotional state before coming to any political conclusions. If you feel angry, ask what got you there. If it was a politician's messaging, question what motivated it. Take a break, take a breath, and come back to the question only when your calmer brain holds the reins.

3. **Political Isolation:** For our brains, the influence chamber is further solidified by an echo chamber. It is easier to be swayed if we never hear from the other side or if we only hear about them from sources within our own groups. In a recent sample of Republicans, a majority believed that the 2020 election was stolen despite extraordinary amounts of evidence and court decisions to the contrary. The Republicans who were able and/or willing to agree that Biden won the election were those who reported talking about politics with a "good mix of Democrats and Republicans."[38] Exposure to diverse viewpoints provides a more solid base from which to interpret the information we hear. It helps us approach political disagreement with curiosity (Why do you feel that way?) instead of certainty (You're wrong and I'll prove it), which opens us up to learning. As a starting point, look closely at your political circles, including those online. Do your social media feeds contain

any viewpoints from the other side? Do you only watch certain channels for political news? And no, clicking to Fox News or MSNBC once a week just to get mad at them doesn't count.

DEMAND MORE OF OUR LEADERS

The best way to protect ourselves from political manipulation is to elect leaders who don't need to manipulate us in order to win power. Though all politicians vie for our attention and try to present themselves as best, not all of them use that influence to turn us against one another.

This gives us some good questions to ask ourselves. If a leader wants our attention, will they tell us details of their policy successes or compromises or alarm us about a terrifying threat to our community? If someone wants to distract us from their own failures, will they explain complex processes of government or scream about someone else's flops? If a leader is trying to steal our power as voters, will they encourage us to vote or tell us to direct our hate toward fellow Americans?

You can actually do the math on this by paying attention to the proportion of a leader's or pundit's statements (in speeches, debates, ads, or tweets) and gut checking how many are about policies versus threats. And how many are facts (provably true or false) versus opinions (just vibes). Literally keeping a running tally can show you just how lopsided this type of rhetoric has become—and give you clues about who's trying to manipulate you.

We are all vulnerable to political influence and persuasion. We can't change that fundamental human nature within us. But if we recognize it and take care to identify those who mean to exploit it, we can own our strength and claim a more powerful say in our democracy.

Our country needs us to. Democracy only works if we can trust our leaders to generally tell us the truth and to work toward bringing us together as a nation. And as much as we may feel powerless, we citizens actually hold the keys. As voters, we can undermine leaders' better motivations by believing whatever they say and ignoring their actions. Or we can assert our greater reason to keep them honest and constructive, to insist that they follow our lead rather than the other way around.

Our human brains, flawed as they are, afford us that power, too.

"The President Should Just…"

Alyssa Farah Griffin

The president of the United States was about to make an infamous, footnote-in-history-books-type gaffe.

I knew it was coming. And I couldn't stop it.

It was Thursday, April 23, 2020. The entire world was shut down, scared, anxious. The United States was in the throes of our first deadly Covid-19 spike; more than 17,000 Americans were going to die that week from the virus.[1] And literally everyone—from senior White House staffers to concerned parents across the country—was desperate for facts: desperate for any semblance of certainty or reassurance. All we knew for certain was that Covid wasn't going to disappear "like a miracle" despite what our commander in chief was telling us.

Just over two weeks prior, I had been named White House director of strategic communications and assistant to President Donald Trump. My main duty was to help craft the White House's message and effectively get it out to the American people. In those dark and early days of Covid, this meant spending my hours—about 16 per day—trying to concoct simultaneously coherent, positive, and truthful communications for a panicked public.

To ensure I was working with the most up-to-date information, most days I sat in on the White House Coronavirus Task Force meeting chaired by Vice President Mike Pence. The task force was made up of senior leaders across government, including principals from the

Centers for Disease Control, FEMA, eight executive departments, and the intelligence community. Their charge was to coordinate the administration's response to the pandemic and make daily recommendations to President Trump about what actions to take to mitigate the virus's wreckage.

The task force typically met for upwards of two hours in the oft-dramatized White House Situation Room, a SCIF—sensitive compartmented information facility—so that classified intelligence and strategies could be discussed freely. Cell phones and smart watches had to be left in cubbies outside, and all participants had to have high-level security clearances. We tackled immediate issues requiring government responses, from where we could source reliable testing equipment, to ventilator shortages, to supply chain breakdowns, to runs on hand sanitizer. The vast majority of the meetings were depressing and overwhelming.

On this day, the task force had two guests: officials from the Department of Homeland Security (DHS) who had been working with military scientists from nearby Fort Detrick. The two DHS guys came to brief the task force on very preliminary results from a few biological experiments they had recently observed. Armed with classified reports and graphs, the officials explained that their very early data suggested that intense heat and humidity could kill the coronavirus. Upon hearing the results, task force members noticeably sat more upright in their chairs. Many quickly made the leap that these findings could maybe, just maybe, lead to a breakthrough in stopping the spread.

Yet the DHS officials stressed over and over that their results were preliminary, hadn't been properly replicated, and hadn't been sufficiently vetted. They were hopeful but didn't want their early findings to be seen as anything more than what they were.

Vice President Pence, usually a very cautious and thoughtful person, thanked them but disregarded their caution. One of Pence's jobs as task force chair was to brief President Trump after every meeting. Too often, he reported the distressing and hopeless status of the pandemic. But the DHS guys had given Pence a rare opportunity to give President Trump what he loved most: good news.

"The president needs to know about this," he told the task force. I suspect that Pence, after spending countless hours hearing of death and illness, also wanted to give potential good news to the public.

I rarely disagreed with decisions Pence made. The vice president had made a name for himself in the West Wing as a cautious voice of reason—an important counter to the often impulsive President Trump. But this time, being intimately familiar with President Trump's knack for . . . overexaggerating, I disagreed. I reminded the task force that we had already faced justifiable public and media blowback for the president recommending unverified and potentially dangerous treatments (Ivermectin or malaria pills, anyone?). With the world hanging on every word we put out, we couldn't afford to stake our credibility on another unproven "remedy."

Again, Pence overruled. With less than half an hour before the task force's daily briefing—watched by millions of people from the James S. Brady Press Briefing Room—he adjourned the meeting, presumably heading in short order to brief the president. I dashed after him, first to his office and then to White House Chief of Staff Mark Meadows's office to make my case. We were joined by acting Secretary of Homeland Security Chad Wolf, the president's trusted senior counselor Kelly Ann Conway, the VP's Chief of Staff Marc Short, and the two DHS officials who didn't wake up that morning expecting to brief the president and maybe change government policy.

"We can't brief POTUS on this," I said to Meadows. "The findings are too preliminary, and we are not at all clear on our message here. Are we saying to the American people to turn their thermostats up to 90 degrees? Are we trying to start a run on portable heaters and humidifiers?"

"I got it," Meadows replied. I wasn't sure if the cryptic remark meant he agreed with me or not. For a moment, it felt like acting Secretary Wolf was on my side. But Conway and Short were in the VP's camp and wanted to take it to the president. I was outvoted.

A few minutes later, the DHS officials were escorted to the Oval Office to present their findings to the eager president. I stood outside the Oval for the five to seven minutes they were in there. I wanted to catch the president on his roughly 45-second walk from the Oval to the briefing room to tell him not to publicly share what he heard. I worried we were going to cause mass confusion at the exact time we needed certainty.

POTUS walked right past me without breaking stride, ignoring or missing my attempts to catch his attention. I followed him to the briefing room, and its big blue sliding door closed. I opted to watch from a stone's throw away in Upper Press, where my office and the White House press secretary's office were located. Then I watched as President Trump did far more damage than I ever could have fathomed.

"There's been a rumor that—you know, a very nice rumor—that you go outside in the sun or you have heat and it does have an effect on other viruses," Trump said from the world's most famous podium. He then turned to Coronavirus Task Force coordinator Dr. Deborah Birx and directed her to "speak to the medical doctors to see if there's any way that [she] can apply light and heat to cure" the virus.[2] Dr. Birx sheepishly nodded, afraid to contradict the president in front of the world. I worked closely with Dr. Birx and hold her in the highest regard. She served her country in uniform as an army doctor, then dedicated her life to fighting infectious diseases, including HIV and AIDS. I'll never fault her for not jumping to the podium to correct the president of the United States, for honoring the chain of command, though I don't envy the position it put her in.

And here's where the wheels fell off.

Previously in the briefing, before the president took over, Bill Bryan, the acting DHS undersecretary of science and technology, had reported strong evidence that disinfectants like bleach killed the virus. Riding the wave of potential cures, President Trump took it 784 steps further by speculating that if disinfectants can kill the virus on surfaces like tables, it only made sense that they could also kill the virus in humans if we somehow mainlined bleach.

"And then I see the disinfectant where it knocks it out in a minute. One minute," Trump said. "And is there a way we can do something like that by injection inside or . . . or almost a cleaning? Because you see it gets on the lungs and it does a tremendous number, so it will be interesting to check that. So that you're going to have to use medical doctors. But it sounds, it sounds interesting to me."[3]

Jaws—Dr. Birx's, the entire White House press corps'—hit the floor. The president of the United States had just told the American people, the world, that they should consider injecting bleach as a potential cure for Covid. And because he was the president, people listened to what he said. Poison control centers saw documented spikes in emergency calls in the days that followed.[4] Even Lysol's parent company had to issue a statement clarifying that "under no circumstance should [its] disinfectant products be administered into the human body (through injection, ingestion or any other route)."[5] I couldn't believe it. And yet, somehow, I could.

The injecting bleach episode is an extreme example of a president making an outrageous and untrue statement and relying on the power of his position to somehow make it true. This is the logical, if unfathomable, conclusion of our distorted and unhelpful expectations of the American president—of presidential power, really. The bleach case, while preposterous, highlights this common myth in our POTUS-crazed political world: that the president wields nearly unchecked power, able to single-handedly steer the course of the nation and world via a perfect combination of charisma, will, and authority. And this false idea leads to ridiculous, infuriating, and sometimes dangerous expectations of our commander in chief.

Trump took this misperception of the president's power and ran; he launched himself unabashed and unconstrained into moments like the bleach one, fueling the illusion that the president could just wave a magic wand, make bleach safe to chug, and voilà, find an overnight fix for a global pandemic under every kitchen sink. It was the extreme use of a myth that preceded him.

These perceptions and resulting expectations, however, are far from reality. The president is not an all-powerful Oz-like figure. Yet over the past century, we all—citizens, voters, Congress, the media—have morphed the president in our collective minds into an omnipotent force that our system never designed him to be. And it has warped what we think is possible, how things are done, and whom we hold to account.

We have come to see the president as the sun of our political universe in a system that was designed for him to be a moon. We expect him to solve every possible problem, from global pandemics to finding that one missing sock. We blame or credit him for things he has very little power over. See how many of these sentiments sound familiar:

The president should just lower gas prices.

The president should just cut mortgage rates back to the low threes.

The president should just turn the inflation dial down.

The president should just fix Social Security.

The president should just close the border.

And on.

And on.

And by extension: When the thing we want doesn't happen, we assume it's only because the president chose not to do it or didn't try hard enough.

All of this has created a power paradox. The American presidency is more powerful now than ever in history. But this increase in power is not due to changes in the enumerated or constitutional powers of the American president. No, it's largely because other actors and branches—namely, Congress—have, both knowingly and unknowingly, surrendered their powers to him (or perhaps by the time you read this, her). For political expediency and sometimes to avoid tough, unpopular decisions, these actors have allowed the president to subsume their constitutional prerogatives—like the power to declare war—and presidents of both parties have been happy to oblige. And every time the president has overstepped without being called out or held in check, it has only inflated the power of the office and solidified the public's expectation that the president can and should just do anything.

The more nuanced reality is that the president is simultaneously the most powerful person on the planet and far more constrained than most people realize. While the president stands as the key figure in our modern system—commanding the world's most powerful military and exercising the loudest voice in every policy decision—his authority fundamentally depends on Congress, the judiciary, and the broader system of checks and balances designed by the Constitution. We might wish for him to just knock heads together until problems are solved, but the interplay among these branches often limits the president's ability to unilaterally implement or change laws. Yes, the president may get some of his followers to inject bleach—and one is too many—but to get a law, a Supreme Court justice, or money to keep the White House lights on, the president needs other officials to agree with him. Or worse, he ignores those other players, leaving us to question whether the system is even functioning as it should anymore.

Our fictitious inflation of the presidency has factual consequences. The more we allow the president to overstep his institutional bounds, the more vulnerable we all become to future Oval Office occupants—some of whom we are sure to disagree with—stretching those powers still further. It's the presidential version of giving a mouse a cookie; the next president is going to want yet another executive order to go with it.

Perhaps most personally, our inflated expectations of presidential power have real, negative consequences for us citizens and the strength of our entire system. Believing and wanting the president to do everything himself leaves us open to charismatic demagogues promising silver-bullet fixes "so fast it will make your head spin." And after he inevitably falls short, we blame him and conclude the whole system is broken. We feel like checking out of our democracy, and maybe we do, which is good for no one.

Understanding the real scope and limits of presidential power requires us to delve deeper into the framework of American governance—to demystify the presidency by examining the specific powers (hard and soft) available to the president, the significant constraints he faces, and the evolving nature of this high office. By exploring these aspects, we can better grasp why relying solely on the president to achieve political goals holds us back. And we can demand a restoration of the essential roles played by other branches of government—roles that they have voluntarily forfeited to the president over time and very much need to claw back.

Powers of POTUS

No author is supposed to say this, but I'm going to because it's that important: Put this book down. Stop reading and google the US Constitution. Find Article II, which outlines the role and powers of the president of the United States. The whole thing is 1,028 words and will take about four minutes of your time. It's worth it.

After reading, most are surprised at just how little time is spent on what has become the most powerful singular position on the planet. Most of the space is taken up explaining how the president gets elected. In fact, the second section of Article II is really the only part that outlines the specific hard powers of the presidency, and it does so in a whopping 322 words, far fewer than the number of words on this single page. Don't mistake brevity for lack of authority, though. Readers will see some familiar items within Article II that have provided the foundation for making the president the focal point of our modern politics. At the same time, some powers we associate with the modern presidency are conspicuously absent.

The constitutional powers of the president are largely broken up into two main buckets: *domestic* powers and powers relating to *foreign affairs.*

On the domestic side of the ledger, the president is the top boss of the entire executive branch, charged with ensuring that all laws are faithfully executed. Although the Constitution doesn't mention or create a single department or agency, the president sits at the top of the organizational chart for more than two million civilians working in executive departments today. For a fun contrast, the entire legislative branch employs about 35,000 people, or roughly the same number as the Department of Commerce.[6]

Next, Article II grants the president the power to issue pardons or grant clemency and commutations to individuals. Additionally, the president alone can make appointments, which in 2024 equals all the 870 federal judge seats for which there are vacancies, 15 cabinet secretaries, and nearly 7,000 other high-level federal positions.

The Constitution allows for the president to call special sessions of Congress and tasks him with updating Congress as to the "state of the union." The president, though, gets to decide how that update is communicated. In 1801, Thomas Jefferson had his clerk read the annual message to Congress, and this "I'll send my assistant" approach continued with every president until Woodrow Wilson decided to break the mold in 1913 and deliver the speech himself.

In powers of foreign affairs, one stands out above the rest: The president is explicitly named commander in chief, which gives him sole control over our nuclear arsenal and allows him to direct the more than two million active duty and reserve troops across the six service branches. The president also has the authority to nominate more than 200 ambassadors to foreign countries and various international organizations such as the United Nations. And as chief diplomat, the president receives foreign leaders on behalf of the United States and is granted the authority to negotiate and sign treaties with foreign nations.

Notice anything missing? Despite the sweeping powers of the modern presidency, the Constitution actually grants the president very little authority to directly impact the one thing we most expect of him: enacting new laws. On this policymaking front, the president is much more dependent than we (and he) appreciate. As many of us learned from *Schoolhouse Rock* (which, by the way, doesn't describe how a bill *really* becomes a law, but that's for another book), Congress writes the bill sitting up on Capitol Hill. And to make it law, the president must sign it. That's where he comes in, and under the Constitution, that's basically where his role ends.

Despite having a 30-car motorcade, the president can't introduce a bill—only members of Congress can do that. Even though he has his own 747, he has no vote on which bills get passed—only members of Congress do. Technically, the president's only hard power when it comes to lawmaking is the power to veto a bill passed by Congress. But even then, Congress has the ultimate ace in the hole—with a two-thirds majority vote in each chamber, Congress can override the president's veto.

Even POTUS's authority over appointments—including his own cabinet—and treaties is constrained by the Senate. Unless a majority of senators agree to his choices for secretaries, ambassadors, and judges, the president becomes the political equivalent of a dude playing fantasy football—he can draft whomever he wants, but the team will never take the actual field. And the threshold for agreeing to treaties is even higher; two-thirds of senators must agree to the president's deal or else the agreement is reduced to a coulda-woulda-shoulda-been for his forthcoming memoir.

This isn't to say that the president is wholly powerless to affect laws. Far from. POTUS has at his disposal a plethora of soft powers—those not explicitly listed in the Constitution—that make him a key, if not the essential, voice in any policymaking debate. The Oval Office, an unmatched Rolodex, Air Force One—all enhance the president's influence beyond the formal, constitutional authorities of the office. The net effect of this prominence is that when the president asks for a particular bill, lawmakers (at least those of his own party) tend to listen and even race to be the member who carries out the president's wishes.

In addition to all these informal trappings of the office, there's one big soft power that we all assume the president can tap into at any time to sway public opinion and, in turn, influence Congress: the bully pulpit. But as we'll see, for modern presidents, the presidential pulpit ain't often so bully.

Polarizer in Chief

The president has an unparalleled public platform, referred to colloquially as the "bully pulpit." When he speaks, the global financial markets move. When he calls a press conference, every cable news outlet covers it live. No other elected official can say the same.

Given that only POTUS can claim a national bully pulpit, we often assume that articulate and charismatic presidents can use it to persuade the public—and by extension, our representatives in Congress—to follow their legislative lead. From FDR's fireside chats to Reagan's sunny optimism to Obama's soaring rhetoric, history is littered with presidents who have used the bully pulpit to change minds and, ultimately, history—or so we imagine in retrospect.

This conventional wisdom is actually revisionist history. As I can tell you firsthand, the presidential bully pulpit does exist, but it's a myth that it is an effective tool of persuasion. Been there, tried that. The truth is, presidents who use the bully pulpit to advance their agenda are more likely to galvanize *opposition* to their goals than support. And the more a president uses the bully pulpit, the more entrenched that opposition becomes. Even FDR's famous fireside chats, remembered as rallying the nation at a time of war and economic collapse, only bumped his approval rating by a *single* percentage point.

This is because, for occupants of the modern Oval Office, being the focal point of American politics is an overlooked double-edged sword. The president can absolutely affect global events with a tweet or a press conference. But even with that power, and perhaps because of it, he is also by far the most polarizing person in the country. *Everyone* has an opinion about the president, and in our polarized times, those opinions are becoming increasingly difficult to change. Put simply, just because you have the eyeballs doesn't guarantee you can change anyone's mind. In fact, the more eyeballs you have, the *less* likely you are to do so.

Presidents feel so central to our politics that we view nearly every issue through a presidential lens. As detailed in Lilliana Mason's chapter, we often motivate our reasoning based on how we feel about a particular party or leader, and especially the president—if we support the president, we will reconfigure, consciously or subconsciously, our views on the issues to match his. If we can't stand him, we oppose whatever he's talking about no matter how much it may make sense. For those we like, we will explain away or minimize criticisms; for those we don't, we will amplify them, even to the point of being more susceptible to misinformation so long as it makes him look bad.

That means you may not necessarily *want* the president to speak up on behalf of your most dearly held priority. If he takes a stance, other players inevitably dig in on their sides more than if the topic had been broached by literally any other politician. As a result, any issue on which the president speaks—school curriculums, vaccination requirements, even sports predictions—becomes easier to oppose, even for those who would otherwise be disengaged entirely. And the harder a president publicly pushes, the more deep-rooted and organized the opposition becomes. As Rep. Jim Cooper (D-TN) put it, "The more high-profile the communication effort, the less likely it is to succeed."[7]

Dr. Frances Lee, a Princeton political scientist and fellow contributor to this book, put numbers behind this phenomenon. She collected a database of more than 4,000 Senate votes on fundamentally apolitical issues that historically enjoyed wide bipartisan support—issues like funding for childhood cancer research or investing in space exploration. She then noted if the current president had taken a public stance on the issue. When the president was silent, the two parties voted against each other only one-third of the time. When the president took a stand, the parties disagreed on over half of the votes despite the issue being apolitical.

Presidents of both parties, eager to put the bully pulpit to use on their own issues, have learned this lesson the hard way. Sometimes their supposed powers of persuasion have even turned previous supporters of a policy into critics. President Clinton, for example, barnstormed the country and Capitol Hill to rally public support for his health-care legislation, nicknamed "Hillarycare" because of the First Lady's leadership on it. The president's team poll-tested every major component of the policy and had numbers that suggested the public would support them. They were also confident they could get GOP lawmaker support because they purposefully used Republican ideas—like letting states set their own standards and requirements for government subsidies. How could Republicans vote against their own solutions? Easily, it turns out. As soon as Clinton took the mantle of these ideas, the same Republican senators who spent years supporting (and campaigning for) the changes turned against them.

President Obama became even more frustrated with congressional Republicans who lambasted his call for an individual mandate within his Affordable Care Act (Obamacare). Republicans loved the idea throughout the 1990s and introduced dozens of bills in Congress with the mandate as a health-care linchpin. Then–Massachusetts Governor Mitt Romney even passed a health-care bill containing the mandate, which many Republicans, including ultraconservative ones, praised as a potential model for a nationwide bill. But when Obama championed the mandate, its previous supporters labeled it socialized medicine. The issue had become polarized by the most polarizing figure in politics, and it was stripped from the bill.

Mandatory testing in schools followed a similarly predictable play-book. Clinton proposed nationwide testing to raise standards in public schools early in his first term. Republicans opposed the initiative, ostensibly because they believed education was a state and local issue, but more because they didn't want Clinton to become the "education president." When George W. Bush took office and called for an even more ambitious testing plan as part of his No Child Left Behind Act, Republicans loved the idea, but Democratic support disappeared.

This pattern of reflexive partisan opposition and flip-flopping has been repeated on issue after issue, from privatized Social Security accounts, to raising the debt limit, to international trade compacts like NAFTA.

The president as polarizer in chief leads to a counterintuitive catch-22 for modern presidents: Take a public lead on an issue and risk catalyzing detractors, or take a back seat, at least publicly, and risk the issue being ignored because it didn't receive the attention and momentum that a presidential push can bring. By keeping a low public profile, presidents may be able to get more done legislatively, but they forfeit their leadership status on the issue and any associated rewards in public approval or legacy. Even worse, if they aren't using the bully pulpit to sell their vision for the country, they risk looking like they aren't even trying.

But even if the bully pulpit were the power source we all think it is, presidents still wouldn't be content with only going the public persuasion route. As commander in chief of the strongest military the world has ever known, steward of the world's largest economy, and representative of 350 million people, the president doesn't take well to the idea of begging for votes from lawmakers who sometimes represent more cows than constituents. Teddy Roosevelt didn't say "Speak softly and carry a swimming pool noodle" when describing his political approach. No, presidents want to use big sticks to get what they want when they want it. And if they can't, history has proven time and time again, they will fashion their own big sticks to get around Congress.

Presidents, as we hear in every campaign, speech, news conference, press release, and tweet, come into office with grand plans. They want to lower taxes, revamp immigration, and even put a human on Mars. But these ambitious agendas almost always run through Congress, and Congress almost always has its own ideas (which, when controlled by the opposite party, is the idea to do everything possible to thwart the president's agenda). And presidents, with a clock ticking on their time in office, have never been content to sit idly on the sidelines.

From the earliest days of the republic, presidents have found creative ways to bypass the obstacles Congress throws in their path. They've become masters of using powers not explicitly granted by the Constitution to achieve their goals. This isn't just about satisfying voters who expect action; it's about presidents seizing the opportunity to lead—even if it means tiptoeing, or sometimes stomping, around the rules. And if the other branches, dazzled as they may be by the president's mythic power, don't push back, POTUS can effectively rewrite federal policy in the time it takes to order takeout.

The go-to tool for this kind of power play? The executive order.

Legislating from the Oval

On the morning of September 13, 1862, at the height of the Civil War, Union soldiers from the 27th Indiana Infantry paused to rest near Frederick, Maryland. As they relaxed in a field from which Confederate troops had recently fled, Corporal Barton W. Mitchell noticed something unusual. At the base of a tree, slouched in weeds, he found an envelope containing three cigars. The road-weary soldier couldn't believe his luck.

But the cigars weren't the real prize. Wrapped around the cigars was a copy of Special Orders No. 191, a crucial Confederate battle plan intended for, but never delivered to, a rebel general.

Forgetting the cigars (for the moment, at least), Mitchell rushed the special orders to his superiors. As the document worked its way up the chain of command, all worried that the orders were fake, purposefully left behind as a feint to lure the Union into a crushing defeat. No one was willing to bet the war on a piece of paper stashed beside a tree.

In a stroke of happenstance that only history can provide, the secret plans eventually made their way into the hands of Colonel Samuel Pittman. Before the war, Pittman was a bank teller in Detroit, Michigan. There, he processed hundreds and hundreds of checks bearing the signature of R. H. Chilton—the very same signature found at the bottom of Special Orders No. 191. Immediately upon seeing Chilton's signature, he knew the document was legit.

With this intelligence in hand, Union General George McClellan led the Union army into the Battle of Antietam. It would be the deadliest single day of war in American history, but the Union prevailed and turned the tides of the Civil War. The success at Antietam provided President Abraham Lincoln the opportunity to do what he had waited for: issue the Emancipation Proclamation, the executive action that declared Confederate slaves "thenceforward, and forever free."

Lincoln did not call his Emancipation Proclamation an "executive order," but it was. In fact, it was the most famous and impactful example of the president of the United States bypassing Congress and changing federal law with the stroke of a pen. But from where did Lincoln's power to issue such a proclamation originate? Despite their frequent use and significant impact, the term "executive order" (or any of its variations) is nowhere to be found in the Constitution. Instead, the authority for what's often called the "power of the pen" originates from the Constitution's "vesting clause." This clause simply vests in the president "executive power," a deliberately vague term that has evolved over time to encompass the wide array of administrative actions involved in managing the government's day-to-day affairs.

This vagueness has produced an eternal debate about the scope of executive power, how the Founders intended it to be used, and what it means for modern presidencies. Constitutional experts generally agree that executive actions are legal as long as they fall within the president's policy jurisdiction (read: matters for which there is a relevant federal department) and within a reasonable interpretation of existing court rulings. (Note that things the president *cannot* do within those bounds include lower gas prices, cut mortgage rates, reverse inflation, fix Social Security, protect abortion access nationwide, or many other moves that some constituents expect him to do.)

These actions—whether they're called orders, directives, or memoranda—are official, legally binding mandates, issued by the president alone, that direct federal agencies on how to interpret and carry out federal law. They carry the full force and effect of law, and unless otherwise specified, they go into effect immediately.

You can see, then, why presidents love these things and why every president but one has wielded the awesome power of the executive order (and the only reason President William Henry Harrison didn't issue one is because he died 32 days after being sworn in). Some presidents, like Teddy Roosevelt, made extensive use of executive orders— he issued 1,081 of them, more than 800 more than the president who issued the most before him, Ulysses S. Grant. Franklin D. Roosevelt took this power to new heights, issuing an astounding 3,721 executive orders during his time in office.

Executive orders have changed the course of history—for better and worse—without so much as a vote in the legislature. FDR's Executive Order 8807 in 1941, for example, led to the creation of a new government agency to oversee defense technology research, ultimately paving the way for the Manhattan Project and the development of the atomic bomb.

Executive orders have also been employed to cement, outlaw, and reinforce discrimination. FDR issued Executive Order 9066 in 1942, which authorized the creation of Japanese internment camps during World War II. With Executive Order 9981, President Truman desegregated the military in 1948, nearly two decades before Congress passed the civil rights acts. Five years later, though, President Eisenhower effectively banned LGBTQ individuals from holding government jobs.

More recently, presidents have used executive orders to legislate from the Oval Office on matters of federal policy they knew Congress couldn't (or wouldn't) legislate on. President Obama's 2012 Dreamer memorandum directed federal agencies not to deport illegal immigrants brought to the United States as children so long as they had no criminal record and were enrolled in school or the military. During his four years in office, President Trump issued 220 executive orders, including Executive Order 13769, more colloquially known as the Muslim Travel Ban. The order put an immediate halt to all refugee admissions into the United States and banned immigrants from seven predominantly Muslim countries from entering the country for three months. Among his unilateral directives, President Biden issued executive orders that mandated Covid vaccinations and testing for businesses with over 100 employees, expanded background checks for purchases of certain guns, and halted the construction of the Keystone XL pipeline (which Trump greenlit via executive order days into his term). These are all huge changes in federal policy.

And don't be fooled by raw numbers of executive orders issued by modern presidents versus their predecessors. It's true that the average number of executive orders issued per year by recent presidents—Obama with 35, Trump with 55, and Biden with 40—pales in comparison to the likes of Coolidge, Hoover, and FDR, who churned out 215, 242, and 307 orders per year, respectively. But quantity isn't the whole story; it's the quality—or rather, the substance—of those orders that really matters.

Take, for example, the difference between an executive order to lower flags to half-staff and one that effectively decriminalizes marijuana at the federal level (as Obama did) or mandates the construction of a border wall (as Trump did). These are not your grandmother's executive orders. So the next time you hear a president or their supporters touting lower executive order counts as a sign of restraint, your first question should be, "Yeah, but what's in those orders?"

THE RISE OF EXECUTIVE ORDERS

Though it's always more complicated, this shift toward more aggressive executive orders can largely be explained by two major political forces: divided government and the nationalization of our American politics.

First, consider the reality of divided government, where the White House is run by one party and at least one chamber of Congress is of the opposite party. In today's political landscape, a divided government is far more common than not. In earlier eras, it wasn't unusual for one party—often Democrats—to dominate both the White House and Congress, sometimes with overwhelming majorities. This made it easier to pass legislation through the traditional *Schoolhouse Rock* route: from Congress to the president's desk. Modern presidents, however, haven't been so lucky.

Even when a president enters office with a unified government, as Obama, Trump, and Biden each did, that alignment rarely lasts beyond the first two years. And with congressional majorities often hanging by just a few votes, the scope of what can actually be accomplished through legislation is severely limited. Frustrated by this gridlock and eager to deliver on campaign promises, presidents have increasingly turned to executive actions to get things done.

The second force at play is the nationalization of politics. There was a time when the phrase "All politics is local" held true, meaning that the issues people cared about most were those directly affecting their communities, like funding for local libraries or whether to implement a tax on grocery bags. But those days are long gone. Today, our politics are highly nationalized. The collective gaze of the public—and the media—is fixed on Washington, DC, and the partisan battles being waged there.

Even local debates, such as curriculum decisions made by local school boards, are now heavily influenced by national political trends and conversations. The political dynamics of DC don't just trickle down to local politics; they dominate it.

And at the center of this nationalized political universe is, unsurprisingly, the president. More than any other political figure, we're fixated on what the president is saying, thinking, and doing.

Recognizing the public's expectations for action, presidents have increasingly chosen to bypass the traditional lawmaking process and instead legislate from the Oval Office. With the clock ticking on their time in power and a public hungry for immediate results, inaction is a luxury they can't afford.

When Congress is gridlocked, unwilling, or simply unable to act, the president proves more than comfortable filling the power vacuum. Yet while executive orders can deliver immediate and powerful results, they also come with significant trade-offs—trade-offs that every citizen should carefully consider when assessing presidential power. The speed and decisiveness that make them so appealing also make them precarious. Presidents who live by the pen can just as easily die by the pen.

Live by the Pen, Die by the Pen

When a president opts to legislate through executive orders, they gain the advantage of immediacy—decisive action that can be implemented with the swift stroke of a pen. But what they gain in speed, they lose in durability. Laws are on the books until Congress decides to take them off (which is rare for many reasons). Executive orders, in contrast, are immediately vulnerable to the whims of the next administration. This impermanence creates a volatile environment of instability and uncertainty, with significant financial, human, and reputational costs for the country.

Take, for example, President Trump's abrupt reversal of President Obama's DACA protections for more than 800,000 Dreamers—young immigrants brought to the United States as children. On an ordinary Tuesday, with a simple executive order, the future of these Dreamers was thrown into chaos. Suddenly, while studying away at school or laboring away at work, they faced the very real anxiety of deportation, the loss of work permits, and the potential separation of families. What was once a source of security became a source of fear.

The financial and reputational costs of impermanent executive orders can be equally significant. On his first day in office, President

Biden reentered the United States into the Paris Climate Agreement—a landmark 2015 treaty aimed at reducing greenhouse gas emissions. Previously, President Trump had pulled the United States out of the agreement at the first possible moment. The back-and-forth nature of this decision-making process—first entering the agreement under Obama, exiting under Trump, and reentering under Biden—created a "snip-snap" policy environment that left both the government and private industry in a state of uncertainty. Billions of dollars had already been invested in low-carbon technologies and electric vehicle production to meet the goals of the agreement. After the United States pulled out and then reentered, companies understandably hesitated to commit further investments, fearing that the policy could once again be reversed after the next election.

The whiplash took a toll on the credibility of the United States, especially with our allies. A similar scenario played out with the controversial Iran Nuclear Deal, formally known as the Joint Comprehensive Plan of Action. This agreement, signed by Iran and the P5+1 group, was designed to limit Iran's nuclear program in exchange for lifting economic sanctions. But since, like the Paris Climate Agreement, it wasn't a treaty, it lacked the permanence that comes with Senate approval. Trump, who had promised to "blow up" the deal if elected, made good on his word by pulling out of the agreement, describing it as "one of the worst and most one-sided transactions the United States has ever entered into."[8]

World leaders, recognizing the potential fallout, pleaded with Trump not to withdraw, with French President Emmanuel Macron warning that doing so "would open the Pandora's box. There could be war."[9] This withdrawal didn't just strain international relations; it also damaged US credibility on the global stage. Our allies feared that other nations might view future agreements with skepticism, wondering whether a deal with the United States was only as strong as the current administration.

The impermanence of executive orders not only has created a land-scape of instability but has also become a powerful tool for presidential candidates looking to make immediate impacts. The promise to reverse a predecessor's executive orders has become a rallying cry on the campaign trail, with candidates often pledging swift action in their first 100 days in office. This tactic allows them to quickly chalk up wins by undoing the policies of the previous administration, appealing directly to their political base eager for change.

So while the early months of an administration are often marked by a flurry of executive action, much of that action involves undoing the work of the previous administration. For modern presidents, their first 100 days have transitioned into playing a game of Whac-A-Mole with the other guy's executive orders—just as fast as one policy pops up, it's smacked back down, and the clock is turned back. And the cycle continues.

A second major trade-off in legislating via executive order is the heightened scrutiny these orders face from the courts. Unlike laws passed by Congress and signed by the president, executive orders are not typically granted the same level of deference. This is because laws originate from the legislative body with the constitutional authority to draft and pass legislation, and they go through a process of public debate and compromise before becoming law. Executive orders skip those steps.

When a president issues an executive order, they're often stepping into territory traditionally reserved for Congress. This leaves the president open to challenges on both the substance of the order and the claim that they are usurping congressional power. Private organizations, state or local governments, or even individuals who disagree with the goals or effects of the executive order can argue in court that it's unconstitutional or that the president doesn't have the authority to take such action.

This scrutiny plays out in courtrooms across the country. For example, when President Trump issued an executive order to divert nearly $7 billion to build a border wall, a federal judge struck it down, emphasizing that "Congress's 'absolute' control over federal expenditures—even when that control may frustrate the desires of the Executive Branch regarding initiatives it views as important—is not a bug in our constitutional system. It is a feature of that system, and an essential one."[10] Similarly, when President Biden extended the eviction moratorium via executive order, he faced immediate legal challenges. The courts ultimately ruled against the administration, with one judge stating, "Our system does not permit agencies to act unlawfully even in pursuit of desirable ends."[11]

Despite the drawbacks, however, the phrase "In my first 100 days, I will . . ." has become a staple of modern presidential campaigns, with candidates outlining their plans to reverse their predecessor's executive orders as a means of signaling immediate change. Much of that action involves undoing the work of the previous administration.

And the cycle continues.

THE DOWNSIDES OF PRESIDENTIAL POWER GRABS

The use of unilateral executive actions to bypass the traditional and constitutional process—debate, compromise, and input from elected representatives—raises concerns about the concentration of power in the executive branch. This concern spans the ideological spectrum, though *when* politicians choose to care about it often depends on which party's president is holding the pen. For instance, Sen. Chuck Schumer (D-NY) complained in 2019, "It is our job here, in Congress, to limit executive overreach, to defend our core powers, to prevent a President—any President—from ignoring the will of Congress every time it fails to align with the will of the President. That is what the balance of powers is. That is what checks and balances is."[12] On the other side of the aisle, Sen. Ted Cruz (R-TX) remarked in 2014, "Of all the troubling aspects of the Obama presidency, none is more dangerous than his willingness to . . . enforce his own policies via executive fiat. The president's taste for unilateral action to circumvent Congress should concern every citizen, regardless of party or ideology."[13] The timing of their constitutional complaints wasn't a coincidence.

Today, the sentiment continues. Sen. Marsha Blackburn of Tennessee expressed it bluntly in a tweet aimed at the Biden administration: "@POTUS, you can't govern with a pen and a phone."[14] Presidential administrations—conservative and liberal—beg to differ.

The rest of us, however, often end up boosting the incentives for executive actions. When citizens grow accustomed to immediate, unilateral action from the executive branch, it changes the expectations for future presidents and how they go about meeting those expectations. Instead of viewing executive orders as a last resort, they are increasingly seen as the go-to method for implementing policy, particularly in a gridlocked political environment where laws via Congress are harder to come by. The media, in turn, amplifies this by highlighting the swift impact of executive orders, reinforcing the idea that strong leadership is synonymous with decisive executive action. The more presidents hear "The president just needs to . . . ," the more they will use their unilateral powers to satisfy the demands.

What's more, lawmakers aligned with the president's party may become more comfortable with this concentration of power, seeing it as an expedient way to achieve their policy goals without the messiness of legislative compromise—they see it as a quick way to get what they want right away. However, this acceptance can lead to a dangerous cycle where each successive president pushes the boundaries further, using executive orders not just to enforce existing laws but to effectively create new ones.

And the reach of presidential power grabs doesn't stop at domestic policy. The same pattern has extended into one of the most critical areas of government: war powers. The Constitution is clear—only Congress has the authority to declare war. Full stop.

The last time Congress officially declared war? 1942.

Yet President Reagan launched a military intervention in Grenada. President George H. W. Bush initiated military actions in Panama and Somalia. President Bill Clinton deployed military forces in Iraq, Haiti, Bosnia, Afghanistan, Sudan, and Kosovo. And Presidents Bush, Obama, Trump, and Biden carried out military operations in 19 countries all without a formal declaration of war from Congress. Even the wars in Vietnam and Korea—conflicts in which more than 100,000 American soldiers died—weren't technically wars because Congress didn't declare them as such. To get around that requirement, presidents from both parties have proven particularly frisky in branding their military operations as anything but, using phrases like police actions and peacekeeping missions.

Or they have relied on Authorizations for Use of Military Force (AUMFs) and stretched their authority far beyond anyone's wildest dreams. In simple terms, an AUMF is Congress's permission slip for the president, as commander in chief, to use military force, typically in a specific situation or against a particular enemy without a formal declaration of war. For example, following the 9/11 terrorist attacks, Congress passed the 2001 AUMF, giving the president the authority to use "all necessary and appropriate force" against those responsible for the attacks or anyone who harbored them. The following year, Congress approved the 2002 AUMF, allowing the president to use military action to "defend the national security of the United States against the ongoing threat posed by Iraq." Targeted authority—not a blank check.

Yeah, not so much. Republican and Democratic presidents ever since have stretched the AUMFs far beyond their original scope and with little to no additional congressional input. The AUMFs, passed over two decades prior and for specific purposes, provided presidents—at least in their eyes—the legal authority to carry out military operations all over the globe. And that's exactly what they've done in Syria, Yemen, the Philippines, and 16 other countries. The 2001 and 2002 AUMFs remain active.

So while the president's use of executive orders to shape domestic policy is certainly concerning, the expansion of presidential power into the realm of war is perhaps even more troubling. It's a trend that should give us all pause as we consider the balance of power in our government—and the role Congress is meant to play in ensuring that no single branch becomes too powerful. As Senate Majority Leader Chuck Schumer said, "Every year we keep these AUMFs on the books is another chance for a future administration to abuse them. War powers belong in the hands of Congress."[15]

Great sentiment, little follow-up.

To date, Congress has largely failed to check such important presidential overreaches. And lawmakers across the aisle will freely admit it. "This process has been the apotheosis of the problem of congressional abdication," Sen. Susan Collins said in a 2020 Senate floor speech. "Through the refusal to exercise war powers or relinquishing the power of the purse, selective oversight, and an unwillingness to check emergency declarations designed to skirt Congress, we have failed. We have failed time and again. We, as a legislative branch, cannot continue to cede authority to the Executive."[16]

She's right.

The more normalized presidential power grabs become, the more we risk moving away from the constitutional framework that was designed to prevent any one branch of government from becoming too powerful. If left unchecked, these trends could fundamentally alter the balance of power in the US government, making the president not just the enforcer of laws but a primary author of laws as well.

This raises serious concerns about the long-term implications for American democracy. If a sidelined (or complicit) legislative branch and an ever-more-dominant executive become the new normal, we might one day find ourselves questioning whether we've traded the careful deliberation of representative democracy for the quick, fragile fixes of autocracy.

Power, Promise, and Presidential Reality

Look, I get it. I was constantly in awe as I walked through the White House, sat in on meetings in the Oval Office, and flew with the president on Air Force One and Marine One—memories I'll never forget. In my work, I saw firsthand how the allure of presidential power often overshadows the complex reality of its limitations. And as a result, we, the public, are drawn to the grand promises of "I alone can fix it" language—a sort of political catnip that convinces us the president can single-handedly solve every problem. But the truth is far less straightforward. The president's ability to enact laws, implement policies, and even lead in a meaningful way is tethered to a web of constraints, many of which are out of his control.

As citizens, we must be wary of the rhetoric that positions the president as a one-man (or one-woman) fix-it shop. When a president's platform is heavy on reversing the other guy's work and light on collaboration with Congress, a red flag is waving. When he promises immediate results, "executive order" alarm bells—including all their trade-offs—should go off. A president's success—or failure—is not just a solo performance; it's an ensemble act that requires the cooperation of the legislative branch, the judiciary, and yes, even the will of the people. When a candidate promises sweeping laws, remember that these are promises tangled in a mess of constitutional checks and political realities. We have to stop falling for it. It only fuels our cynicism when he inevitably fails to follow through on all his promises.

At the same time, we have to understand that presidents—of both parties—will always look for ways to skirt the system and get things done on their own terms. So, then, what happens when the president overreaches, which is all but guaranteed? In today's polarized climate, we already know the opposition party is going to be crying foul. But that's not enough for meaningful accountability—the president's own party holds the most power in keeping him in check.

Unfortunately, all too often, we see a dangerous acquiescence from a president's political allies, who find it politically expedient to let overreach slide. They excuse the behavior, try to explain it away even though they know better. This is not just about giving the president a free pass; it's about eroding the very institutions that are supposed to safeguard our democracy. When one party allows their president to stretch the limits of executive power, it sets a precedent for the other party to do the same when they get their turn in the White House. The result? A never-ending game of "whataboutism" where the rules are constantly bent until they're broken beyond repair.

The lesson here is simple: If we want our presidents to stay in their constitutional lane, it's up to us, and especially our elected leaders, to hold them accountable. Whether it's investigating wrongdoing or reining in executive orders, oversight requires good faith from all sides. Just as Nixon's fall from grace came when his own party turned against him, today's presidents must know that their power is not absolute and that their actions will be scrutinized—by friends and foes alike.

Finally, as tempting as it is to fixate on the drama unfolding in Washington, don't forget about the politics closer to home. Your state and local governments are the ones debating the issues that hit closest to your everyday life, and they're often more responsive to your input than the far-off federal behemoth. By turning your attention to these levels of government, you'll find that you have not only more access to decision-makers but also a greater ability to influence outcomes. And who knows, you might even discover that your local school board meeting is where the real action is—at least compared to the latest Beltway brouhaha.

Yes, the president may wield significant power, but it's far from unchecked. By understanding the constraints of the office, holding our leaders accountable, and engaging locally, we can ensure that our democracy remains strong, balanced, and resilient.

True power in a democracy lies not in the hands of one person, one leader, but in the vigilance of many who dare to demand better.

"Members of Congress Don't Do Anything"

Rep. Derek Kilmer

As members of Congress, it's strange being part of an organization that is less popular than head lice, colonoscopies, and the rock band Nickelback (apologies, Nickelback fans). We constantly hear the dismay and frustration from constituents across the political spectrum. Our family members hear it from neighbors at the grocery store. Even my kids have heard it in the school cafeteria: "What the heck do members of Congress do anyway? Why don't they spend less time posturing for the media and more time doing their jobs? When was the last time they made any actual laws? And why do they need so much 'recess'?"

Between the government shutdowns, partisan standoffs, and occasional scandals (here's looking at you, George Santos), it often looks to the public like members of Congress just don't do anything beyond bickering with their colleagues. Maybe it looks that way to you, too.

Much of that unpopularity is well earned. Indeed, Congress—as an institution—has persistently punched below its weight.

But while some of the discontent is earned, there are also misperceptions and myths that drive much of the grumpiness directed at Congress. Big and—from the vantage point of someone who has experienced the dysfunction firsthand for over a decade—unhelpful ones. These misconceptions fuel much more than kitchen-table conversations and jokes at the expense of members of Congress. They add up to an exasperation that often drives people to throw up their hands and disengage entirely. If you don't see any (or enough) action on the issues you care about most, you might conclude that the members must be wasting their time. You hear Congress is on yet another recess and presume the members are off vacationing in Cabo (seriously, that was only Sen. Ted Cruz, and it was just that one time).

And believing that, you might deem Congress a lost cause and decide to spend your energies elsewhere. If your representatives aren't even doing their jobs, then why should you wear out your keyboard and speed dial asking them to address bigger issues that matter to you?

I can understand that, believe me. But stay with me.

When I was a kid, my dad used to say there was a difference between being busy and being productive. It is undeniable that Congress is not as productive as it should be (or as any of us want it to be). But it is also true that members of Congress actually *do* a lot. The truth is that the vast majority of lawmakers I know work 70-plus-hour weeks, and even more when we're back home in the district. And it's not just busywork. A lot of that work is, in fact, quite productive. You just don't see or hear about it (Matt Fuller's media chapter in this book will tell you more about why).

The confusion lies in the fact that what we're doing with all those hours is not exactly what you expect we'd be doing. In fact, the job of being a member of Congress isn't even exactly what you may think it is. It's really several jobs at once. Making laws is obviously one of them—but only one of them. We are simultaneously lawmakers, representatives, constituent services providers, communicators, and overseers of the public and private sectors, as well as members of a broader political party. The demands are relentless and impossible to fulfill. There literally isn't enough time to do them all.

But I'm not here to lament lost sleep or overwhelming demands (cue the voters' tiny violins). I'm here to let you in behind the curtain, to show you what members of Congress actually do all day—and how you could help us do it better.

In the pages that follow, I'll do my best to give folks the straight skinny on life in Congress, addressing the six most common misperceptions that I hear (other than the one that I get my congressional salary and health insurance for life—also NOT TRUE!) about how we do (or don't do) our jobs.

Armed with that inside knowledge, I hope you'll be ready to shed the myth of congressional do-nothingness and see the discouraging headlines within the bigger picture of genuine action by your representatives. All of which equips you to spot the levers you can and should pull as constituents to help make Congress, and our government more generally, work a little bit better.

Misperception #1: Members of Congress Barely Pass Any Laws

I will confess at the jump that, to my chagrin, Congress hasn't passed laws on some really important things that require action. From immigration to school shootings, I can give you a long list of matters on which I'd like to see Congress do more.

At the same time, what voters perceive as a "do-nothing Congress" actually gets a fair number of legislative pucks into the nets.

When the Covid-19 pandemic struck, there was real and justifiable fear from folks in my district. I heard from small business owners who were unsure how their businesses would survive. I heard from physicians who couldn't get personal protective equipment and whose hospitals were overrun. I heard from people who had lost their jobs and from teachers and school administrators trying to figure out how to reopen and address learning loss.

Had Congress done nothing, the consequences would have been catastrophic. Instead, Congress quickly passed legislation to help small businesses stay afloat; extend unemployment benefits for folks who lost their jobs; provide assistance to state, local, and tribal governments as well as school districts; and deploy resources to medical providers.

Congress passed four separate relief bills, with varying provisions and amounts of funding attached.

But a review of media coverage shows far more stories about the delays in negotiating these bills than the actual contents of the bills themselves. There was more coverage of gridlock than grants. More of bickering than benefits. More of standoffs than small business assistance. (I'd keep going, but I've run out of alliteration.)

And Congress doesn't just legislate in response to a crisis. It also occasionally addresses big problems that, simply put, need to be solved.

For example, after years of talk about infrastructure, Congress finally passed an infrastructure law in 2021. That legislation—supported by overwhelming majorities of Democrats and Republicans—resulted in the most significant investment in roads and bridges since the creation of the interstate highway system. It provided funding to get rid of lead pipes and develop clean water projects. It helped connect people to the internet.

Or how about the 2022 passage of the Inflation Reduction Act, which empowered the federal government to negotiate for lower prescription drug prices under Medicare for the first time, reduced health-care costs, and invested $783 billion in clean energy and climate measures (the largest investment in climate action in our nation's history)?

Or the 2022 CHIPS and Science Act, a bipartisan law that made historic investments in domestic manufacturing and scientific research?

Or the 2022 Honoring Our PACT Act, which expanded health benefits for military veterans exposed to toxic substances while serving?

These significant laws all passed within a three-year period. That's a significant record of accomplishment.

And yet a Gallup survey taken prior to the 2022 general election put congressional job approval at just 21 percent—among the lowest numbers on record since Gallup began asking the question.

What's going on here?

Undoubtedly, some of the discontent reflects a real failure to make progress on some big issues, such as immigration reform. (For an explanation of those shortcomings, check out my colleague Representative Pascrell's chapter on how perverse incentives have made gridlock electorally and politically rational.)

That said, some of the frustration reflects the TV version of what happens on Capitol Hill. More often than not, voters hear from the media about gridlock and dysfunction—not progress. Even when the media covers new laws, they tend to provide more coverage of laws that spark political disagreement. Indeed, research by Mary Layton Atkison found that an important law is likely to get five times more media coverage if it's a close vote than if it gets strong bipartisan support.[1]

Some bills can be bipartisan and get pretty much zero attention. Let me give you an example of one I worked on that found a fun path to bipartisanship . . . and zero media coverage. I had a college friend who worked for a nonprofit helping low-income individuals build assets. He told me his nonprofit had been working with a Harvard economist and had discovered some challenging truths.

First, their research found that asset-poor people often didn't have savings accounts. And even if they had savings accounts, asset-poor people often didn't make deposits. Second, they found that asset-poor people disproportionately gambled and played the lottery. And third, they found that if you could somehow take the excitement of gambling and playing the lottery and apply it to saving money, you could influence savings behavior. So they came up with an idea called prize-linked savings accounts.

The concept was simple: Every time you made a deposit, you would earn a chance for cash prizes. Your money would never be at risk. Rather, the financial institution would use some of its marketing budget and, rather than running ads on radio or TV, offer cash prizes.

Their research turned up two key insights about this. One, offering cash prizes for savings deposits was an amazingly effective tool for helping people build assets. People were far more likely to open this kind of account and make deposits into it.

And two, it was completely illegal.

But prize-linked savings accounts weren't illegal for any particular reason. They were just uncharted territory that existing regulations hadn't anticipated. So my office worked with a coalition of organizations and wrote a bill to allow these kinds of accounts.

To advance the legislation, I needed a cosponsor—ideally a Republican on the Financial Services Committee (which oversees banking) who could help usher it through. So I looked at the committee roster and saw a guy named Tom Cotton from Arkansas who had worked for the same management consulting firm that I worked for after grad school. Tom (now a senator) is an incredibly conservative guy. But I figured I'd give it a shot.

I remember approaching him on the House floor. I said, "Tom—we both used to work at the same firm." And then I gave him the whole pitch: "Harvard economist. Amazing research. Really impactful. Helps people save money!"

When I was done with my pitch, Tom stared at me silently for about 10 seconds.

When someone stares at you for 10 seconds, it can be the most romantic moment of your life—or the most awkward. In this instance, it was the latter.

But after this silence, Tom said, "So what you're saying is . . . you'd like to introduce legislation to eliminate unnecessarily onerous financial regulations that prohibit financial institutions from offering innovative products that would enable people to be more self-sufficient and less reliant on the government."

And I thought about it for a second and said, "Sure!" I mean, for me it was about helping poor people save money. But if it meant he'd be willing to work with me on it, I had no problem with him signing on for those reasons.

It was a Kilmer-Cotton bill in the House and a Sherrod Brown–Elizabeth Warren–Jerry Moran bill in the Senate. It passed both chambers and was signed into law by President Barack Obama. And now financial institutions across the country offer prize-linked savings accounts that help asset-poor people build assets.

That legislative effort never made cable news (I'm not even sure it made the *Tacoma News Tribune* in my district), but it was an example of good legislation—and of the little things that Democrats and Republicans do together.

Even legislation that is maligned as a misuse of time—like legislation to rename post offices—can be meaningful. In 2020, I passed a law to rename the post office in Bremerton, Washington, after John Henry Turpin, the first African American chief petty officer in the history of the US Navy (and a longtime Bremerton resident). When we held the ceremony and placed a plaque in that old post office, more than 100 residents showed up, including leaders of the NAACP and other civil rights organizations who celebrated a trailblazing leader in Black history. A stroke of a pen in DC didn't feel like a waste of time to the people in Bremerton or his family.

In other words, despite seemingly endless examples of dysfunction, members of Congress do actually pass some laws. Not as many as we'd all like, to be sure. But buried beneath the conflict-ridden front pages, signs of legislative life can be found for those who just know to look.

Misperception #2: When Members of Congress Are in DC, All They Do Is Raise Money for Their Reelection Campaigns

As was the case with misperception #1, there's a little bit of truth to this assertion. In fact, if Casey Burgat had asked, I would've happily written a book with him about the problems with our campaign finance system. (I could share a stunning number of fundraising jokes with you—but it will cost you.) According to the campaign finance reform advocates at Issue One, candidates in toss-up races have to raise $15,000 *per day* to have a fighting chance in their election. So it's safe to say that—particularly for members in swing seats—far too much time is dedicated to fundraising.

Having said that, the notion that representatives are solely spending their days dialing for dollars fails to account for the other activities members of Congress engage in. In addition to being lawmakers, we are representatives who must speak to and on behalf of our constituents. To do this well—and to ward off potential complaints that a lawmaker has lost touch with his constituents—members must constantly meet with citizens, hear their plights and dreams, and turn those disparate interests into tangible results. We host town halls, meet with stakeholders and experts, and communicate our policy goals in local and national media.

Often that's through legislation, but other times, it's community-level work as constituent service advocates. This means helping veterans access their hard-earned benefits, assisting Social Security applicants through cumbersome red tape, and responding to the thousands and thousands of messages from voters who rightfully expect a response from the representatives who work for them.

Don't believe me? Let me throw some statistics at you.

My office, for example, responded to more than 130,000 emails, calls, and letters; attended more than 800 meetings and local events; and resolved nearly 1,800 constituent pleas for help—in 2022 alone. And not an email or letter with my name on it went out without my review and approval. I personally attend 5–10 events in the district pretty much every single day I'm home. And before you develop another misperception, let me point out that those stats (which should be on the back of my baseball card) are pretty standard for me. I'm a busy guy whether it's an election year or not.

The to-do list doesn't stop there. There is also the constitutional duty to conduct oversight of the executive branch and nefarious activities within the private sector. For example, when I met with navy leadership to understand why they shuttered the labor and delivery services at my region's naval hospital, I was fighting for my constituents. When I asked Defense Department leadership about the decision, I recounted a meeting I'd had with a female service member who had suffered a miscarriage because of the inadequacy of services in our region. Though I wasn't "passing a law," I was trying to hold decision-makers accountable and make change for the people I represent.

In addition, each member sits on an average of more than five committees and subcommittees, each generally meeting at least weekly to debate and amend legislation, hear from expert witnesses, and root out waste, fraud, and abuse in public spending.

The sum total is a cyclone of a schedule that barely leaves time for sleeping or eating, let alone fundraising.

For the sake of illustration, I give you my calendar on Thursday, March 23, 2023, a day I was in DC:

7:00 a.m.: Wake up and get rolling. Most days my alarm buzzes at 6:00 a.m., but on the 23rd, I had a later-than-usual start. I generally eat some granola with blueberries and pound two cups of coffee (caffeine helps me handle the three-hour time difference when I'm in DC).

8:00 a.m.: Walk to the Longworth House Office Building.

8:30 a.m.: Call with one of my colleagues. I kicked off with a conversation with a colleague on the Appropriations Committee, giving them a heads-up about questions I'd be asking in a subcommittee hearing on health services for military service members.

9:00 a.m.: Meet with the leaders of a port in my district. One of the most important parts of my job is hearing from my constituents. In my office, we try to prioritize constituent meetings. In other words, if you flew all the way from Washington state to meet with me in DC, then I'm going to do everything I can to make time for you. In this meeting, we discussed efforts to secure federal funds for a new terminal (which our port successfully got!).

9:15 a.m.: Meet with the head of a high school skills center from my district (and her son). We had the chance to catch up on some of the workforce training the school was providing. And the principal's son really liked all the Star Wars PEZ dispensers in my office. Nerds unite.

9:30 a.m.: Walk briskly to the Rayburn Building for a meeting of the Interior & Environment Subcommittee. On this day, I had three subcommittee meetings all scheduled roughly between 9:30 and noon. I do a lot of brisk walking when I'm expected to be in three places at once.

9:35 a.m.: Attend Interior & Environment Subcommittee hearing. At my first of three hearings that day, we heard from the leadership of the US Forest Service. The Forest Service is tasked with managing forests across our nation, including the Olympic National Forest in my district. On the Olympic Peninsula, we aren't getting what we need from the Forest Service to keep forests healthy and support our mill infrastructure. I asked the agency's chief about his plans to address these problems. I would've liked to stay and hear more from the Forest Service chief, but I was also expected to be in two other hearings at the same time, so . . .

9:55 a.m.: Walk briskly (a.k.a. run up three flights of stairs) to the Defense Subcommittee hearing.

10:00 a.m.: Attend Defense Subcommittee hearing. Recent changes to the Military Health System have resulted in downsizing several military treatment facilities, including Naval Hospital Bremerton. As mentioned, the closure of labor and delivery services has come at an extraordinary cost. This is where I asked Defense Secretary Lloyd Austin and Chairman of the Joint Chiefs General Mark Milley how they plan to improve health care for service members in my region. When I was done with my question, I would've liked to stay and hear more from our military leaders, but I had yet another subcommittee meeting at the same time. So . . .

10:58 a.m.: Walk somewhat briskly a few doors down. Thankfully, my next subcommittee meeting was right nearby, so I didn't have to risk pulling a hammy.

11:00 a.m.: Attend Energy & Water Subcommittee hearing. For my final meeting in the subcommittee trifecta, we met with Secretary of Energy Jennifer Granholm. I represent the Department of Energy's only Marine and Coastal Research Laboratory. The marine energy research lab in Sequim, Washington, plays a critical role in driving our regional economy and conducting research focused on confronting climate change. I asked Secretary Granholm a question to better understand her views on the role of water-related energy (and to make sure she knew how to pronounce "Sequim").

12:30 p.m.: Attend New Democrat Coalition Mental Health and Substance Use Disorder lunch. After the hearing, I rushed to the Capitol Visitor Center for a meeting focused on mental health and substance issues. The New Democrats are a coalition of roughly 100 pro-innovation, pro-growth, centrist Democrats. Over lunch, we met with the director of the Office of National Drug Control Policy, the director of the National Institute on Drug Abuse, and the assistant secretary in charge of the Substance Abuse and Mental Health Services Administration. I raised a specific concern with them about ensuring that our service members and veterans are getting the care they need when they need it.

1:15 p.m.: Meet with Fawn Sharp, vice president of the Quinault Indian Nation and president of the National Congress of American Indians. Then, I ran back to the Longworth Building to meet with a leader of one of the 12 Native American tribes in my district. The Quinault Indian Nation is experiencing sea-level rise and pursuing federal resources to move their village to higher ground. Vice President Sharp and I discussed the challenges the tribe was facing in accessing those resources.

1:30 p.m.–2:15 p.m.: VOTES. I dashed to the Capitol for a series of procedural votes related to an education bill. (Before most major bills, we have to vote on a "rule" that governs debate and consideration of amendments. This may seem small, but I try not to miss votes of any kind.)

2:15 p.m.–3:00 p.m.: Three more meetings. I then walked briskly back to the Longworth Building and met with the Bipartisan Policy Center, my policy staff, and a group of professors advocating for research funding.

3:00 p.m.: House Administration Committee Oversight hearing. Then I ran up one floor and down the hall to the House Administration Committee Room for a hearing in which we discussed Congress's response to the Covid pandemic.

4:00 p.m.–5:00 p.m.: Four constituent meetings. I walked briskly back to my office for a flurry of meetings with folks from our district. It started with advocates for early learning from Tacoma and Bremerton with whom I discussed the importance of adequately compensating Head Start teachers. Then I met with leaders from an innovative Tacoma manufacturer, board members and staff from housing authorities in our region pushing for affordable housing funding, and leaders from our state Conservation Commission. If you're doing the math, four meetings in one hour means 15-minute meetings. That may not feel like a lot of time, but I've discovered that you can cover a lot of terrain in that time—and make sure people feel heard.

5:15 p.m.: Speak to the Pacific Northwest Waterways Association. Then it was a brisk walk to the basement of the Capitol building, where I gave a speech to the Pacific Northwest Waterways Association and took some of their questions. After several years in this job, I now have some good jokes about ports and waterways (but I only tell them after I get a little pier pressure).

5:30 p.m.–7:15 p.m.: More votes. Then, I walked briskly back to the House floor and did some more voting. Usually, my staff also sends me to the House floor with a hefty "to-do list" that often involves inviting colleagues to cosponsor certain bills.

7:45 p.m.: Back to my apartment. I ended my day with a quick dinner and then spent some time returning phone calls from folks in my district and preparing for the next day.

10:00 p.m.–midnight. According to my phone, I walked 22,323 steps (briskly) on this day (including spending an hour on the elliptical at 10:00 p.m.). Then I cleaned up, called my kiddos, and hit the hay.

Honestly, this was a pretty average day for me—and you'll note not a *single* hour devoted to fundraising.

To be clear—and as you'll read in the campaign finance chapter—there are certainly members that have to do *a lot* of fundraising. New members (who usually start with nearly empty campaign accounts) and members from swing districts who are fighting for their lives have far greater demands to raise money. Indeed, research by Issue One found that the average member of Congress who stood for reelection in November 2022 raised about $2,800 per day for their campaigns. Freshman members raised an average of about $3,900 per day. And incumbents in races rated a "toss-up" by the Cook Political Report raised about $7,200 per day.

What does that mean?

Well, if you're in one of those toss-up seats, you spend far more time raising money than the typical House member. That means more time dialing for dollars and attending fundraising events (e.g., receptions where you chat and collect checks over breakfast tacos, lukewarm lunches, or in the evening, wine). It means your days involve a lot less of the committee hearings and constituent meetings that I mentioned above. Instead, your schedule builds in a lot more time for entertaining people at fundraisers and being a telemarketer. That's a messed up system and a sad trade-off.

For average members, though, while fundraising is a part of life, it's not omnipresent the way it's assumed. I typically attend a fundraising lunch every week or two (generally attended by a handful of supporters). Or a reception where I snack on room-temp appetizers and kibitz with supporters.

And in general, an incumbent (or a member of his or her campaign team) will need to make some calls inviting people to those events. That can take several hours per week, but it's not the dozen or more hours facing our most electorally endangered colleagues.

You may notice, however, that one thing besides fundraising is on my schedule in force. I had three subcommittee hearings—all with senior administration officials testifying—at the exact same time. This leads to another misperception.

Misperception #3: Members of Congress Often Skip Their Committee Meetings and Miss Votes

Unfortunately, my clone didn't make it to work on March 23, 2023, so my seat in the subcommittee room was often vacant.

Was I playing hooky? Was I just being lazy?

No and no.

I was at one of my two other committee hearings.

If this sounds like a bad way of doing business, you're right.

While committee rooms are meant to be the places where members of Congress learn, discuss thorny issues, and develop policy, the scheduling mess has meant that they are more often the places where members airdrop in right before it's their turn on the dais, make a five-minute speech that they can put up on their social media accounts, and then run to their next committee hearing. This is why if you flip on C-SPAN (bless you), you'll often see committee hearings with many empty chairs.

It doesn't need to be this way.

The first problem is that Congress simply isn't in Washington, DC, enough. In 2022, Congress was in session for 65 full days and 66 travel days. Figure 1 illustrates what the congressional calendar looks like in an average month.

What does that mean exactly?

Well, most weeks, members of Congress fly in on a Monday or Tuesday and have votes at 6:30 p.m. The next two days, they have a mix of committee hearings and votes on the House floor. And on Thursday or Friday, Congress holds floor votes sometime between 10:00 a.m.

Figure 1: Congressional calendar in an average month

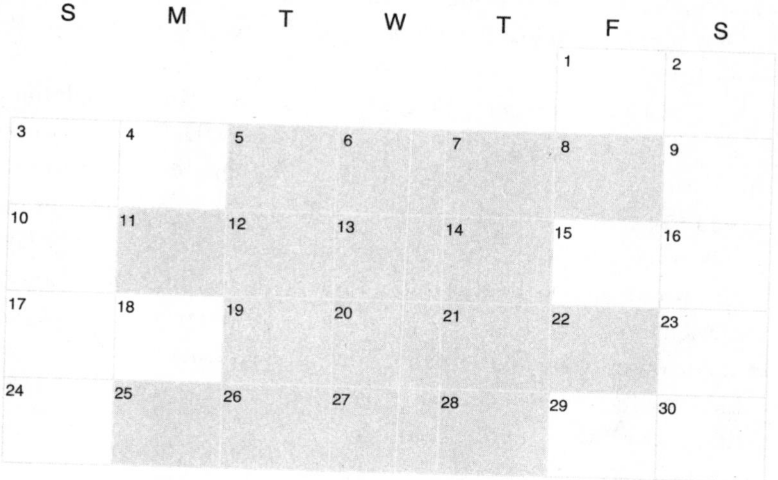

S	M	T	W	T	F	S
					1	2
3	4	5	6	7	8	9
10	11	12	13	14	15	16
17	18	19	20	21	22	23
24	25	26	27	28	29	30

and noon, after which members head back to their districts until the next week. That happens about 30 weeks out of the year!

What are the consequences of that pattern?

For one, members of Congress often spend more time with flight attendants (who are usually delightful) than in committee hearings. Additionally, because committee hearings generally only happen on the full days, you're often trying to pack 10 pounds of committee hearings into a 3-pound bag.

But there's a second problem as well. There's currently no good method of de-conflicting committee hearings. As much as every member hates this schedule and knows firsthand how it prohibits productivity, we still haven't fixed it.

So how do we solve this? For one, there would be value in having more full days and fewer travel days. Staying in DC one extra day per week might be a bummer for my kiddos, but it would be a boon to congressional productivity.

Another proposal is to use technology to deconflict hearings where possible. A central portal could help committees try to schedule around potential conflicts for their members.

But there would also be a benefit in putting guardrails around when certain committees could hold their hearings. After all, every high school in America has figured out how to arrange scheduling to avoid conflicts (because my kids can't take two classes at the same time). Most members—perhaps not committee chairs—would love a schedule in which certain committees could *only* meet on Tuesdays in the morning and other committees could *only* meet on Wednesday in the afternoon. While this might limit some flexibility for a committee chair scheduling a hearing, it would mean far more members of their committee could actually show up. And when they did, they could actually stay in their seats—listening and learning rather than walking (briskly) to another hearing.

Misperception #4: When Congress Isn't in Session, Members of Congress Are on Vacation

The term "congressional recess" might lead people to imagine their members of Congress swinging on the monkey bars or playing freeze tag (though given the ages of many members, this could cause a concerning number of broken hips). In recent years, the time between DC sessions has become known instead as the "district work period."

That's more like it. And I want to emphasize that middle word—WORK.

The district I have the honor of representing includes more than 710,000 people and covers just under 7,000 square miles! It's my responsibility to make sure I am representing people in every corner of the district. That's meant showing up in every nook and cranny of it. As a general practice, if more than eight of my constituents are gathered somewhere, I'll be there.

Sometimes, my schedule involves reacting to invitations. For example, when the head of the Asia Pacific Cultural Center in my district invites me to speak at a groundbreaking for more affordable housing, I'm there! When the pastor at Emmanuel AME Church invites me to join his parishioners on Sunday morning, I'm there! When the local Rotary Club or Kiwanis Club asks for a legislative update, I'm there!

Other times, my schedule is filled with proactive events that my team and I have scheduled. We use the district work period to hold town hall meetings. We pull together roundtables of veterans' groups. We visit local businesses to learn about the challenges they face (we call those visits "Kilmer at Your Company," which I think is pretty catchy). And we find opportunities to highlight legislation we are working on or projects we are pursuing funding for in the Appropriations Committee.

Again, the details of an individual day may say it best. So I give you August 10, 2023:

5:00 a.m.: Wake up. I get up early to get in some exercise, and then—just as I do in DC—drink a couple of cups of coffee, eat some breakfast (always granola and blueberries), and hit the road.

6:00 a.m.: Drive to Bainbridge Island. As a resident of Gig Harbor, Washington, I end up often driving an hour or two to get to my constituents. Sometimes it can take three or four (or more!) hours.

7:45 a.m.: Meet with the Bainbridge Island Oatmeal Club. To start the day, I joined the folks at the Bainbridge Island Oatmeal Club for a working breakfast to update them on the goings-on in Congress. Yes, this is a real club, and yes, there is oatmeal. And yes—it's fantastic.

9:00 a.m.: Drive to Port Orchard while calling with constituents. Often, when someone from my region contacts my office about a problem with their VA benefits or their small business is in crisis, I reach out personally to hear their story and see how I can lend a hand. Sometimes that happens when I'm in transit.

10:00 a.m.: Meet with one of our regional community health centers. It was National Community Health Center Week, so I visited a community health center to celebrate the important work they do to provide access to primary care and mental health services in my neck of the woods.

11:00 a.m.: Speak to one of our local chambers of commerce. I was the guest speaker at the monthly meeting of the South Kitsap Chamber of Commerce. I pounded a burger when I got there, gave a legislative update, and then thanked the chamber and local small business leaders for their efforts to keep and grow jobs in our region.

12:30 p.m.: Drive to Bremerton.

1:00 p.m.: Meet with Kitsap Homes of Compassion. I stopped by this awesome organization that works to provide safe, affordable, permanent housing through comprehensive support services for those experiencing homelessness or housing insecurity. They took me on a tour of one of their homes.

2:30 p.m.: Conference call with a hearing aid clinic and audiology practice from my district. These two companies provide hearing aids and services in Kitsap County to primarily nonmilitary federal employees with work-related hearing loss. I heard their concerns about new rules related to hearing aid reimbursement.

3:00 p.m.: Speak at the Veterans History Project. Next up, my office partnered with the Library of Congress to give local veterans an opportunity to tell their stories. Created in 2000 by Congress, the Veterans History Project provides veterans with a platform to share and preserve their personal narratives about their time in uniform and help Americans understand military service and its importance to our country's history. That day, I got to interview an army veteran in front of a room full of community members who had signed up to record the stories of local veterans.

5:30 p.m.: Head home.

6:00 p.m.: Chow time! During the summer, I make it a priority to have dinner with my kiddos as much as possible. On tonight's menu: spaghetti and meatballs!

7:00 p.m.: Catch up on letters. If you call or email and ask for a response back, you'll get one. Today, I wrote a few letters to constituents who wrote about everything from broadband access to affordable housing to restoring salmon populations.

10:00 p.m.: Bedtime. That's a wrap! Time for bed. Up early the next day for another full day!

I could've given plenty of other examples. Like on August 11, when I started my day with a tour of the US Geological Service's Marrowstone Marine Field Station to learn about their Puget Sound recovery efforts; met with community leaders at the Port of Port Townsend's Boat Haven Main Breakwater Replacement Project, one of my office's federal funding requests; and ended the day with a visit to the Port Townsend Shipwrights Co-Op, a local full-service boat shop.

What's the goal of all these meetings? A cynic might say these are all photo ops to help a member of Congress get reelected. The truth is that there are a lot of reasons for a member's in-district meetings and events.

Sometimes, the purpose of these events is to listen and learn. Sitting down with folks grappling with local challenges informs the policy work I do and the votes I take. When we visit a local project for which I am pursuing federal funding, it often gives me useful information that can make me a better advocate for that funding.

Sometimes, it's to develop relationships with partners. When I sit down with a city council or tribal council, it's because I want to understand their challenges—and want them to know me well enough to reach out when they need help.

Sometimes, it's to inform. When I meet with a local Rotary Club or chamber of commerce, it's aligned with my commitment to being available, accessible, and accountable to my constituents. In nearly every meeting I have, I remind constituents that they can reach out to my office for casework help (more on that below).

Sometimes, it's to say thank you. I visit local businesses to say, "Thanks for doing business in our community." I visit local nonprofits to say, "Thanks for contributing to the vitality of our community and helping us solve problems together."

Misperception #5: When Members of Congress Don't Pass Bills, They're Ineffectual

Inevitably, during a reelection campaign, a member of Congress will hear an attack from an opponent saying something along the lines of "Congressman X is ineffective. He's only passed two bills in the last five years." This is your opportunity to spot a myth in action.

Now realize for a moment that in the entire calendar year 2023, Congress only passed 27 bills into law.

That does indeed sound abysmal. And it's a sign of legislative dysfunction. (Though the bipartisanship chapter in this book explains why the numbers don't tell the whole story.)

But is it a sign your individual member is ineffective? Not necessarily.

While passing a stand-alone bill (including one focused on helping asset-poor people save money) can be a big accomplishment, the reality is that there are a lot of ways in which a representative can demonstrate effectiveness—and spotting them can help us all be more thoughtful judges of our elected officials' job performance. Here are a few of the big ones.

LEGISLATING

The largest employer in my district is a naval shipyard that services submarines and aircraft carriers, employing thousands of workers. On occasion, those workers get sent overseas, most commonly to Yokosuka, Japan, where they maintain our forward-deployed ships. I learned that when American workers went to Japan and worked overtime, they weren't getting paid overtime. And as we dug into it, it became clear that fixing this problem would require an act of Congress.

If you search the record of bills signed into law, you won't find one entitled "The Paying Shipyard Workers Overtime When They Work Overtime Overseas Act." But I did change the law to get the workers the pay they deserved.

How?

I fought to get the change as part of a much larger bill—the National Defense Authorization Act.

Over the years, I've managed to pass significant legislation as part of defense bills, tax bills, and spending bills. It has involved working directly with committees and advocating for priorities to be included. And these successes will never show up on a scorecard.

Each year, Congress also passes spending bills (almost always far later than it's supposed to). But those spending bills provide an avenue for directing funding to programs and projects to benefit constituents. For instance, during my tenure in Congress, I've more than doubled the amount of funding directed to the recovery of my region's most iconic body of water, Puget Sound. In recent years, through "community project funding" (what used to be called "earmarks"), I've secured funding for affordable housing projects, investments to help coastal tribes move to higher ground, economic development projects to revitalize downtowns, and public safety upgrades.

CONDUCTING OVERSIGHT

Members of Congress can often make big changes simply by conducting oversight of the executive branch. Asking questions—in public hearings or letters to agencies—can often yield significant outcomes.

For example, I heard from a rural hospital in my district, Olympic Medical Center (which also happens to be the hospital in which I was born). Several years ago, the Center for Medicare and Medicaid Services (CMS) established a new rule known as "site-neutral payment policy" that significantly cut Medicare payment rates for hospitals that provide care through a network of off-campus clinics. These cuts stood to slash Olympic Medical Center's reimbursement by nearly $50 million over 10 years. Consequently, the hospital announced it would be unable to expand primary care and surgical services in a nearby town, make critical investments in medical equipment, and hire new staff.

For four years, I had meeting after meeting with CMS. I introduced them to hospital officials to hear them explain the consequences of the change in policy. I wrote letters and made calls to reverse the policy and restore payment rates to ensure the hospital could provide quality care.

Four years later, CMS rolled back the cuts for rural safety net providers like Olympic Medical Center. That new rule has meant big things for the bottom line of that rural hospital—and may actually help keep its lights on. And it didn't require passing a bill.

CONVENING

Members of Congress can also play an important convening role. For example, after decades of conflict, I pulled together leaders from the timber industry and the conservation community to figure out how to manage the national forest in my district in a way that works better for our economy and our environment.

In the years that followed the creation of the Olympic Forest Collaborative, we've been able to move forward with multiple timber sales designed to responsibly increase harvest levels in the Olympic National Forest. We've also been able to avoid persistent litigation. And it didn't require passing a bill.

SOLVING CASEWORK PROBLEMS

Half the staff in my district office does what we call casework. In a nutshell, casework involves solving problems on behalf of constituents. We've worked with dozens and dozens of military veterans who have been denied the benefits or recognition that they deserve. In fact, one of the best days I've had in this job was getting to pin a Purple Heart on a man who was wounded during the Vietnam War. When he reached out to my office, he explained that getting his Purple Heart would help him heal some of the wounds people couldn't see. When my office looked into the situation, we learned that he was injured on a classified mission in Laos. Over a series of months, we got his mission declassified and got the military to review his injuries, and I got to pin a Purple Heart on him in front of his family and friends.

We've even brought people back from the dead! We had a constituent who told our office that Medicare had qualified her as "deceased" (and, as it turns out, it's really hard to get your health care when they think you're dead). We worked with that constituent and managed to bring her back to life! And none of this very tangible assistance resulted in new laws.

Misperception #6: Congress Just Keeps Getting Worse—and There's No Hope on the Horizon

I admit I still have hope for Congress. Not a blind belief, like Kevin Bacon yelling at rioters in *Animal House*, that "All is well." Not a Pollyannaish view that, despite evidence to the contrary, there are no reasons to be concerned. But hope.

Why?

Well, for one reason, I've actually seen some progress!

A little over five years ago, then-Speaker Nancy Pelosi called me to lead a committee called the Select Committee on the Modernization of Congress, which—based on the name—sounded like it was the IT help desk. But it became known as the Fix Congress Committee. It had a simple mission—make Congress work better for the American people.

The committee covered a lot of issues that have fueled the unpopularity of Congress and hindered progress. The committee went to work on some of the topics I touched on in this chapter—such as the congressional calendar and committee hearing conflicts.

We analyzed—and made recommendations—related to other areas as well. For example, we looked at how Congress can better use technology to solve problems. Recognizing the important role that staff plays, we made a bevy of recommendations to help Congress recruit, retain, and develop staff and promote staff diversity so that the folks who work in Congress are representative of our country.

We dove into the arcane rules and procedures related to the budget and appropriations process and proposed changes that could reduce shutdowns and restore the authority of Congress as the Founders intended in the Constitution.

And we even studied how to improve the culture of Congress to reduce some of the partisan dysfunction that bedevils the institution, leaning on the expertise of political scientists, organizational psychologists, management consultants, and even marriage counselors (I confess, I thought about also consulting an exorcist).

Our committee—in the midst of presidential elections, pandemics, insurrections, and other chaos—managed to pass 202 recommendations to make Congress function better. At this point, nearly a third of them have been implemented, and another third are on their way to implementation. And we are trying to get that other third out of the parking garage.

Some of those changes have made a real difference. For example, the revolving door of poorly paid staff has long diminished congressional capacity and left the institution overly reliant on lobbyists for expertise (see the lobbyist chapter for more insights on this very misunderstood problem). Delinking staff pay from member pay now means that senior staffers with substantial expertise can stick around and continue to share their knowledge with Congress rather than taking their talents to K Street. When Speaker Pelosi implemented a pay floor of $45,000 and Congress created a fund to pay interns, it meant that junior staffers were no longer being nickeled and dimed—and congressional offices were no longer overly reliant on bringing on the children of wealth who could afford to intern or take an entry-level job.

In addition, Congress implemented a recommendation to restore the ability of members to direct funding toward projects and programs in their districts (what used to be called "earmarks") but with accountability measures and reforms to prevent abuse and waste. Why does that matter? Well, rather than making funding decisions the sole purview of unelected folks in marble buildings in Washington, DC, members of Congress—who are closest to the challenges facing their districts—can direct funding to address those challenges. As a consequence, in my district, communities struggling with homelessness and housing instability are getting resources to build more affordable housing. The local food bank that was stretched to the brink during the pandemic is getting some extra support.

And there have been some other changes that may be less noticeable and may take time to demonstrate impact.

During our work, I connected with a football coach who had taken over a team with a corrosive culture and turned it into a healthier, winning culture. I said, "Coach, what do you do when you have players on the team trying to sabotage the team?" And he said, "Well, I cut 'em." And I said, "We don't really have that option." And then he said, "Well then, I bench 'em." And I said, "We don't really have that option either." And then he asked me a question: "How do you do new player orientation?" And I said, "You know, it's funny you ask that."

In many respects, new Congress member orientation works entirely the wrong way. Much of the orientation process is an exercise in keeping the two parties from talking to each other. In fact, some members tell stories of arriving and seeing signs that directed Republicans and Democrats to separate buses and then separate rooms. When I shared this, the coach told me, "Derek, I don't know a lot about Congress, but I think you ought to stop doing that."

So one of our 202 recommendations was to stop doing that.

Last year, the orientation process involved Democrats and Republicans going through orientation together for the first time in three decades.

To be clear, that is *not* going to fix Congress overnight. However, I do believe that some of the relationships formed through that process, and the tone that sets, over time should make a difference in the institution.

Now, someone could look at our record and mockingly say, "Hey, bang-up job, Kilmer. Congress is clearly fixed!" Obviously, that's not the case. We still need to implement many of the Modernization Committee's reforms—and tackle other big ones, such as the manner in which district boundaries are drawn, members are chosen in primaries, and campaigns are financed. Reforms that would reduce the likelihood of extremists getting elected and eliminate impediments to bipartisan collaboration.

But I'm reminded of a conversation I had with the House chaplain during the 15th or so round of votes for Speaker of the House in January 2023.

I saw her on the House floor, and I said, "Pray harder!" And she put her hand on my elbow and said, "Just imagine how bad things would be if I wasn't praying this hard."

That's sort of how I look at the work of the Modernization Committee. And my sincere hope is that—over time—you're going to see some positive change because of that work.

Ditching the Congress Misperceptions

So what do these misperceptions mean to you?

The reality is that some of the misperceptions *about* Congress actually exacerbate many of the problems *with* Congress.

For one, the notion that members of Congress don't do anything discourages making any investments in the institution. When people feel like a product is a failure, the last thing they want to do is put more money into it. Similarly, when the public holds Congress in such low esteem, the easiest thing for members of Congress to do to score political points is to treat Congress like the piñata at the party—to knock it down rather than lift it up. Indeed, when Newt Gingrich became Speaker of the House in 1994, he cut committee budgets substantially, eliminated an office in Congress dedicated to understanding technology policy, and reduced funding for offices to pay their staff. The consequences were stark. Ever since, committees have been outgunned by lobbyists. Congress has struggled without the capacity to keep pace with technological change. And congressional staffers have short tenures, leaving offices in a frequent state of flux, struggling to build the brainpower to solve big problems.

The ability of Congress to solve big problems *requires* some smart investments in staff and technology to navigate 21st-century challenges.

As citizens, we need to be stewards of our institutions—to be what former Cabinet Secretary John Gardner referred to as "loving critics." We should do all we can to improve the institution—not simply through criticism but through care and investment. And as citizens and voters, we should reward the lawmakers who do the same.

In the meantime, don't believe all the myths you hear. Take the time to sift facts from fiction so you're set up to spot what's really going on. Then roll up your cuffs and push your representatives to move in the right direction. And while you're at it, perhaps, "Pray harder!"

"The Supreme Court Has Become Too Political"

Stephen I. Vladeck

The Supreme Court's public approval has plummeted to record lows, dragging its once-sterling reputation down with it. Just before the court's fall 2023 term, Gallup found that only 41 percent of Americans "approve" of the court. Worse, fewer than half of Americans have even "a fair amount" of trust and confidence in what Alexander Hamilton promised would be "the least dangerous branch." For the 50 years prior, over two-thirds of the country had at least a fair amount of trust in the highest court.[1]

When did it change? It fell below 50 percent only in 2022—shortly after the justices overruled *Roe v. Wade* and eliminated a constitutional right to pre-viability abortions. It hasn't risen above 50 percent since.

Ask a typical SCOTUS hater what's so objectionable about the institution, and they're likely to tell you that the court has become "too political." This generally means a couple of things. One, that, unlike in the past, modern justices are essentially extreme partisans in robes rather than the neutral arbiters we expect them to be. And two, that the court's rulings are, more than ever, political acts intended to benefit one party over the other rather than faithful applications of neutral legal principles.

It's easy to see where that impression comes from. The obvious culprit is the nomination and confirmation process for justices, which has become one of the hottest battlefields in the partisan political wars. In 2016, the Republican-controlled Senate blocked President Obama's nomination of Merrick Garland without so much as a hearing. In 2018, Justice Brett Kavanaugh's confirmation was narrowly approved along almost strict party lines. And in 2020, Justice Amy Coney Barrett's rushed confirmation saw all 52 Republicans voting in favor and all 48 Democrats opposed.

The recent confirmation battles not only condition Americans to view the court as a political piñata; they have also left us with a court divided along ideological lines that perfectly mirror the political parties of the president who appointed each justice. This is the first time in history with perfect partisan alignment between the two branches. The last conservative Democrat retired from the court in 1993. The last liberal Republican stepped down in 2010. This division was evident in the court's most recent term, where it issued 32 nonunanimous decisions. Although that number is not high by historical standards (the court used to hear far more cases), what was unusual was the *frequency* with which the justices divided in a particular way: Across those 32 cases, the most common lineup featured the six Republican appointees in the majority and the three Democratic appointees in dissent. And the runner-up wasn't close.

It's not just that the court is splitting along partisan lines in the greatest number of cases; it's that those cases tend to be the court's most significant rulings. From abortion and affirmative action to religious liberty and redistricting, the loudest critiques of the current court focus on the six Republican justices and claim that they are sacrificing legal principle (and, through it, the court's credibility) in favor of doing . . . whatever they want—precedent, public opinion, and prudence be damned.

Yet the indictment that SCOTUS has become too political rests on an assumption that rarely gets questioned. It assumes that, in some bygone kumbaya era, things were different. The court was better and could be trusted because justices of yesteryear were above (or, at least, aloof from) politics. They kept their personal views quiet and considered cases with cold judicial neutrality. In other words, they stayed in their lane, which is to just "call balls and strikes," as Chief Justice John Roberts famously described his would-be job at his 2005 confirmation hearing.

That idea certainly does sound nice. Only one minor snag: It's completely false. The belief in an apolitical judiciary is a myth—and a dangerous one. The Supreme Court has never been above politics. Even more to the point, the Supreme Court *shouldn't* be above politics. And if anything, the view that the court is *supposed* to be above politics has helped precipitate the true crisis facing the Supreme Court today.

That true crisis is not the one we think of whenever the press reports another divisive SCOTUS decision. It is that, to an extent that we have never seen in American history, the justices are not accountable to the other branches of government, especially Congress (or really, to anyone). Nor do they believe they should be. Justice Samuel Alito said this quiet part out loud in a July 2023 interview with *The Wall Street Journal*, asserting that "no provision in the Constitution gives [Congress] the authority to regulate the Supreme Court—period."[2]

Alito is wrong as a matter of text (Article III of the Constitution expressly authorizes Congress—and only Congress—among other things, to make "regulations" of the Supreme Court's caseload). He's wrong as a matter of history (he himself holds a seat created *by* Congress in 1837). And he's wrong as a matter of common sense (without congressional approval, the court would have no money, no building, no staff, and no ability to do much of anything). The Constitution envisions an independent judiciary to check majority tyranny, but it doesn't allow for tyranny by unelected judges.

And yet the *more* we indulge the myth that the court should *not* be political, the more we overlook how politics have historically been the key constraint on the court and its justices. The counterintuitive solution to the court's legitimacy crisis is to reintroduce politics—that is, the *right kind* of politics—not to reject them entirely.

The Supreme Court Has *Always* Been Political

When I mention the word "politics," you're likely thinking of fights between the parties, naked grabs for power when one team is in charge, and all the worst types of contemporary gamesmanship. That's not what I'm talking about here. Our politics—the type that the courts have been enmeshed with since the start—are the debates about who holds which powers in society. Some call this "high" politics (in contrast to the "low" politics of contemporary partisan divides). But whatever the term, the idea is the same: that the way our institutions assert their powers and seek to empower and constrain one another is very much "political." To pretend that the court, as one of the three branches of government, should somehow be above these discussions is both wrong and unhelpful. The court is made up of justices with political opinions, nominated by presidents with political opinions, and confirmed (or not) by senators with political opinions. Plus, we *need* them to decide questions about our political relationships—that's one of their most important roles. In these ways, the courts have always been political.

Recently, we've drifted away from this shared understanding. It's no coincidence that this shift coincides with the court increasingly overstepping its bounds of accountability. Or that while that has been happening, public trust in the judiciary as an institution has dropped to an all-time low.

A quick trip through the court's origins helps put into proper context the moment in which we find ourselves.

The Constitution created the Supreme Court but left almost all the details (and the personnel) to be filled in by the political branches. Not only does the text of the Constitution provide that justices will be nominated by the (politically accountable) president and confirmed by the (politically accountable) Senate, but the Constitution also leaves to those branches everything from how *many* justices there will be to the nature and size of the court's caseload to the justices' salaries (which can't be *diminished* once they are fixed). In all these ways, the Constitution directly involves politics in the court by ensuring it's made up of politically chosen judges who can only exercise their powers with the approval of the political branches and other government institutions.

That's the obvious sense in which politics have always been part of the Supreme Court. But there's a more subtle sense that, in many respects, is even more important: how the justices use politics in their decision-making, including how they shape and time their rulings to manage the court's relationship with the rest of government and society.

The less obvious sense is perhaps even more important because it shows where the seemingly untouchable power of today's court came from.

If everyday Americans know one thing about the court, they know it has the authority to declare laws to be unconstitutional. That's the court's superpower. But that power wasn't explicitly provided by the Constitution. Nope, the court only has it now because it asserted its existence in the landmark 1803 decision in *Marbury v. Madison*. That ruling cemented the power of "judicial review"—that is, the court's power to invalidate laws or executive actions on the grounds that they are unconstitutional. But there's a lot more to the story—and it's all about *Marbury*'s politics.

The story begins in the aftermath of the election of 1800, in which the two Democratic-Republican candidates, Thomas Jefferson and

Aaron Burr, tied for the most Electoral College votes—a result that sent the election to the House of Representatives. Knowing that one way or the other, a Democratic-Republican would soon be president, along with a Democratic-Republican-controlled Congress, the outgoing party—the Federalists—sought protection in the courts, creating a slew of new federal judgeships, which lame-duck President John Adams and the lame-duck Federalist-controlled Senate quickly filled. Just as we see today, when a party knows they are headed for the exits, they burn the midnight oil trying to install their own people—especially in jobs with lifetime appointments—to minimize the changes the incoming party can make.

Naturally, not long after Jefferson entered the White House, the new Congress repealed the lame-duck bill creating these new judgeships. This move touched off a massive constitutional confrontation and a test case known as *Stuart v. Laird*. How tenuous was the young Supreme Court's power at this early moment in American history? Well, while *Stuart* was pending before the court, Congress simply eliminated the court's entire 1802 session (again, a sign of Congress's ultimate authority over this independent branch). Although the measure was spun as a harmless housekeeping change to the court's calendar, everyone understood the not-so-subtle message Congress was sending.

Enter, Chief Justice John Marshall (a cousin of now-President Jefferson, by the way). Instead of addressing the constitutional question in *Stuart* and deciding whether Congress could dismantle the courts—or risking making a ruling Jefferson might ignore, which would neuter the court's power—Marshall chose option C: He avoided it altogether and answered an entirely different question. When the court sat again in 1803, in *Stuart*, it decided a different (and less significant) question than the one the case ostensibly presented. Instead, Marshall enshrined the principle of judicial review in a case about the nerdiest of questions—whether Congress could give the Supreme Court the power to decide, as a trial court rather than an appeals court, cases other than those specifically mentioned in Article III of the Constitution. The great irony of using *Marbury* this way is that the constitutional problem Marshall identified was that Congress had given the Supreme Court too *much* power. Even those most suspicious of Marshall's motives couldn't object to a decision in which the justices voted unanimously to limit their power.

In retrospect, what is striking about Marshall's efforts in *Stuart* and *Marbury* is how profoundly *political* they were. Although the background was full of partisan tension between the Federalists and the Democratic-Republicans, Marshall's politics were *institutional*—about establishing the court's power over the other institutions of government in a way that, in the short term, limited the court's power over the other institutions of government. The actual *text* of the relevant statute and the Constitution made brief appearances, but the real point was to structure the relationship among the branches in a way that, in Marshall's view, was best for the young country as a whole. That's politics of the highest order.

And to that end, in *Stuart*, Marshall sidestepped a major decision because the consequences of either potential outcome would have been massively destabilizing for the young constitutional system. And in *Marbury*, Marshall used a strange technicality and ignored key judicial principles to establish the court's power to strike down laws, an authority the Founders nowhere explicitly gave to the court. The scholarly consensus is that *Marbury* was "a political masterstroke"— and, just as importantly, that that was a *good* thing.

The politics of *Marbury* simultaneously allowed the court to cement its power of judicial review going forward while accommodating the political reality that the court circa 1803 was not *really* in a position to strike down whatever statutes it wanted to. Rather than *not* establish that power (in which case, the court would have been ignored) or establish it in *Stuart* (in which case, the court would have been destroyed), Marshall understood the need to walk a political tightrope—to preserve the court's power in the long term while keeping the other branches of government content with how it exercised power in the short term. Indeed, the court only struck down one other act of Congress before the Civil War, subtly conveying that it would use its power of judicial review rarely and responsibly. How times (and our expectations) have changed.

We could tell a remarkably similar story about the Watergate tapes case—*United States v. Nixon*. The Watergate special prosecutor had issued a subpoena to obtain President Nixon's secret recordings of Oval Office conversations. Nixon refused, claiming that his confidential, internal communications were protected under executive privilege. The conflict went to the Supreme Court.

The case was of enormous political importance *regardless* of how the court ruled—one side was going to praise the court, and the other was going to trash it. But as in *Stuart*, both possible rulings risked shifting the balance of power too much toward or away from a specific branch of government; either the court or the president was going to emerge too strong.

The court, recognizing this, did not ignore the conditions on the ground or the critical need to maintain the government's legitimacy, deeming these considerations too "political." Instead, once again, it compromised.

In an 8–0 ruling, Chief Justice Warren Burger (a Nixon appointee) recognized *both* views. He wrote that while the Constitution *does* protect certain executive branch communications from compelled disclosure, in this case, the special prosecutor's unique interest in accessing potentially incriminating evidence overrode that executive privilege.

Judging strictly on the basis of its legal analysis, most experts agree the court's opinion in *Nixon* is a mess. It's awash in contradictions, unnecessary holdings, and patently unpersuasive arguments. And yet the *Nixon* decision is generally viewed in a positive light—as an example of the court living up to its highest institutional responsibilities. In a 2016 speech, then-Judge Brett Kavanaugh counted it as one of the "greatest moments in American judicial history."[3]

That assessment has nothing to do with the court's reasoning—and everything to do with its political impact. Nixon's camp had considered refusing to comply with an adverse Supreme Court ruling, but the fact that the court was unanimous and that the only opinion was authored by Nixon's handpicked successor to Chief Justice Earl Warren poured cold water on the idea. In other words, what made *Nixon* one of the "greatest moments in American judicial history" wasn't its reasoning; it was its politics. Not because Democrats prevailed over Republicans, but because the court found a way to issue a ruling that best preserved the effective functioning of the government—without tilting the scales too far in one direction.

Similar politics played out in *Brown v. Board of Education* (which ended legal segregation) and other landmark cases where the court prioritized unanimity or cross-ideological majorities over unassailable legal analysis. In these vital cases, the message the court sent was more important than the specific reasoning that it provided. We know the justices didn't all *agree* with every word the court wrote in each case. What matters is that they agreed that speaking in one voice in those cases was a *central* part of the American political enterprise; these rulings were about the court as an institution, not the justices as individuals. These courts understood that the politics of the ruling—how it was perceived and put into effect—took precedence over their own personal preferences.

If we were being purists about the idea that politics should never enter SCOTUS decisions, we would think it unbecoming of the court to factor such concerns into the results it reaches and the reasoning it adopts. In the "balls and strikes" view, the court should only concern itself with the "correct" answer to the legal question presented and ignore everything else. I disagree. These cases are not *departures* from the "rule of law"; they are the epitome of it. They reflect a nuanced and complicated understanding of the delicate role we need the court to play in our system. A Supreme Court that, throughout its history, did whatever it wanted, whenever it wanted, without any regard for its relationship with the other branches of government, would have been a court that provoked those branches into narrowing its jurisdiction, cutting its budget, and perhaps even declining to enforce its decisions. To take one especially prominent example, it's hard to imagine that President Eisenhower would have sent the army into Little Rock, Arkansas, in 1957 in order to enforce the court's ruling in *Brown* if the court had spent the preceding decades running roughshod over the other branches of government. Institutional politics thus not only *constrain* the court; they also empower it. The idea that an institution so designed and so constrained should nevertheless pay no attention to high constitutional politics is . . . self-defeating.

That doesn't mean that all political decisions by the court are necessarily good ones. Some of the most infamous Supreme Court decisions can be criticized for the same reasons that we glorify *Marbury*, *Nixon*, and *Brown*. For instance, the infamous *Dred Scott* decision—which ruled that slaves were property, not people—was a transparent attempt to *settle* the political future of slavery in a single judicial ruling. Chief Justice Roger Brooke Taney and his majority ruled that because slaves weren't people, they couldn't seek relief in the courts. Ergo, no more court cases questioning slavery. Taney's politically myopic (and racist) overreach backfired. Instead of calming things down, it simultaneously angered the abolitionists in the North (who bitterly opposed slavery) and further fractured the Democratic Party into proslavery and antislavery groups. This division helped clear the path for Abraham Lincoln's victory in 1860, and the Civil War soon followed.

Similar criticisms apply to *Bush v. Gore*, the infamous end of the 2000 presidential election. Even if we accept Justice Scalia's defense that "someone" had to settle who won Florida's 27 electoral votes and, thus, the election, the court's 5–4 decision along ideological lines was quite clearly "political," this time in the partisan sense where conservatives ruled for conservatives. The court tried to cover itself by claiming that the ruling only applied to that one case, but that caveat only made it look *more* like cutthroat partisan politics—rather than a neutral principle to be applied in all future cases, including when it might help Democrats.

What separates *Marbury* and *Nixon*, on one hand, from *Dred Scott* and *Bush v. Gore*, on the other? Context is key. A ruling feels like a significant institutional decision when the Supreme Court acts together, with all justices, from all sides, in agreement. But when only some justices, particularly those with similar partisan political views, make a ruling for the whole country, it can seem less like a reasoned high-level judgment and more like just another partisan dispute dressed up in legal robes. Both of the Supreme Court's 2024 rulings in support of former President Trump—keeping him on the ballot in Colorado and recognizing at least some immunity from criminal prosecution for his alleged role in January 6—are guilty of these unfortunate optics, among lots of other shortcomings.

The answer isn't for the court to *not* be political; it's for the court to be *responsibly* political and not partisan. For much of our history, we had a court that *was* responsibly political. The harder question is when (and why) that changed.

The Modern Court: Too Much Power, Too Little Accountability

As should hopefully be clear by this point, the "politics" to which I have been referring are reflected not just in how the Supreme Court decides cases but in how it interacts with the other branches more generally. Historically, the courts have been involved in politics not just through their decisions but also by joining broader public debates about their role within the system itself.

For 200 years, the courts were active participants in an ongoing debate about their own role in our government. That conversation was significantly different from today because it also involved Congress and the president—the courts themselves were just one voice, and hardly the most powerful or untouchable of the three. And that conversation was profoundly influenced by and attuned to the politics of the moment. That healthy balance of powers carried on into the 20th century—until a heavy-handed law, passed 100 years ago, began to turn the tables.

Up until then, Congress had historically used its various powers to regulate the court in many ways, both big and small. This included controlling the court's caseload, deciding when and where it sat, setting its budget, determining which cases it could hear, and even managing when and how justices could retire—not just in general but in the specific cases of at least two of the court's members.

Congress used these powers not just to ensure that the court's decisions loosely reflected its preferences but to influence the court's direction more broadly. In short, Congress acted, or threatened to act, when it wanted to remind the court of its proper role. For example, when Congress wanted to prevent the court from deciding a major case testing the constitutionality of military governments in the South during Reconstruction, it took away the court's power to hear that particular dispute *after* oral arguments had concluded. The court later ruled (read: admitted) that Congress had the power to do so. And when Congress wanted to nudge Justice Ward Hunt off the bench after he suffered a paralyzing stroke in the early 1880s but refused to step down, it passed a bill directed solely at him—promising full benefits if he would resign within 30 days. He did. Congress pulled the same move a few decades later with Justice Joseph Lamar. And of course, we already saw the example of Democratic-Republicans canceling the court's entire 1802 term.

Beyond what Congress actually did, there's also a rich history of justices responding to even the hint of congressional intervention. When Justice Abe Fortas resigned in 1969 in the middle of an ethics scandal (which paled in comparison to more recent SCOTUS antics), it was because he feared the possibility that Congress would use the episode as a pretext not only for impeaching him but for attacking the court more generally. When Justice Owen Roberts changed his crucial vote on important constitutional cases in the middle of FDR's New Deal—an event known as the Constitutional Revolution of 1937—it wasn't a coincidence that Congress was at that moment discussing plans to expand and weaken the court. Just by *debating* FDR's so-called court-packing plan (not even passing it), Congress helped bring about Roberts's "switch in time that saved the nine."

In all these respects, Congress used levers as a way to keep the court—and the justices—generally in line. But Congress's most important lever is its power to sit on its hands. The Constitution protects the justices' salaries from being cut, but nothing else. In fact, the court depends on Congress to fund its building, security, computers, clerks, and everything in between. For fiscal year 2024, the justices' salaries accounted for less than 2 percent of the court's $151 million budget request. If Congress wanted to, say, leave the remaining $148 million out of its next budget, it's not clear how the Constitution would stop it.

Before you gasp in alarm at the thought of today's Congress pushing the Supreme Court around, pause to remember that they are the only ones who can. And they are, at least, subject to public scrutiny and reelection. If Congress refuses to play its role in the delicate dance of checks and balances, there's no other entity with the levers of power to hold the court accountable. If the court achieves complete independence—as many have called for—it also means they become insulated from any kind of accountability at all.

At the same time, the court is not only beholden to Congress; its ability to function requires the president's support, as well—as the Eisenhower example noted above underscores. The point is that, historically, the separation of powers has been a three-way street, with the court both constrained by and constraining the other branches of government.

This is also why public confidence in the court has historically been so central to its ability to hand down unpopular but important decisions. The less credibility the court commands among the people, the less likely the elected branches are to enforce its rulings. Like parents giving their teenagers more freedoms because they've proven trustworthy, judicial independence has historically been *facilitated* by judicial accountability, not undermined by it.

It turns out that the seeds of the court's supreme power had actually been planted many years before *Brown*, or Fortas's ouster, or Roberts's "switch in time." But they sprouted and grew slowly, and it took decades for the rest of us to notice.

The change began with the passage of one of the most important judicial reform efforts in American history, culminating in the Judiciary Act of 1925. The bill is better known as the Judges' Bill because it was spearheaded and largely drafted *by* judges. At the heart of the Judges' Bill was a vision championed, most prominently, by Chief Justice (and former President) William Howard Taft. Taft believed that the court's role in our system was to serve as a constitutional court—above and apart from the fray of ordinary judicial business—and not, as had been true since the founding, as a supreme court of appeals. Put simply, Taft wanted the court to have more power over the other branches and, ironically, used Congress to get it.

To help achieve that vision, Taft pushed for two major reforms aimed at making the court more independent. First, Taft sought to get the court its own building—so it would *physically* be free from the political branches. At that time, the court met in the US Capitol, a clear signal that it was literally beneath Congress in more ways than one (it had sat in the basement until 1860). Second, Taft pushed for Congress to give the court more control over its own docket—determining which cases it would and wouldn't decide. At the heart of these reforms were two overlapping ideas: that the court needed more power and that the court needed that power to come *from* the political branches.

It's no coincidence that what law professors generally view as "modern" constitutional law followed shortly on the heels of the Judges' Bill. Armed with the power to pick and choose the cases it would decide, the Supreme Court quickly turned toward issues with deeper impacts and cases with broader ramifications than what had comprised the bulk of its earlier work. The court started deciding fewer cases—but also *bigger* cases. Critically, though, the "big" rulings were also largely *popular* ones—such as the slow but steady application of different parts of the Bill of Rights to the states, and not just the federal government.

While all that was happening, Congress has gradually abandoned the use of its powers over the judiciary to mold the courts and hold them accountable. For example, Congress hasn't altered the size of the court since 1869. It hasn't altered the court's calendar since 1917. It hasn't messed with the justices' pensions since 1937. It hasn't held out on pay raises for the justices since 1964. And it hasn't meaningfully altered the court's docket since 1988—and when it did, Congress effectively ceded complete control to the justices, finishing the work Taft and the Judges' Bill had started. These are just the big-ticket items; there are lots of smaller and subtler ways in which Congress used to nudge the court but doesn't anymore.

The result is a dangerous combination: At the same time the court has grown *more powerful*, it has also grown *less accountable*. Justices no longer need to worry, as Justice Fortas did, about Congress stepping in if they don't address their own misconduct. The court no longer needs to worry, as Chief Justice Marshall did, about its decisions being ignored by the political branches. And justices no longer need to bother considering the political context or impact of their decisions because the court is seen as untouchable by enough elected officials to give credence to that view. This is why Chief Justice Roberts can decline an invitation to appear before the Senate Judiciary Committee out of concerns for the "separation of powers and the importance of preserving judicial independence."[24] It's also why Justice Alito can tell *The Wall Street Journal* that "no provision in the Constitution gives [Congress] the authority to regulate the Supreme Court—period." He's wrong, but it probably *feels* like he's right. And *he* definitely feels like he's right, which is most important.

It has taken time for the consequences of this disengagement to become visible, but they are increasingly undeniable. The court today is deciding fewer cases through written opinions than at any point since the Civil War. More and more of the court's most important work instead comes through unsigned (and usually unexplained) orders—because no one is telling the justices which cases they must hear or how to hear them. It's like telling kids they get to choose what homework to turn in; we can't be surprised when they choose to do less (and do more of it anonymously) than ever before. As a result, entire categories of disputes, like cases about the scope of the Fourth Amendment's protection against unreasonable searches and seizures, have disappeared from the court's docket—and few outside lower courts or researchers have noticed. An equally disturbing trend, which I detail in my book *The Shadow Docket*, is that the court is using unsigned and unexplained orders more today than at any point in history—even as it nods toward the need to be transparent by at least *posting* those unexplained orders to its website. This is a deeply problematic shift in the way justices exercise their authority, but they can do it because they face and fear no direct consequence. In short, the court isn't just deciding fewer cases; the typical ruling is less transparent than ever.

That unaccountable mentality also comes across in alarming personal behavior by Justices Thomas and Alito—especially their shoddy compliance with ethical and financial disclosure rules and norms. Justice Alito failed to recuse in a case that produced a multibillion-dollar windfall for a hedge fund owner who had recently taken him on a luxury fishing trip to Alaska. Justice Thomas failed to disclose all kinds of financial support from conservative benefactors—one of whom publicly admitted that he "didn't know" if he would've shown the same hospitality to Thomas were he not on the court. But unlike in the days of Justice Fortas, there is no sign that anyone in a position to influence the court is going to do anything about it—which may help explain why the responses from Thomas and Alito have been so combative, defending their conduct and criticizing those who have raised questions about it. They know, despite their behavior, they won't face any real consequences.

Thus, the real significance of Alito's statement on congressional powerlessness over the court is not that it's correct according to law or history but that it reflects the contemporary reality—what the world looks like when a critical mass of justices are no longer looking over their shoulders. And that is what makes this current moment in the Supreme Court's history unique—and uniquely problematic. Today's Supreme Court is not, and does not think it ought to be, accountable to the other branches of government—in ways that shape which issues the justices rule on, what they decide in those cases, and how they behave more generally both on and off the bench. One can trace a pretty direct path from the fading of institutional politics in the court's day-to-day interactions with the other branches of government to the mess we're dealing with now.

The Dangers of an Apolitical Court

If you're aghast at the court's extreme decisions, made largely along partisan lines, you have good reason to be. A number of SCOTUS decisions in recent years have been brazenly partisan—advancing long-term planks of the Republican Party's political platform. From the court's 2022 decision overruling *Roe v. Wade* (and eviscerating a federal constitutional right to pre-viability abortions) to the 2023 ruling ending race-based admissions preferences in higher education to the 2024 ruling reversing 40 years of deference to administrative agencies, the problem with all the rulings that divide the court's Republican appointees from the Democratic appointees is how many of them perfectly align with things contemporary Republicans support and contemporary Democrats oppose. While they may fairly be labeled partisan decisions, don't call them "too political." Because the logical consequence of that is to insist that the court should be completely apolitical, and that belief is part of what has gotten us the legitimacy crisis we have today.

In recent years, calls for an apolitical court have often been repackaged through the lens of judicial courage, or the idea that judges should follow their legal principles *wherever* they lead. The basic gist, which appears in public comments from judges themselves, is that so long as a judicial decision is "correct" (whatever *that* means), it shouldn't matter if it is "unpopular."

I have no problem with judicial "courage" in the abstract. A big reason why we have unelected judges in the first place is so that they feel free to make politically unpopular decisions. In this way, they preserve the ability of federal courts to stand as a bulwark against the tyrannies of the majority.

But even if we could agree on a definition of the concept—and that is a mighty "if"—judicial "courage" isn't the absolute good we think it is. Politics cuts both ways, and when "courage" becomes hubris or willful blindness to the broader impact of court decisions, it cuts badly. Public support for the courts is crucial for their ability to make unpopular decisions. Precisely because the courts will issue some important rulings that go against public opinion (like *Brown*, at least at first), it is essential for federal courts to be politically responsible and act accordingly. Indeed, there tends *not* to be a lot of public support for expanding the rights of criminal defendants. But the Warren Court, in particular, was able to give more substance to the Fourth, Fifth, Sixth, and Eighth Amendments *because* it was broadly credible.

Throughout history (at least until recently), Supreme Court justices applied their "courage" selectively, considering the societal context of each decision and its potential impact on the health of our democracy overall. One powerful reflection of this debate involved the dilemma faced by judges (and justices) tasked with enforcing the Fugitive Slave Acts of 1793 and 1850—especially those jurists who were personally opposed to slavery as an institution. As Professor Robert Cover noted, the dilemma these judges faced was not between their personal opposition to slavery and the "right" legal outcome; it was between hostility to slavery and the highest of high politics—the very real belief that the preservation of the Union turned on the enforcement of these compromise (and compromised) laws in those cases in which there was no reasonable legal basis for refusing to apply them. In other words, the dilemma was the risk for these jurists that letting their personal preferences influence their interpretations and applications of the relevant statutes would literally tear the country apart.

It turns out that this is an inherent tension in judging (and in law, more generally)—when should the institution take precedence over the issue? And the best anyone can do is to understand that this tension inheres—and to try not to tilt (or be responsible for tilting) the scales irrevocably to one side.

That's the tension Chief Justice Marshall navigated in *Stuart* and *Marbury*. It's the tension Chief Justice Warren navigated in *Brown*. It's the tension Chief Justice Burger navigated in *Nixon*. And against that backdrop, arguments encouraging judges to be "courageous," or to not shy away from handing down "unpopular opinions," are missing at least half of the point. In a system where federal courts' power—and public faith in our government overall—relies on public acceptance of their rulings, decisions that frequently go against public opinion or undermine public confidence risk weakening judges' ability to make more "courageous" or "unpopular" decisions in the future. Put another way, a court that believes it should *not* be "political" is a court that is likely to act in ways that undermine the public's confidence—and, ultimately, its legitimacy.

The point is that justices should care about maintaining public confidence in the court *and* faithfully interpreting the law—it has to be both rather than either-or. That doesn't mean that the court should do whatever is most popular. But it does mean that there is a very serious risk to issuing too many decisions (or publicly alarming behaviors) that the public opposes. The upshot is that the court *needs* to be political, in the best sense of the word—not just to preserve its own legitimacy but to keep our democracy healthy overall.

Make the Courts Political Again

If you've made it this far, then you've hopefully been persuaded of three points: First, the court has *always* been political, which has long helped its relationship with the rest of government and its ability to fulfill its constitutional role. Second, as the court has become *less* politically attuned in recent years, it has also become *less* accountable—in ways that have made it far easier for the justices to abuse the powers that they accumulated during earlier periods of more responsible behavior. And third, a court that—like the current one—throws those considerations to the wind does so at serious risk of undermining its own constitutional role and, with it, the health of our whole constitutional system.

With those points in mind, keep an eye out for opinion pieces or even news stories that frame the Supreme Court in unhelpful terms:

that pitch "judicial independence" as an absolute and any push for legislative reforms as an "assault" on that independence, that defend unpopular rulings by the justices *on the ground* that they are unpopular, or that otherwise try to suggest that the court errs whenever it takes anything into account besides the text of the law it is interpreting. These are all variations on the same flawed theme—that the court should be totally divorced from politics. That's the *problem*, not the solution.

So how could making the court more political restore the accountability it clearly needs? The answer depends on understanding different types of reforms that are increasingly being tossed about to "fix the court."

Perhaps the most aggressive option is to "pack the court." This involves changing the court's ideological composition by "expanding" the court to 13 justices by passing a law to add four new seats to the bench. The justifications for this vary. Some say the court needs more justices to match the growth in the number of circuit courts (something Congress did from 1789 to 1801 and 1802 to 1866). Others are more transparent in their goals: The court needs to be packed to get more liberals on the bench as retaliation for the political machinations of 2016–2020.

Changing the size of the court is clearly within Congress's constitutional authority. In fact, only Congress can do it and has done it seven times (when Congress first set up the Supreme Court in 1789, it had only six justices). But these calls are the most overtly *partisan*, since they are intended not only to limit the power of the current Republican-appointed majority but also to give that power to a more ideologically balanced court. And it's hard to see how that could ever be possible without a Democratic trifecta that includes a filibuster-proof majority in the Senate—and perhaps not even then.

Even if court-packing could be done, it might make matters worse. The main problem with that move is that it would only strengthen the view of the court as a tool for partisan power. We would probably land in a "race to the bottom"; the next time Republicans have a trifecta, they'd add 8 seats to the court. And then Democrats add 12. It wouldn't be long before the court would have 75 justices and no credibility—where no one benefits except those who want to damage the court as an institution.

Another sort of reform that gets a lot of airtime these days is the kind that would change not the court's composition but its power. For instance, "jurisdiction-stripping" (to prevent the court from deciding certain types of cases), requiring a supermajority vote of the court before the justices can invalidate government action (a measure that the House of Representatives actually passed in 1868, only to have it die in the Senate), or proposals to impose a higher standard of review in certain cases. These moves all circle around the same basic idea: that Congress can and should reassert its ability to keep cases away from the court and/or restrain the court from acting against the democratically elected branches.

The devil is really in the details in this category. Congress has pretty broad power over the court's jurisdiction (there's a debate as to whether that power is total; I'm of the view that it probably isn't). And Congress also has broad power over how the court interprets statutes, regulations, and other texts besides the Constitution itself. The tougher question about these reforms is whether they would actually work. The stronger the reform, the fiercer the constitutional objections would be.

For instance, a law barring the Supreme Court from striking down any gun control regulation on the ground that it violates the Second Amendment would raise grave constitutional questions. One that limits when and how the court can hear such cases may not, but at the expense of actually making an impact. Plus, if reformers push too hard, the justices themselves could rebel. The court could bypass a supermajority requirement by pulling the judicial equivalent of price-fixing:

agreeing internally that any time a majority votes to strike down a law, a supermajority of justices will agree with at least that part of the decision. And changing the rules for how the court interprets statutes and regulations assumes that the justices will follow the new rules; they haven't been great about following the old ones.

The tension here is between impact and viability. Outside of literally amending the Constitution, any change would likely have to be (significantly) less than 100 percent effective in order to be accepted as constitutional. At that point, the question becomes whether the benefit is worth the cost (and, it should be said, the political capital). Especially because these reforms would likely involve a Democratic majority in Congress and a Democratic president trying to limit a Republican-controlled court, it's not hard to imagine how such efforts will be spun, fairly or not.

This leads to the third option: reforms designed to make the court more accountable without changing its composition or reducing its formal power. There are a lot of examples here, but these would include (1) expanding the court's mandatory docket so that the justices *have* to decide more cases, including cases they are not choosing for themselves; (2) appointing an inspector general to provide meaningful oversight of the justices' compliance with financial disclosure and ethics rules; (3) using Congress's power over the court's budget to demand more transparency and accountability with respect to *how* that money is spent; and (4) at a more basic level, more congressional engagement in the court's day-to-day work and decision-making processes—including hearings about specific cases, investigations into allegations of misconduct, and so on.

None of these is as visible or, at least to this point, as popular as more dramatic changes to who's on the court or how much power it has. In that respect, they won't have nearly the short-term impact for which many of the court's critics are clamoring. Nor will they prevent the current court from taking the cases that at least four of the justices want to hear or directly stop the court's majority from doing . . . whatever it wants to do . . . in those cases.

But it's possible that those realities can be viewed as a feature, not a bug. Reforms with more subtle, long-term effects on improving the court's role and respectability are less partisan. That makes them more attainable and less damaging. And it gives them the potential to strengthen the court's credibility and restore its image as a responsible and balanced branch of government, as it was at earlier points in our history.

Whichever flavor of reforms suits your taste, the relevant point is that the way to fix the court by making it more political is for Congress to reinsert itself into more of the court's decision-making. Congress won't always make the right decisions. But the messy, occasional dialogue between branches will help maintain their balance of power and legitimacy far better than today's one-way monologue, where one very powerful branch answers to no one. And if citizens don't like how their representatives are overseeing the court, they can vote them out in two years. Without that oversight, the citizens get to weigh in on the work of unelected, lifetime-appointed judges—well, never.

These efforts start with *you*. After all, if it's going to take reengagement by Congress in the work of the court to accomplish the right kind of reforms, it's going to take informed citizens—and voters—who *prioritize* such reengagement to impel Congress to act. But it's not just about calling or writing your representatives; it's also about the conversations you have at home and with your friends. The more we *talk* about the court in these kinds of institutional (as opposed to partisan) terms, the easier it is to persuade those whose partisan preferences differ from our own that there's still a problem worth a solution.

After all, if, like me, you believe that our constitutional system depends on a legitimate and strong court, then it should be obvious both that the current state of affairs is undesirable and that many of the proposed "fixes" might end up making matters worse. We can't expect the court to always do what we *want* it to do. But we should expect the court to act as a balanced part of the federal government, not as an untouchable authority with unchallengeable decisions.

Simply put, if the real problem with today's court is a lack of accountability, fixing that requires creating the conditions in which justices of *any* ideological stripe will think beyond themselves and their times before they act.

Changing who's on the court won't, in itself, make the court more accountable.

Imposing term limits won't, in itself, make the court more accountable.

Taking away the court's power to decide specific cases or interpret particular texts won't, in itself, make the court more accountable.

The way to make the court more accountable is to demand that our elected representatives engage with the court as an institution, with the justices' behavior, and with their workload. The exact same court with the exact same powers would act differently with the specter of Congress insisting that the justices wield those powers more responsibly.

That would be a much *more* political court than the one we have today—and the health of our constitutional system would be better for it. And that's no myth.

"Politicians Are Bought and Paid For"

Rep. Steve Israel

In January of 2001, I walked the gilded halls of the Capitol, humming the theme from Frank Capra's *Mr. Smith Goes to Washington*. I'd just been elected to the US Congress, representing Long Island. I felt chills as I took in the rotunda, the National Statuary Hall, and the House chamber. My boyhood dream had come true.

I was blissfully unaware that I was about to confront an unpleasant reality. The Democratic Congressional Campaign Committee (DCCC)—the party organization tasked with supporting Democratic incumbents and candidates to the House—wrangled all the new members together as soon as they stepped on the premises to deliver a strict set of instructions. First, hire a political action committee (PAC) director to turbocharge our fundraising. (PACs are organizations that pool campaign contributions and then contribute to political campaigns.) Since PACs could legally donate more money to our campaigns than individual voters, they were essential to our reelection bids.

And second, raise $10,000 a week. Every week. Otherwise, as an incumbent in a competitive congressional district, my dream of serving in Congress would not last long.

We weren't the only ones. Newly elected Republicans received similar instructions from their party leaders. I learned early that there is only one area of instant bipartisan agreement: raise money.

Far from the resplendent white marble of the Capitol, I soon found myself shuttled into a "call room." Since it's illegal to fundraise within Capitol walls, members do their financial dirty work a few blocks away in a less auspicious building. Gray fabric cubicles. Flickering fluorescent lights. Members of the US Congress reduced to glorified telemarketers. For 10 to 15 hours every week, I would cold-call donors, delivering my well-honed 60-second pitch to raise the money required to stay afloat in politics and address the pressing issues I sought to tackle as a legislator.

I'd envisioned long hours spent on the House floor in great debates with partisan foes, hashing out hard-fought compromises and passing legislation that would improve the lives of my constituents. The reality was a financial arms race that would lead me to spend over 4,200 hours dialing up donors during my 16 years in Congress. That's almost half a year of my life.

Fundraising felt unnatural at first, but over time, I got better at it. I worked my way up the Democratic hierarchy of Washington, eventually becoming chair of the DCCC in 2011. That meant it was my job to . . . how should I phrase this . . . strongly encourage my colleagues to keep their campaign war chests filled. What qualified me for this job? Well, to climb the partisan ladder in Congress, you need to stand out among your colleagues in a variety of areas. Party leaders are effective policymakers, equally comfortable debating the intricacies of environmental protection regulations and wrangling the votes of their colleagues. They're also talented communicators, able to command attention on the House floor and, more importantly, on television and social media. But crucially, they're torrid fundraisers, bringing in millions for the party and, if they're smart, supporting their fellow members in tight races.

I'd like to believe that I was chosen as DCCC chair simply for the staggering eloquence of my floor speeches and my thoughtful positions on foreign affairs. But in a role focused on raising and distributing money across hundreds of candidates running nationwide, something tells me that my fundraising abilities were a factor.

I'll put it this way: In the 2022 midterms, Republicans and Democrats combined had over $8.9 billion in spending. That money has to come from somewhere.

I became chair of the DCCC just a year after the Supreme Court flung open the floodgates of campaign fundraising with its landmark *Citizens United* decision, which gutted the constitutional support for many campaign spending regulations. I found myself tasked with reading the same fundraising riot act to new members that I'd heard 10 years earlier, but the amount they had to raise each week had sky-rocketed and only kept rising with each election cycle. By the time I left office in 2017—undefeated and unindicted, an accomplishment in this era of politics—I was telling candidates in competitive races that they had to raise $30,000 a week. This was not how I expected or hoped elections would work. It was the unfortunate reality of our political system. To win elections and legislate solutions to voters' problems, we had to commit ourselves entirely to a *Dr. Strangelove*–esque financial arms race.

If $10,000 a week took 10 to 15 hours, how many hours do you think legislators are now required to spend dialing up donors each week? While not a direct multiple of three, it's not that far off.

The end result of this fundraising Olympics is 535 overworked politicians struggling to keep their perches on Capitol Hill and a critical mass of voters observing that their legislators seem to spend more time raising campaign funds than smoothing their potholes. It's no surprise that many of these voters have come to believe one of the defining myths of this era of politics—that their legislators' votes are bought and sold by high-value donors.

Voters see the staggering campaign fundraising totals flash across news screens and assume it's bribery. Many imagine a smoke-filled back room where an all-too-eager special interest lobbyist slides a gobsmackingly large check across the table to a member of Congress. That lawmaker then stands up in the House chambers the next day and casts the purchased vote. It's a depressing image—one that suggests our politics is entirely rigged against you, the voter.

But having served in Congress for 16 years and as chair of the DCCC for 4, I can tell you that the imagined story just isn't true. Sure, there are always exceptions—California Rep. Duke Cunningham was actually jailed in 2006 for selling earmarks, and New Jersey Sen. Bob Menendez literally hid gold bars in his basement freezer in one of his several bribery scandals—but those examples are few and far between. The reality is that campaign cash *does* buy something, but it's not votes. What donors want and get from their big-money contributions is simple: access to members of Congress.

And this access is a real problem—allowing the wealthy to bend the ears of the politically powerful in a way that most voters just can't—but it works differently than the myth depicts. Even the heroes and villains of this story aren't right. Your elected representative isn't trying to corrupt themselves by taking campaign cash. They just know they have no prayer of getting sent back to Congress for another term to help fix your health care or lower your taxes if they can't pay for expensive advertising and a campaign ground operation. And the vast majority of interest groups donating to a candidate aren't trying to break our democracy. They're trying to make sure they have equal face time to rival interest groups. The closer you look at this system, the more misery—and dollars—you find.

The sliver of hope here is that if you're willing to dispel the myth that campaign cash buys votes and instead work to understand the complex shadow game of legislative access, you can find ways to change this system yourself. Seriously. Because once we learn how campaign finance really works in Congress, we can figure out how to reform this broken system into one that works for every American.

Inside the Campaign Cash Machine

In my early days as a congressman, I found myself discouraged by the meager turnout of my fundraisers. They were not elegant affairs held in smoke-filled back rooms but rather quick sojourns to whatever cost-effective restaurants were within a half-mile walking distance from the Hill. There, I would munch on the obligatory soggy egg rolls or slightly rancid artichoke dip while listening to the handful of PAC donors that showed up.

At one point in those early days, I leaned over to my fundraising consultant and complained about the sparse crowd. He reminded me that we'd raised $30,000 from this one-hour event and said, "It's not the quality of the crowd but the quantity of the dollars." That's what political fundraising is: expending as little time, energy, and sanity as possible to extract as much cash as possible to keep your campaign afloat.

Let's step back and lay out a few basics of the American campaign finance system. First, there's very little systematic about it. The United States is overwhelmingly protective of freedom of political speech (see: Amendment, First), which it has historically defined as dollars, which has led to a more freewheeling approach to campaign fundraising compared to other Western democracies (which, by contrast, often publicly finance their elections). In the past several decades, court cases like *Citizens United* have dramatically curtailed the ability of the government to regulate campaign donations, leading to a flood of cash into our elections. That said, there is a regulatory framework—and the Federal Election Commission (FEC)—dedicated to preventing the abuse of campaign cash.

So what does all that mean for you? Well, you can easily donate up to $3,300 (as of this writing) to a candidate's committee each election cycle.

The candidate then can take your money and buy advertising, pay campaign staffers, and open field offices. Or you could donate up to $5,000 to a PAC, a tax-exempt organization, which can then donate a small amount of money directly to candidates or spend unlimited amounts itself in support of a candidate, likely blanketing the airwaves with its own ads. Or you could donate $500 million (let's pretend you have $500 million) or more to a Super PAC, which has no limits on receiving donations but cannot donate to an individual candidate. Instead, since a Super PAC can spend unlimited amounts independently, they'll use your $500 million to run their own ads in support of that candidate, thereby electing them to just about any political office you like. Super PACs are a relatively recent phenomenon, having emerged after two 2010 legal decisions: *Citizens United* and *Speachnow.org v. FEC.*

If you're really feeling creative, maybe you'll make a dark money organization (a nonprofit, tax-exempt group) that can likewise raise and spend unlimited amounts as long as its political spending is less than 50 percent of its annual budget. As added fun, dark money groups don't have to disclose their donors, which is a nice perk if you're perhaps a reclusive billionaire or a foreign country that isn't on our holiday card list (I see you, North Korea). You may notice that this summary began sanely and ended with the potential for a financial hijacking of the world's leading democracy. That's part of the *real* trouble with American campaign finance.

And if you're not just a voter on the sidelines but an elected official yourself? Well, start raising money—your election and your future career prospects depend on it. If you want to rise up your party ranks, land on plum committees, and legislate on pressing national issues, you need to get out your list of contacts and shake out some cash from the couch cushions of every human you've ever interacted with in the course of your life. This will be the arms race you'll engage in every single day of your political career until its conclusion (usually either retirement or being outspent in your reelection bid).

I'm not painting you a rosy picture. But we have to understand how this big framework actually plays out behind the scenes, beyond the myth, to build a better system for our democracy.

Money Talks, but Does It Sway Votes?

Contrary to what you might think, the PAC donors at my soggy-egg-roll lunches were not hard-charging insiders trying to wield their financial might to change my vote. They represented interests in business or social issues and hit five to six fundraisers a night to get face time with a legislator and discuss the policies they cared about. Rather than paying to persuade us of new positions, their checks were the price of access to political decision-makers—just as campaign donations are today. And donors, now as then, largely meet with elected officials who already agree with them or, at least, feel neutral toward them. This is a critical difference between the fact and fiction of campaign finance. Donors typically don't intend (or bother to try) to bribe someone into doing something they otherwise wouldn't. Whatever their priority issue, their checks go to the already converted to keep them in the flock rather than convince them to join it. Your job as a member of Congress is to nod along through these one-hour events, make pleasant political small talk, and get out with your integrity intact.

Crooked? Rarely. Take, for example, teachers' unions. In 2021–2022, their PACs spent $4,098,442 in donations to candidates. Guess how much of it went to Democrats? $4,067,442. And to Republicans? A paltry $24,000. In almost the same year, 2022, the National Rifle Association (NRA) donated almost $8 million to candidates. Guess how much of it went to Republicans? Every last cent.

In these meetings, donors regularly bring up political issues, without asking—or even hinting—for your vote on something. And sometimes, by virtue of being experts in their fields, they can offer genuinely useful information on deeply niche policymaking issues (see the lobbying chapter in this book for more details on true lobbyist influence in DC).

For example, I sat on the House Financial Services Committee for one term, despite the fact that my experience in financial services existed only in my occasional use of an ATM. As I sat on the committee dealing with intricate regulatory questions on capital markets, banking, and consolidation, I knew where I stood on the broad issues based on my bedrock values. But like any member of Congress, I was also constantly trying to decipher the details in an area where I held little preexisting expertise.

At one point, I held an event with an insurance PAC and learned of a pressing fear within that industry that there would be a run on insurance in the event of a mass, 9/11-esque terrorist attack. Without a federal backstop, private insurance companies simply didn't have the cash reserves to ensure everyone would get their payout. My staff and I later researched the issue and worked with colleagues on both sides of the aisle to pass the Terrorism Risk Insurance Act in 2002 to create that very backstop.

That law doesn't exist solely because some insurance PAC mentioned it to me, but my access to an industry executive did allow me to better understand the nuances of its necessity and set me on a path toward thinking more deeply about it long term. As legislators face a dizzying array of issues to tackle with every law, they need access to expert opinions, and sometimes those seeking to gain access with donations can provide them.

Many legislators have clear red lines over what money they're willing to accept. In my time in Congress, I categorically refused to take checks from the oil, gas, drilling, and mining industries and gun organizations like the NRA. It was an easy promise to uphold—these PACs weren't looking to waste their money on me anyway. (It's like saying you refuse to go on a date with Heidi Klum. She wasn't going to ask you in the first place. Keep that in mind the next time you hear your representative boast about refusing donations they were never going to be offered.) These donors already knew where I stood and chose instead to donate to whoever was running against me. Many members also have their own policies on who they'll meet with, donor or not. There were times when a PAC or individual expressed interest in donating to me, but I simply felt uncomfortable with the prospect of being associated with them. So I'd politely turn them down.

Despite these restraints and the often-overlooked positive effects of donor meetings, we shouldn't be sanguine about this practice. Money doesn't buy votes, but it does cause problems. And more frequently, it's a pernicious force rather than a positive one in our politics.

Among the chief reasons is that access may not equal votes, but access does accrue influence. Those you hear from the most have a way of making themselves heard the most. And if you're only talking to people who can write donation checks for $5,000 a pop, you're talking to people with $5,000 problems rather than $5 problems. That's a bubble. Many members of Congress work to break out of that bubble—talking to working-class voters in their districts, holding town halls, working diligently on constituent casework—but it's not easy, especially with the ever-demanding legislative schedule in Washington.

The consequence of all this is not that Congress is corrupt but that money in politics is often corrosive. When the House and Senate tackle thorny problems of economic regulation, health care, and the social safety net, they're doing so with powerful corporations and special interest groups in their ears, rather than a Long Island coffee shop barista who desperately could use a hike to their minimum wage salary. Working people are too often left out of this process; the wealthy and well-connected aren't. So what do you get? A political system that more often works for the wealthy and well-connected than anyone else.

The Access Arms Race on Capitol Hill

Among the most glaring illustrations of the access arms race is the practice of PAC check drops. In a manner not unlike a dentist preparing to drill into the molars of an all-too-eager patient, I was routinely tasked with sitting in my DCCC office for hours on end, greeting representatives from PAC after PAC as they dropped off their checks for Democratic campaigns, usually in amounts averaging about $15,000. These donors walked into the room, handed over the check, and lingered for 20 minutes of conversation. In another office building not far from mine, the chair of the National Republican Congressional Committee was simultaneously collecting checks from the PACs supporting the GOP.

Often, these donors have something on their minds long before entering the room. I distinctly recall receiving a lobbyist for a pharmaceutical company and listening to their diplomatically delivered critique of my comments slamming the industry on a national cable news show. The pharma PAC didn't try to change my policy opinion—they knew they'd only be wasting their breath and cash—but they did leverage their face time with me to make a substantive case that my rhetoric ignored some of the real challenges to research investments in potentially lifesaving drugs.

The reality is that—as is the case with most political disagreements—they had a legitimate point, even if I still thought they were wrong. Their donation was not an effort to buy my vote or anyone else's. But it did get them in a room with me to make their case and attempt to make me more open-minded to their positions long term. That's the goal with this access. Get in a room. Make real conversation. Keep those in power on speed dial.

Meanwhile, by contrast, the millions who would benefit from reforms within Big Pharma had no easy way to cram into my office at the DCCC. That's the problem: Big money develops a gradual soft power advantage on Capitol Hill that can subtly shape policymaking. Voters are right to be wary of this influence, but they shouldn't misconstrue it as something as extreme as corrupt vote buying.

The High Costs of Winning Elections

If you wonder why lawmakers put up with this charade, allow me to take you behind the curtain. When I wasn't receiving PAC donors as DCCC chair, I was coordinating the fundraising apparatus for congressional races across the country. In that capacity, it was sometimes my job to play bad cop to candidates who were avoiding their call time. As we tracked our candidates' fundraising numbers, we'd notice when the money was lagging and place a call to the campaign manager. They would inevitably tell us if the candidate wasn't putting in the work and my intervention was required.

One day, I brought in a highly respected candidate who'd served in the Armed Forces in Iraq. We stood together on the balcony of my DCCC office, about four long blocks from the Capitol. The view in this lower rent district wasn't exactly luxurious: a power plant spewing steam. Literally. I told the candidate frankly that it would cost him $3 million to win his race. With three-quarters left in the cycle, I broke down how much he'd have to raise by month, week, day, hour, and minute. If he wasn't going to put in the time required, the DCCC wouldn't invest in him, and he might as well pull out of the race. I never enjoyed this part of my job, but candidates had to know the reality of their races. We couldn't afford to waste resources on anyone who wasn't giving their all to win.

This war hero who'd fought in heavy combat looked at me as though he'd seen a ghost. Taking gunfire in battle was perfectly acceptable to this man, but the prospect of spending hours upon hours coldcalling rich donors was a form of torture. Despite my pump-up speech, he couldn't bring himself to do the work. He ended up losing his race. And he would have been a great member of Congress.

That's what our campaign finance system does to dedicated public servants. If you think the voters at home are frustrated, just imagine what politicians feel. This is one reason there's such a brain drain nowadays from politics. Many potentially great lawmakers look at the fundraising grind required to get elected and balk. Perhaps even more don't come from wealthy backgrounds or carry Rolodexes of big-money donors and conclude that they just don't have a chance to win. Money is the great barrier to entry for public service in our country.

I'm being plain here about my frustration with the fundraising paradigm in Washington. So why did I remain committed to the chief fundraiser role? To explain, I'll tell you about my worst day as DCCC chair. It came late in the 2014 election.

I woke up at the crack of dawn to catch a plane from New York to Los Angeles, where I was scheduled to fundraise with some of the most competitive California candidates. One was incumbent Rep. Ami Bera, who was locked in a white-knuckle race in CA-7 against then-incumbent Rep. Doug Ose. At 6:30 a.m., I received a call from Kelly Ward, executive director of the DCCC.

She informed me that the Republicans had reserved $2 million in TV ads against Bera. To keep parity and give him a chance in the race, we'd have to come up with $2 million of our own to shovel onto the California airwaves. That meant pulling out of another congressional race altogether. After deliberating over which candidate we'd be painfully forced to abandon, Kelly and I made the decision, and I resolved to call the candidate when I arrived at my hotel in California.

Just when I got there, though, I received another call from Kelly, informing me that the Republicans had reserved $2 million against Bera. I thought she must have been sleep-deprived—we'd just had this conversation. But instead, Kelly explained that the Republicans had countered our counter of $2 million with another $2 million. This was now a $4 million problem. There was no way we could find another $2 million of our own to match the Republicans again. If we were lucky, other outside groups would make up for the shortfall. In one of the most expensive media markets in the country and under a financial avalanche from the GOP, Bera would need every penny he could get to survive. In November, after over $9 million had been spent between the two candidates, Bera narrowly did—squeaking by with a victory of less than a single percentage point.

The process wasn't pretty. The shuffling of dollars was unpleasant, even grimy. But to elect a thoughtful, effective congressman who shared my party's values on issues like health care and climate, every last dime was essential.

Influence Beyond the Dollar

For all the insanity of the campaign finance system, there's another, less conspicuous but even more powerful mechanism by which outside organizations wield power in our politics. In this invisible marketplace, campaign cash isn't leveraged for influence or vote bribing. What's leveraged is the collective power of you, the voter, through these organizations. From unions to business associations to the NRA, the biggest power of these organizations isn't financial; it's electoral.

Often, the great motivator for members of Congress meeting donors is not to deposit a check into their campaign account but to avoid alienating key allies for reelection. On both the left and the right, outside organizations wield clout not through their dollar power but through their manpower—offering huge troves of voters and volunteers.

Back to my friends and allies at the teachers' unions. Their PACs donate millions of dollars a year to campaigns, almost every cent of it to Democrats. But while Democrats are certainly happy to accept some extra money for their campaigns, the real heft of these unions resides in the three million members of the National Education Association and the almost two million members of the American Federation of Teachers. These are reliable voters who can power a member of Congress to reelection and keep a campaign humming with volunteers to phone bank and knock on doors. The platform and branding of these unions also offer opportunities for candidates to get their names out there, appealing to voters well beyond their membership rolls.

On the right, the NRA holds a similar strength. While Republican members of Congress are certainly thrilled to have some extra money in their campaign coffers, the priority is not extracting this money from the NRA—it's keeping the more than five million members of the organization happy, energized, and voting. If the NRA decides it doesn't like a legislator, they have enormous power to shift NRA members' opinions of them through their publications, phone banks, and endorsements. NRA candidate grades alone can shape an entire primary—on both sides. Just as Republicans like to flaunt an A grade from the NRA, Democrats love to show off an F. Interest groups don't need to make donations to wield influence; they just need to possess the power to tank someone's reelection.

I learned this early in my tenure in Congress, when I was involved in a partisan squabble over President Bush's proposal to provide a prescription drug benefit as part of Medicare, known as Medicare Part D. The trouble was that I was on the opposite side of my own party on this issue. You weren't supposed to agree with George Bush about anything as a Democrat, especially as we barreled toward a hotly contested 2004 election.

But this was one of the exceedingly rare areas where I actually agreed with the Republican administration. In my view, it was just good policy. And I'd said as much on the campaign trail—over and over again. I wasn't about to break a campaign promise simply because it delivered a legislative victory to President Bush. So I continued to support it.

One day, I was at an event with senior citizens when an elderly man asked me a question: "How do you know Art Linkletter?" For those of you born after 1940, Art Linkletter was a popular TV game show host. When you went to visit your grandmother—or goodness, your great-grandmother—she probably had Art Linkletter on TV while she was waiting for the cookies in the oven to brown. But I told the elderly man I'd never met Art. Without skipping a beat, he informed me that Linkletter knew me—he'd been on TV telling senior citizens to vote for me.

Little did I know that the American Pharmaceutical Association had hired Linkletter to do a commercial for all the Democrats who crossed the aisle to support Medicare Part D. That's the power of money in politics. One day, I'm just another Democratic member of Congress, who most senior citizens couldn't pick out of a lineup. The next, I'm beloved by grandmothers and grandfathers because a powerful organization used their financial weight to back me to their huge membership.

In that case, I'd actually been rewarded for bipartisanship—but this dynamic more frequently does the opposite (see Representative Pascrell's political gridlock chapter in this book). And it leads to one of the profound problems of our present system: that while PAC donors don't try to buy anyone's votes, they do use their access and influence to eventually harden legislators' positions and discourage compromise. Lawmakers can find themselves increasingly rewarded by powerful organizations for refusing to stray from their positions. This system causes either paralyzing fear or overwhelming stubbornness in legislators due to the potential of massive outside spending for or against them. Every amendment becomes a battleground.

Put yourself in a lawmaker's shoes. For the sake of argument, let's say you're a mainstream Democrat in a purple district who wants commonsense gun regulation. Does it make sense to go out on a limb for a gun control bill that you know won't pass when the NRA will then tag you to be ousted? If you do, you'll lose your seat to someone acceptable to the NRA. You'll be out of a job, and your replacement won't accept any gun regulations at all. When you're in such a lose-lose position, the default action becomes inaction.

As voters sit at home witnessing congressional inaction on so many fronts, the quickest, easiest explanation is the myth that campaign cash is buying votes. It's an efficient, emotionally satisfying conclusion to draw—everyone's corrupt! But the reality is something more nuanced and perhaps more disquieting. We've allowed the financial and organizing power of outside organizations to gain such an outsized influence in our politics that there's never a need to buy votes in the first place.

The Dark Influence of Dark Money

We're not quite done yet. I mentioned dark money earlier as a mechanism for massive political fundraising. It's also a powerful weapon wielded *against* bipartisanship. In simple terms, certain organizations can run political advertisements (or more often, hit pieces) and donate to other PACs *without* disclosing their donors because of their IRS status. These organizations can't buy access to lawmakers but can bomb the airwaves with hundreds of millions of dollars trying to influence the American voter without any accountability whatsoever. Unlike campaign ads, where a candidate must face the camera and heartily say "I approve this message," you will never know who is approving this onslaught of messages. It's a private, behind-the-scenes nuclear arsenal for those seeking to keep lawmakers in their ideological corners.

I first realized the power of dark money by watching television at home in Long Island. As I sat in my den, trying to decompress from a long week of congressional duties and, of course, fundraising, I sat up as a burning Israeli flag flashed across the television screen. It was a withering political ad arguing that to protect the state of Israel, you must vote Republican.

I wondered if it was directed at me—someone who'd long been at the forefront of supporting Israel in Congress—or perhaps a Democrat in a neighboring district. Either way, this was my media market, and I was not going to allow an ad like that to go unaddressed.

I called up my campaign manager and demanded to know who ran the Emergency Committee for Israel, the organization the ad cited as its funding source. My campaign manager looked into it and found . . . nothing. It was a dark money group. There was no way to discover who was donating to them or their motives. To this day, I have no idea who ran an attack ad suggesting that Israel was soft on, um, Israel.

Dark money attack ads like that one hold a dangerous power in our politics—and they're one of the essential mechanisms by which our broken campaign finance system crushes bipartisanship. There's no buying of votes here, but there is the wielding of money as a blunt weapon to cull those who stray from the ideologically pure herd. If millions of dollars can suddenly be dropped on your district without warning or trace to denounce one of your policy positions, you live in a constant state of fear that if you drift too far from your party's consensus, you might find yourself drowning in a sea of attack ads—without even knowing if they represent a set of legitimately angered voters or one pissed off billionaire. (Not to mention the national security implications when dark money comes from foreign adversaries seeking to sow discord in our democracy.)

Imagine you're a member of Congress taking a series of votes on a tough issue—let's say tax exemptions of religious groups—and all of a sudden, you're inundated by dark money ads denouncing you as hostile to voters of faith. How are you supposed to know if you've failed to represent the popular interests of your district or if you've simply run afoul of wealthy groups? If you're a typical member of Congress, commissioning a spate of polling is an expensive—and often inaccurate—endeavor.

And once again, no one has tried to buy your vote. No act of corruption has occurred. But there has been a fundamental corruption of the political process.

Breaking the Chains of Campaign Cash

So what do we do about all this? More importantly, what can you, reader of this book, do to change a political system where politicians are forced to spend more time chasing dollars than your vote? First, you can abandon the myth that campaign cash buys votes. When a candidate stands on a debate stage and accuses their opponent of being bought by a campaign donor, you can recognize it as the grandstanding it is and instead look for candidates seriously interested in campaign finance reform. That leads me to the second thing you can do: Change this system yourself. Honestly. The answer resides in the same place it always does in a democracy—at the ballot box.

If voters are willing to demand their elected representatives change their positions on these issues and take long-overdue action, politicians will take note. This isn't as simple as it sounds. We're talking about turning campaign finance reform into a decisive electoral issue—one that drives voters to the polls and elicits sustained organizing and pressure campaigns. For the latter, that means calling up your representative, writing letters, and knocking on doors, repeatedly over time. This is politics, the old-fashioned way. But with new tools at our fingertips.

For all the political concerns engendered by social media (from life-and-death misinformation to my former colleagues resorting to painfully awkward TikTok dances for clicks), there's a real opportunity for a grassroots movement to pick up steam online without the high-dollar advertising that campaign cash is hoarded to pay for.

What I'm suggesting here is a campaign to change how we campaign in this country. And despite the cynicism that has been drilled into us in this hyperpolarized political era, the truth is this still is a campaign we can win. Here's what we should try to get done:

First, let's talk about what could be instituted tomorrow to effect real change: executive orders. **The president should mandate shareholder disclosures of all corporate political expenditures.** This would mean that if you own any stock in a company, you'd get a regular report detailing every political donation made by that company. Doing so would create greater accountability for major corporations seeking to use their financial might to influence Congress.

We also need to shed some sunlight on dark money. **Every campaign ad, no matter who pays for it, should require an explicit disclosure identifying the funding source and a QR code that links to that source.** A law requiring this would be fantastic, but again, the president could make this happen on a Tuesday with an executive order.

Long term, we need to think about more wholesale challenges, such as **publicly financed elections, stricter limits on money bundling by PACs, a dark money ban, and candidate spending limits**. These would require big changes in law. I'm not going to sugarcoat it—this stuff has zero chance of passing right now. But as the only Western democracy that allows this frenzied, unlimited spending in our politics, we need to work toward commonsense reforms to restore confidence in the integrity of our government. It starts with you demanding sensible campaign finance solutions rather than relying on myths that discourage you from taking action.

Politicians only have an incentive to change this system if they know voters will evict them from office for sitting on their hands.

Recognize the power in this—fearing for their seats means that lawmakers will go where there are the most votes. It's how they stay there. Without that pressure, members of Congress are perpetually attempting to fight financial fire with financial fire. The only way to topple this house of cards is to shake up the entire House.

"Lobbyists Are Evil"

Quardricos Driskell

It's funny how a pair of socks can change your life.

Actually, it was a pair of *missing* socks that changed mine.

On a sweltering Sunday in August 2012, I stepped into a historically Black Baptist church in rural Flint Hill, Virginia. Churches are and always have been a second home to me. At that time, I was an assistant pastor in Alexandria, Virginia, right outside Washington, DC. But on this day, I had been invited to preach to Flint Hill's congregation of local churches, a big deal for me at the time. I dressed impeccably, going sockless under my loafers to stay cool. Though young, I had preached to large congregations, so I knew I was ready to deliver the good news to this rural community.

Upon arrival, I realized this was not just any rural church. The host pastor, Rev. Donald Simpkins, wasn't just any preacher. He was the moderator for the Northern Virginia Baptist Convention and a known bigwig in our Baptist circles. And here I was, a young assistant pastor in my mid-20s, standing before him like I'd just stopped in on my way to a country club Easter buffet.

Rev. Simpkins looked me up and down, clearly disturbed. I could see the doubt—or was it disappointment?—in his eyes. He quickly escorted me to his study and sat me down, and the interrogation began.

Rev. Simpkins grilled me about my theological education, my church affiliations, and my upbringing, all in a tone that was more trial than small talk. Finally, he zeroed in on the real issue: "Why aren't you wearing socks, and why did you think this was appropriate?" His voice carried the weight of every expectation I'd failed to meet, and I suddenly realized the magnitude of my wardrobe malfunction. It wasn't just about socks—it was about respect, tradition, and the unspoken rules of the pulpit.

By this time, my appointed sermon time was only minutes away. I felt certain the reverend was going to show me the door before I spoke a word to his flock. But instead he said, "I'm going to let you preach this time, but next time you need to be properly attired."

As I stepped up to the pulpit, Rev. Simpkins sat so close behind me that I could feel his presence looming, as if ready to pounce at the first sign of heresy—or perhaps the first sight of ankle bone. I don't even remember what I preached that day, but I'll never forget the look on his face when I finished. He smiled, laughed even, and exclaimed, "Boy, you can preach in my pulpit anytime!" From that moment, we became friends, and he became a mentor, always pulling up my pant cuff at church functions to check for socks.

In 2019, two years after I became senior pastor at my church in Alexandria, I learned that Rev. Simpkins had passed away from prostate cancer—a disease that disproportionately affects African Americans and veterans like him. Rev. Simpkins had served in Vietnam, and as a health-care lobbyist in DC, I was all too familiar with the disastrous connection between Agent Orange and prostate cancer. I knew that one in five veterans can expect to be diagnosed with prostate cancer in their lifetime, and they are twice as likely as the general population to die from it; the rates are even higher for Black veterans exposed to Agent Orange.

I also knew that, at the time, routine screenings were not a standard practice in Veterans Administration clinics, even for those dispro-portionately affected by prostate cancer, such as Black veterans like Rev. Simpkins. As I spoke with his son at his funeral, my worst fears were confirmed: Rev. Simpkins's death could have been prevented if only his cancer had been caught sooner. He was only 65.

Rev. Simpkins's death made my work even more personal than it already was. He had ministered and served his country, only to be failed by the very system that should have protected him. His death was a stark reminder of the disparities in our health-care system, particularly for those who have given so much.

This was the moment when my two ministries collided.

On one side, there was my Christian ministry, rooted in the commitment to improving people's lives, giving hope, and helping them cope with life's pains. On the other side was my lobbying ministry, which I view as making democracy better—improving the federal republic as our Framers intended, flawed as it may be. Both callings, though seemingly worlds apart, are deeply connected. Both try to make every soul feel seen, heard, and cared for. And in both, I serve as an intermediary and translator for their hopes, dreams, and fears.

At the time, I was leading government relations at the American Urological Association, working on legislation to increase prostate cancer screening for men at higher risk, like Rev. Simpkins.

His passing became the impetus for my work on the Veterans Prostate Cancer Treatment and Research Act, a bill that would create a comprehensive clinical pathway care program within the Veterans Health Administration. For more than three years, I lobbied members of Congress and managed political contributions to key members of the congressional Veterans Affairs Committee, which would largely author the bill. In every conversation, I carried Rev. Simpkins's story with me.

When President Biden signed the bill into law in 2021—officially instating a clinical program that included early detection and screening for populations with known high-risk factors—I contacted Rev. Simpkins's family to let them know that my efforts were in memory of their father.

There are so many policy stories that don't end like this. Stories of people who want policy changes—whose lives literally depend on it—but don't have the time, capacity, or expertise to effectively push that change.

I've seen this over and over, on issues ranging from school shootings to child trafficking to prescription drug costs. Groups of people may organize around a critical goal, earn TV news appearances and big donations, and march on Washington in huge numbers. And despite all this, they fail to achieve what they need most: a change in law.

The reason is fairly simple—they don't have the right advocates. They have the motivation, the powerful stories, and even broad public support, but they're missing the crucial elements—the right conversations with the right people, using the right language—that turn passion into policy.

In short, they need lobbyists. We all do.

In Defense of the Scarlet "L"

I tell my students often that everyone is represented whether they realize it or not. Their response typically runs something like: *"Lobbyists?!"* Many assume lobbyists are the main reason our government is so broken, so dysfunctional. Lobbyists are the swamp rats of DC, corruptive mercenaries for hire, armed with cash to bribe lawmakers for votes to ensure their conglomerate overlords can buy yet another bigger yacht at the expense of the American people. They're the problem, not the solution. (How close am I to your perception?)

I know firsthand that nearly everyone hates lobbyists because I am one. I often joke that I should be forced to wear a scarlet "L" to warn folks not to come near me. With such anger toward my ilk, it's no surprise that "Drain the Swamp" became an effective rallying cry in Donald Trump's 2016 run for president. Barack Obama did the same thing, in nicer language, in his 2008 campaign, saying, "I intend to tell the corporate lobbyists that their days of setting the agenda in

Washington are over." Any candidate looking for an automatic applause line only has to mention how tough he or she will be on special interests once elected. In a rare case of bipartisan agreement, Americans across the board hate special interest groups and view lobbyists as corrosive influences, using money and shady maneuvers to steer legislation to serve their self-interest over the national interest.

Yet I proudly tell people that I am a part of the swamp!

I can understand why lobbying looks that way from the outside. Anytime you mix money and influence, you instantly enter the territory of our worst perceptions about politics and shady politicians. Yet speaking as someone who sees the practice from the inside—including its good, bad, and ugly—I can tell you that assumption is just simply wrong.

This isn't to say that lobbyists and special interest groups aren't powerful in American politics; they are (some more than others, as we'll discuss). Or that lobbying causes no problems. But there is a tremendous and dangerous gap between what the average American *thinks* a lobbyist does—including their role, influence, and tactics—and what they *actually do* in Washington, DC.

The truth is that lobbyists and politics are as intertwined as log-ins and forgotten passwords. As long as governments have been around deciding things, people have grouped together to add volume and organization to get more of what they want. It's how you get things done in a democracy. You need friends. You need advocates. And in a diverse country as big as ours, there will always be a need for an intermediary between the people and lawmakers: conduits who organize and promote the many competing interests to lawmakers while everyone is off living their busy lives. Just as in a courtroom where a plaintiff needs a prosecutor and a defendant needs a defense attorney, in politics, you need advocates to plead your case in the language of the industry. In politics, these intermediaries are lobbyists, and they are vital to representation. They ensure all sides of an issue are heard—though, to continue the courtroom analogy, some lobbyists, like some lawyers, are more skilled (and much more expensive) than others.

Consider a fundamental issue like the minimum wage. On one side, you have employers, often represented by business entities like chambers of commerce or the Business Roundtable, who want to keep wages lower. On the other side, you have workers, typically represented by labor unions, who fight for a bump. Although these camps may look like opponents, the relationship between employers and workers is symbiotic: Without employers, there are no jobs; without workers, there's no production or profit. The debate over wages is crucial for both to survive. If wages are too high, employers might shut down due to insufficient profits. If wages are too low, employees struggle to make ends meet. Both sides have legitimate self-interests, and the debate is necessary without labeling either as inherently wrong, greedy, or unethical. Lawmakers weighing these questions need to hear from advocates for both parties in order to understand the issue in full and attempt to develop a sensible national policy that weighs all the considerations.

Those advocates are called lobbyists.

Plus, lawmakers *need* them, but also not for the reasons you think. It isn't the cash (though not many will turn down the campaign donations). Lobbyists are valuable and influential because of the *information* they can provide to overburdened legislators and inexperienced staff who can't possibly be expert enough on all the issues we expect them to solve.

Because of this reality, everything—every issue, company, or organization—affected by governmental decisions has representation in DC, largely through special interest groups and lobbyists. When we think of special interests, though, we mostly think of those advocating for things we don't like. Big tobacco. Pharmaceutical companies. The gun lobby. Oil conglomerates. These four make up the Mount Rushmore of most despised lobbyists. But the ACLU, AARP, the Nature Conservancy, Environmental Defense Fund, NAACP, the National Organization for Women, the Anti-Defamation League, labor unions, cancer patients, parents wanting fewer school shootings, and electric bike advocates also have lobbyists working to be heard on their issues, too.

We all have interests, and to us, the ones we care about the most are special. For things we support, we are relieved when our voices are heard in the halls of power. In fact, we wish they were even more effective and had even more resources to be heard by more people with the power to do something.

So unless you plan to pack up and move to DC to be a full-time advocate for all the issues you care about, let's admit we need lobbying and lobbyists. Admitting this is an important first step to fixing the very real problems within the lobbying industry. Because as much as it's necessary, the lobbying system in the United States is far from perfect. We have huge disparities in access and influence between lobbyists, and it biases our laws as a result.

The disproportionate strength of corporate versus everyday interests lobbying shops is enormous. Like a sumo wrestler versus a toddler in a tug-of-war, the outcomes of many policy battles are predictable and predictably unfair. And we need to fix it. To do that, we first need a much clearer picture of the role lobbyists play in our system. Most of all, we need to get past the well-intentioned knee-jerk calls to ban them from the system entirely.

From Eavesdropper to Advocate

I was always a proud nerd and an old soul. For as long as I can remember, I've been fascinated with history and government. As a kid, I could regularly be found with a newspaper in my hand, asking questions with no provable answers—for me, the conversations, the people, were the point. And yet I never planned to join the ranks of America's most misunderstood profession.

My journey into lobbying began in Atlanta, where my mother was a force to be reckoned with—one of those unstoppable ladies who seemed to have a hand in everything. She was deeply committed to making a difference, and Atlanta, with its thriving Black middle class, was the perfect backdrop for her activism.

Thanks to her, I grew up rubbing elbows with some serious movers and shakers, like Maynard Jackson, the first Black mayor of Atlanta (or any other major Southern city). Picture this: a nosey kid wanting to sit at the adult table, but not being allowed. I eavesdropped on their high-energy conversations and prayed no one would notice me and tell me to go do something more age-appropriate. I was just a fly on the wall, soaking up every word and loving every minute of it.

When I was in middle school, my spark for civics turned into a full-blown blaze, thanks to my mother. She took on the role of treasurer and co-campaign manager for a local state house race, backing Regina Davis, a young woman taking on longtime incumbent Tyrone Brooks—a seasoned civil rights leader. Regina didn't win, but that campaign was my crash course in the nuts and bolts of politics. I was the kid tagging along to every meeting, passing out leaflets, and grasping every nuance as if my future depended on it. My mother's commitment showed me that this wasn't just about supporting a candidate—it was about making a real difference through what that candidate could achieve.

In high school, I threw myself into every leadership opportunity I could find—youth leadership programs, Boys State, the City of East Point youth council. By the time I got to college, I was knee-deep in student government and active in the Morehouse Republicans. As a junior, I landed an internship at the Georgia General Assembly, working for Ed Harbison, chair of the Georgia Legislative Black Caucus. I remember sitting in his office, answering phones, responding to constituent letters, and praying the office AC would keep up with the Georgia humidity. I watched, day after day, as people came in and out to meet with the senator.

These folks were always impeccably dressed—a personal kryptonite, I'll admit—and they had direct access to the lawmakers. My job was to politely inform hopeful visitors that, regrettably, Mr. Harbison's schedule was tighter than a drum and there was no room for a meeting. And yet, somehow, these other people were getting in.

Finally, I asked an office colleague, "Who are these people?"

The answer: They're lobbyists. And I knew immediately, "I want to do that."

As a college student wanting to make a difference through policy, that seemed like the pinnacle of influence. I quickly learned that a lobbyist's job was to shape legislation, to influence the very policies that govern our lives. It sounded fascinating and impactful—and it didn't hurt that the perks (Did I mention they were impeccably dressed?) were pretty appealing, too. Here was a path to combine my passion for politics with my aim to improve people's lives. My own kind of ministry.

Debunking the Lobbyist Stereotype

We've all been inundated with tales, both real and Hollywoodized, of lobbyists sleazebagging the legislative process. Characters like "Casino Jack" Abramoff, famous for bribing legislators and getting rich off his Rolodex of politicians, are seared into our public perception of the profession. Everyone with the lobbyist title is tarnished by these scandals. So I knew I was entering a universally loathed profession. But I also know from my decades of experience that frauds like Abramoff and his cronies are the exception, not the rule. Most lobbyists actually care about the causes they represent.

Let's address the $4.27 billion[1]—the amount spent on lobbying in 2023 alone—elephant in the room right from the start. This figure covers lobbyist salaries, travel, office rents, and yes, campaign donations. Just for comparison, Americans spent about $26 billion on Valentine's Day purchases in the same year.[2]

Still, $4.27 billion is an undeniably gross amount of money. But despite the sticker shock of the amount, anyone who works in policymaking—including lawmakers themselves—will admit that it isn't the cash that makes lobbyists influential. It's their information. They have it. Lawmakers need it. And a valuable market is created. As a point of proof, around 70 percent of lobbying organizations don't contribute a dime to political action committees (PACs). So the next time you hear jaw-dropping figures about lobbying expenses, keep in mind that most of that money is actually spent on the people doing the lobbying, not on piles of campaign cash given to candidates.[3]

How can lobbyists have information that Congress—the most powerful legislature in the world—doesn't? Put simply: Congress is overwhelmed.[4] Not only does it not employ enough or the right kind of in-house experts, but the number and depth of issues on which Congress is expected to be expert is utterly impossible.

Each representative has an average of three policy aides. As a lawmaker or one of their few staffers, you've got to stay on top of everything from climate change to cybersecurity to agricultural policies—at the devil-in-the-details knowledge level required to write complicated legislation. On any given day, staffers may have to author the best policy for deterring Belarus from attacking Ukraine, incentivize the expansion of manufacturing jobs in the Rust Belt, and reduce factory emissions into drinking water. The more the policy demands of the job increase, the less the 26-year-old legislative staffer with nine issues in her portfolio (true averages, by the way) is able to keep up with the research and drafting. It's like studying for a final exam in every subject, every single day. But instead of the pressures of a grade that you'll forget about as soon as you're handed your diploma, lives and jobs (including your own) depend on your decisions.

Members of Congress simply don't have the staff or informational resources at their disposal on all the issues on which they make monumental decisions. In these many cases, they do what all of us do when we need information: They find it from a trusted source so they can move on to the next problem in their inbox. In Congress, this means from lobbyists with whom they already agree on the issue. For example, on the complex question of how to regulate power plant emissions, both liberals and conservatives need expert advice. But a liberal probably seeks that advice from environmental protection advocates, while a conservative asks coal industry lobbyists.

Lobbyists enter this equation not with bags of cash but with binders of knowledge. Compared to congressional offices, lobbying shops are well staffed with experts—from data scientists to researchers to former practitioners—whose job is to be the authoritative voice on a few selected issues. Notice how I said a few issues: not the average of nine that a congressional staffer is assigned or the infinite number we expect our lawmakers to thoughtfully legislate on. This laser focus on a smaller set of topics allows for a more in-depth expertise that is the source of the true and genuine influence of lobbyists in DC. They are the specialists in a business that requires and rewards specialization.

It may, understandably, feel backward that outsiders are feeding essential information to policymakers. But the reality is that these outsiders are the ones with the expertise on complicated, nuanced issues. They help lawmakers become the experts we expect them to be, when they could never realistically possess all that knowledge on their own.

How about a corollary? If you need brain surgery, are you cool with your general practitioner whipping out the drill on your dome, or do you want a known expert for your particular condition? For things that matter, having just a general sense of what to do isn't good enough. No, you want the person with the track record, the experience, the earned knowledge to identify the right course in an unpredictable environment. And members don't have this level of knowledge in everything they need to take votes on. If there's a proposal to build a nuclear waste site in your neighborhood, do you want your representative to wing it on the science or take advice from an actual nuclear waste specialist? If a cyberattack threatens to cripple essential services, do you want your senator—average age of 64, by the way—to lead the government's defense strategy, or would you rather they listen to cybersecurity experts who have worked on the issue for decades and dealt with similar crises?

In a constantly evolving, complex, interconnected world, lobbyists act as the crucial bridge between the public and private sectors. They are educators, translators, interpreters, and liaisons. They ensure that lawmakers hear from those who are most affected by the decisions made in Washington, DC. Consider the CHIPS and Science Act, a 2022 law that invested $280 billion in research and domestic manufacturing of semiconductors (hardware used in nearly every electronic device in the world). The act was considered vital to our national security because without domestic manufacturing of these vital parts, the United States would become increasingly reliant on our "frenemy," China, to supply them.

Private sector experts and those who would ultimately produce the semiconductors were called on to inform Congress of how best to write the incredibly complex legislation. No singular individual was expert enough on all the related aspects to author the 394-page bill, given its intricacies across dozens of industries and technologies. Though ostensibly a bill about semiconductor manufacturing, the legislation touched on nearly every aspect of the global economy, including supply chains, blockchain standards, coastal acidification, waste disposal, nuclear fission technology, and projects involving the weaponization of space. A single misplaced or forgotten phrase could have scuttled or sidetracked one of the law's priorities. One of the law's 60-plus provisions, for example, created a new fund to help incentivize the private sector to work with the National Science Foundation to train the next generation of engineers who will work on semiconductors. Below is the dense language used in the legislation to create such a fund—and remember, this is just one paragraph of a nearly 400-page bill:

> There is established in the Treasury of the United States a fund to be known as the "Creating Helpful Incentives to Produce Semiconductors (CHIPS) for America Workforce and Education Fund" (referred to in this subsection as the "Fund") for the National Science Foundation for microelectronics workforce development activities to meet the requirements under section 9906 of the William M. (Mac) Thornberry National Defense Authorization Act for Fiscal Year 2021 (15 U.S.C. 4656).

The law created more than 25 similar funds, each with its own prioritized recipients, overseers, statutory eligibility requirements, and outlined metrics of success. To inform the process, hundreds of experts—academics, practitioners, and yes, lobbyists—testified at more than two dozen hearings and worked with congressional committee staff and lawmakers to draft a passable and overwhelmingly bipartisan bill both parties championed as a huge success.

This process happens constantly on all matters before the legislature, and lobbyists are at the policymaking table throughout. They might provide a background crash course for lawmakers and staff, reports on the latest relevant research, detailed policy papers that offer specific options for legislative fixes, or questions for witnesses appearing before a committee. And yes, lobbyists provide actual draft legislation that can be introduced by lawmakers the second it hits the office printer tray. Staffers actually love this because they don't have the time or knowledge to draft the complicated language themselves (case in point: the language of the CHIPS Act above).

The information that lobbyists provide and Congress loves isn't always policy related, either. Because of their much fatter wallets, lobbying shops can run expensive political polls—down to the district level—that give lawmakers data-backed insights on how (and how much) certain populations feel about an issue or potential solution. Relatedly, special interest groups can offer lawmakers insights from their focus groups that lead to small but incredibly impactful differences in how issues are framed, discussed, and accepted. The seemingly semantic language changes from "pro-choice" to "reproductive rights" and from "global warming" to "climate change"—small differences in words that made enormous differences in support—didn't come by accident; they were largely developed by special interests looking to broaden support.

Finally, lobbying groups often use their resources for electoral purposes, such as phone banking operations for or against a certain politician or distributing literature to citizens about how a lawmaker is viewed on a certain issue. The most famous example of this is the National Rifle Association's "report card" that gives all sitting members of Congress a grade on their gun control stances; because of the NRA's huge membership, conservatives work hard to earn A's, while liberals wear their F's as a badge of honor. Just as Representative Israel mentions in his chapter on the real influence of campaign cash, lawmakers work hard to keep their party-aligned interest groups happy so they don't risk their big memberships being turned against them.

Put simply, lobbyists do a lot of the homework that allows lawmakers to look smart and stay just informed enough to get through their hearing, press conference, or vote or to be a leading voice on an issue of importance to them. It's a win-win, symbiotic relationship: Lobbyists get their agendas in front of legislators, while legislators get the detailed, up-to-date info they need to do the job they can't do on their own. The cliché that "Information is power" is true for making laws, too.

Think for a moment about the kind of information that moves you, and you'll quickly recognize that the expertise lawmakers need to fully grasp an issue is not just technical; it's human. Just like the story of a single child with a cleft palate can convince you to donate money when a raft of statistics cannot, elected officials need help to turn the technical and abstract into the personal and the tangible. That is also lobbyists' job.

One of the best tactics we use to personalize issues to those in power is to organize "fly-ins." Here, instead of informing lawmakers ourselves, we literally fly in people—practitioners, patients, survivors—from across the country to voice their policy wishes and warnings to lawmakers and staff. Not just one person, but a lot of people, to flood congressional offices with real human stories. Because unlike stacks of signatures or form letters that an intern receives and shreds within hours, Congress can't ignore us if we're in front of their faces.

Early in my career, I organized impressive groups of first-hand experts—more than 300 patients, caregivers, widows, and families—who had been deeply affected by prostate cancer. I was one of two lobbyists for the organization ZERO—The End of Prostate Cancer. These annual events were more strategic than a big march on the Washington Mall that draws TV cameras but delivers no legislative change. They were targeted and purposeful. I asked parents, children, nurses, and doctors to make their case to specific lawmakers for specific changes in law, regulation, and congressional attention.

And I took on the responsibility of preparing these advocates to effectively engage with and influence members of Congress. I taught them how to navigate the complex legislative process and communicate their experiences in a way that would resonate with policymakers and their young staff. These volunteers came armed with personal stories and experiences that underscored the urgent need for policy changes around early detection and screening for prostate cancer. They described how their families were torn apart by their dads' preventable death or how deeply they had to go into debt for treatments. Stories can move policymakers just as powerfully as they move all of us!

These grassroots fly-ins laid the groundwork for my later work organizing grass-top fly-ins, where I focused on connecting key health-care leaders with influential members of Congress. These high-level meetings played a crucial role in getting the Veterans Prostate Cancer and Research and Treatment Act across the finish line. As an experienced lobbyist, I knew to target Rep. Neal Dunn (R-FL-02), a member of Congress who was also a urologist. To do that, I forged relationships with his staff and visited his district. When the bill needed a Senate companion, I met with Sen. Jon Tester (D-MT) and attended a fundraiser for a chance to talk with Sen. Jerry Moran (R-KS), empowering him with stories like that of Rev. Simpkins. When I met with members of Congress in the law's drafting stage, I brought key prostate cancer urologists, VA urologists, and veteran service organizations to make sure the bill was inked just right. This was a change that the United States and our veterans deeply needed, but it took experts, advocates, and lawmakers working together with a skilled lobbyist to make it happen.

Trust, Truth, and Influence

The fact that Congress relies so heavily on lobbyist information to get the job done naturally opens quite a few cans of worms for those skeptical that lawmakers aren't always working on behalf of "we, the people." You yourself may be asking, "Doesn't that leave our representatives incredibly vulnerable to biased, misleading, partisan, or outright manipulated information?"

Yup.

And here we come to the crux of the *true and very real* problems of lobbyist influence: the risk of biased information and the financial disparities between lobbying organizations. Lobbying for nonprofit organizations versus for-profit clients presents stark differences, particularly when it comes to access and influence.

And I have lobbied for both.

While lobbying for ZERO, I often found myself on the outside looking in. The nonprofit world, despite its noble cause, often lacks the financial resources that can open doors in the political arena. This reality hit home when I, at a later stage in my career, became a more corporate lobbyist managing a PAC for the American Urological Association. It was the PAC's deep pockets that allowed me to spend the $2,500 or so that it cost to attend that critical fundraising lunch for Sen. Jerry Moran. I knew that Senator Moran was the ranking member of the Senate Veterans Committee, and I needed him to sponsor the bill. So I strategically attended a fundraiser where I was the only health-care lobbyist. This provided me with direct access to get to know him while discussing the specifics of the bill—access I wouldn't have had in my earlier years working for the nonprofit.

Listen, as a corporate lobbyist, I have been on yachts with members of Congress, dined at Michelin-star restaurants, and stayed at some of the finest hotels. The disparities are clear: Nonprofit lobbyists typically have to work much harder to get lawmakers' attention, relying heavily on the passion and personal stories of their advocates rather than financial contributions. In contrast, corporate lobbyists often have the means to participate in high-profile events where we can directly engage with influential members of Congress. This difference underscores the challenges nonprofit lobbyists face in trying to compete.

Does that mean, however, that well-resourced lobbyists get to walk a tightrope of truth on behalf of clients with a policy agenda? No. We lobbyists know better than most that an expert-deficient legislature provides fertile ground for unscrupulous actors to exploit lawmakers' dependence on their information. Many believe this is the dark side of lobbying—a murky realm where bad-faith actors peddle false information to achieve their ends regardless of the public good. In this version of DC—one in which Kevin Spacey is likely playing a lead role—the assumption is that lobbyists can, and regularly do, lie to accomplish their policy ends.

We can't. Well, some do—but they don't last long.

There's no denying that the lobbying profession, like every profession throughout history, has its share of bad apples who can't overcome the immediate but fleeting rewards that accompany the easy way out. But, and hear me out on this, most of us understand that our reputation in this business, especially in the bubble that is Washington, DC, is the currency that purchases the most valuable commodity in making laws: access. Without the access our name provides, it doesn't matter what information we have—we aren't getting in the room where it matters to present it. And without trust, access evaporates.

Plus, think about it from the lawmaker's point of view: They are putting their reputations—and their political futures—on the line when they publicly speak on an issue or take a vote on a bill. Knowing this, they rely on known and trusted brokers. They block unknown numbers just like you do.

As a lobbyist, my credibility is crucial for sustaining my influence and effectiveness, much like a journalist's reputation for accuracy and fairness earns loyal readers. The relationships I've built—both as a young lobbyist in the nonprofit sector and later as a corporate lobbyist—have proven invaluable. Early on, while working for nonprofit organizations like the prostate cancer advocacy group, I had to rely on building deep, meaningful connections with lawmakers and their staff. These relationships were forged on trust, shared values, and the authenticity of our cause. Despite the limited resources and access I had then, the genuine rapport I developed became a cornerstone of my professional credibility. Years later, lawmakers remember the work I did, the causes I championed, and the sincerity with which I approached every issue. The respect and trust I earned during that time remain intact. It's how I stay valuable.

If a lobbyist (or staffer, for that matter) becomes known for peddling crooked, misleading, or falsified information, their access to decision-makers is shut off, and their value plummets. They become toxic to lawmakers who fear being linked with the next Casino Jack. No organization or company that deals with Congress will want to jeopardize its standing by hiring or employing a fraud. A lobbyist's influence—and thus their value—comes from being the go-to person for reliable, justifiable, and verifiable answers. This reputation hinges on accuracy and trustworthiness, especially when it means telling lawmakers, staffers, and clients exactly what they don't want to hear—that the most trusted information doesn't support their objectives. As one former Republican representative turned lobbyist told me, "Besides time, what's the one thing I can't get back if I waste it? My reputation." The vast majority of us lobbyists agree.

The sad thing, however, is that too many modern lawmakers aren't interested in unimpeachable, perfect information. No, they *want biased* information that supports their partisan stances. They actively seek it out and use it to substantiate their preexisting beliefs and justify their decisions. And special interest groups are, of course, happy to oblige. Lobbying shops with enough cash are increasingly opening up their own nonpartisan but definitely partisan research shops, staffed with impressive CVs, to pump out findings to support the organization's points of view, which Congress uses as justification to do what they always wanted to do in the first place. It's an echo chamber of prepaid confirmation bias that would make even the most aggressive social media algorithm jealous.

As a citizen, you can spot these fake think tanks in a few different ways. First, always follow the money. As nonprofits, every think tank must make financial statements publicly available—they aren't as entertaining as John Grisham, but they tell you the organization's main funding sources. If the organization is primarily backed by a specific industry or political group, that's a red flag that their research might be biased. Also, review the backgrounds of the board members and staff. If they have strong ties to a particular lobby or political party, their "nonpartisan" label might be just for show.

The rest of us take truth as our utmost responsibility. But even if principled lobbyists don't outright lie, it is still true that lobbying is advocacy, and advocacy has a point of view. When there are arguments both for and against a particular policy, I am naturally going to emphasize the ones that serve my clients. And that's why we dearly need to level the playing field of access and influence to ensure that all points of view are heard equitably.

Certain industries and issues, because of their limitless bank accounts, are able to open more doors and provide lawmakers with more vital information than others—and that gives them more influence. To be blunt, the industries many people hate—pharmaceuticals, tech giants, insurance, and Wall Street—represent the top four biggest lobbying spendings. Pharmaceutical companies spent just shy of $400 million lobbying (nearly 10 percent of all money spent lobbying) in 2023 alone. With those resources comes the trifecta for influence in DC: access to advocate for your preferred outcomes (which can often mean no change at all), funds to employ and retain in-house experts to produce the information Congress craves, and the money required to hire and pay a whole lot of lobbyists.

The nonprofit sector just can't compete. And the tilted playing field affects who Congress is listening to and, ultimately, what laws they choose to change. As political scientist Lee Drutman, one of the leading voices in the lobbying industry, writes, "Today, the biggest companies have upwards of 100 lobbyists representing them, allowing them to be everywhere, all the time. For every dollar spent on lobbying by labor unions and public-interest groups together, large corporations and their associations now spend $34. Of the 100 organizations that spend the most on lobbying, 95 consistently represent business."[5] For the public interest groups, it's like trying to win a cooking contest with a toaster.

Striking the Balance for a Fairer Democracy

The very real struggle—and the important one for our democracy—is to design a system where the special interests of the few don't outweigh those of "the people." This is where we absolutely do need reforms, and lobbyists are the first ones to admit it. There are a few key places to start.

First and foremost, we need to get past the knee-jerk calls to ban lobbyists from the system entirely. Not only is this impossible, but it's been tried in partial form—and it backfired. As he promised, President Obama signed an executive order on his first day in office prohibiting registered lobbyists from serving in his administration and working on issues for which they previously lobbied. President Trump issued a similar executive order for his administration. But because we can never reasonably remove lobbyists from politics, this well-intentioned "solution" led to a drastic 30 percent reduction in the number of registered lobbyists, while the amount of money spent on lobbying continued to skyrocket.

In other words, the lobbying continued but just went unreported. Formerly registered lobbyists became consultants, doing the same work but with far less transparency and accountability. Just as Prohibition produced an explosion of black market alcohol and an accompanying rise in crime, banning political lobbyists drove the services underground and left the public more in the dark than ever about their work. This is good for no one except those cashing the lobbying checks.

Recognizing that we cannot and should never get rid of special interests in policymaking, the goal should then be to level the lobbying playing field so that all interests have equal access to decision-makers. With equal access, we get closer to the democratic ideal that the best-supported argument—rather than the argument with the best access—wins out.

The counterintuitive solution put forward by Drutman and others? More lobbying, not less.

The greater the diversity of thought informing the process, the better chance we have to represent all perspectives. This means it cannot simply be about who has the most money to hire well-connected lobbyists or fund "impartial" research organizations. One potential solution is to use public petitions to guarantee congressional responses—meetings, hearings, floor debates, even votes—if and when a certain signature threshold is met (100,000 signatories, for example). Understanding that Congress must respond to a well-organized interest would create an incentive for those to invest in grassroots mobilization and engage more citizens in the democratic process. This approach could help ensure that the voices of ordinary people are heard alongside those with deep pockets.

Congress could also create a cadre of publicly funded "civic lobbyists" whose job it is to represent the public on a predefined set of issues. Think of these as political public defenders; their job is to advocate for their client when their client doesn't have the resources to hire their own representation. Relatedly, Congress could pass legislation that requires lawmakers to provide equal time and access to organizations that don't receive donations from for-profit entities. They could also require that any for-profit organization formally lobbying Congress spend a certain amount of its budget on community enrichment and civic education efforts. Or they could develop a match system whereby nonprofit organizations receive a five-to-one boost in public funds to help offset the financial advantages currently enjoyed by for-profit firms.

At the very least, Congress could update its transparency requirements for all organizations and individuals lobbying lawmakers, including publicly available and up-to-date meeting schedules, disclosure forms, dollar amounts associated with the lobbying effort, and details on the issues or legislation being discussed and with whom. This would ensure that the public knows exactly who the lobbyists are, who is paying them, and what they are paying them to do. Sunshine is, after all, the best disinfectant.

In my view, though, the key reform to limit the informational influence of special interest groups is a wholesale reinvestment in Congress itself. To ensure that lawmakers and committees are able to maintain the requisite in-house expertise required to proactively legislate (and oversee the private sector for nefarious actors), Congress simply needs more resources—financial, technological, and human. Such an investment would require much more money to hire more legislative staffers and pay them comparable wages to compete with the private sector and those who are lobbying them. Staffers responsible for writing policy on banks, Wall Street, or taxes, for example, are currently paid 50 percent less than those working in those fields for private companies. The ratio is even worse for staff addressing technology innovation or regulation, where they are competing with tech giants like Meta and Google for the same employees. For those considering a career in these fields, working for Congress never even crosses their minds.

While any system carries the risk of being exploited, the dangers of maintaining the status quo in our advocacy system are far greater. To ensure our democracy truly represents all its citizens, we must take decisive action so that those with wallets big enough to double as life rafts don't have the only seats at the table. By promoting diverse and balanced advocacy, we can strengthen our democracy and make it more reflective of the people it serves. I strive to do this every day.

After all, a stronger republic is built not on the exclusion of interests but on the inclusion of diverse voices working together for the common good. Our definitions of the common good are often wildly different, but the beauty is that our system allows—even encourages—such disagreement.

In the end, it's not the absence of conflict but the freedom to navigate it together, with equitable representation, that truly fortifies our democracy.

"Term Limits Will Fix Our Broken Congress"

Dr. Casey Burgat

On a warm spring day in May 2023, a throng of tourists, photographers, and reporters stood outside the US Senate steps with their cameras fixed on a silver Lexus creeping to a halt. The car's passenger door creaked open as several young staffers, clad in ill-fitting suits, rolled up a black wheelchair to help Sen. Dianne Feinstein (D-CA)—then 89 years old and a 30-year Senate veteran—make her way into the Senate. Feinstein was returning from a nearly three-month absence due to complications from shingles. And onlookers were eager to get a glimpse of the senator to determine if her deteriorating health would continue to impact her ability to carry out her duties.

Once in view, the senator appeared frail. Her hands trembled. "Where am I going?" Feinstein asked, to no one in particular, as she was transferred from the car into the wheelchair and guided inside the Capitol. A few months and several reports of similar states of confusion later, Feinstein had to be uncomfortably directed by Sen. Patty Murray (D-WA) during a hearing of the Appropriations Committee. The clerk had called Feinstein's name several times to register her vote.

"Say 'Aye,'" Murray whispered to Feinstein. She repeated the directive twice more.

Feinstein suddenly sprang into action. But instead of voting, she began reading from her prepared remarks, prompting an aide to whisper that the time for statements had passed.

"Just say 'Aye,'" Murray whispered once more.

Finally, Feinstein complied.

Those questioning the mental capacity of aging members of Congress have as many examples as those horrible caramel candies they put in their congressional office treat bowls. There's a storied tradition of senators and representatives overstaying their welcome well past the point when they should have retired and gone to spend more time with the grandkids. There's even a clue in the very name of the Senate that this is an institution for old people: The word "Senate" comes from the Latin word "Senex," meaning "old man."

A similar "Senex" moment came the day before the Feinstein-Murray episode. Senate Minority Leader Mitch McConnell (R-KY)—the chamber's fourth oldest member at 81—froze midsentence at a news conference, blankly staring ahead for a painful 30 seconds before concerned aides ushered him away.

These very public occurrences have served as megaphones for the many calls to finally adopt one of the most popular—and misguided—reform ideas in American politics: congressional term limits. This evergreen idea wins fans across the ideological spectrum and has been introduced in every Congress all the way back to 1943. Advocates are convinced that term limits are a silver-bullet remedy—perhaps the only one—for a broken, ineffective, even corrupt Congress. Not only would they prevent lawmakers from serving while senile, the thinking goes, but they would magically free our politicians to represent the will of the people rather than the moneyed special interests.

Based on those arguments, I'm in! Or at least I would be, if only those things were true. But once you actually dive into the issue, the assumed benefits of term limits turn out to be a myth. In fact, term limits would be a dumpster fire for Congress and American politics more broadly. If we imposed term limits in real life, instead of seeing a Capitol full of fresh-faced new lawmakers racking up policy wins for their constitutions, you'd witness a Congress even more like *The Jerry Springer Show*—and even more unable to fulfill its critical role—than the one we have today. It's long past time to stop falling for the fantasy. Let's break down why.

The Popular Case for Term Limits

Only one in five Americans approves of Congress, a depressing historical low. Traffic jams and cockroaches receive higher marks.[1] Literally. Citizens—liberal, conservative, and indifferent—see Capitol Hill as an inaccessible, ineffective waste of space that has lost all touch with the average American. I'm willing to bet you feel this, too. You feel unheard and drowned out by the swampy modes of business in Washington. You see lawmakers as ambitious and self-interested, far more worried about feathering their own nests than doing what's good for the country. You aren't alone.

This is why nearly 90 percent of citizens want to throw the bums out by passing a constitutional amendment to limit the number of terms members of Congress can serve. Although proposals vary, the most popular scheme—sponsored by Rep. Ralph Norman (R-SC) and Sen. Ted Cruz (R-TX)—would cap House members at three terms (6 years) and senators at two terms (12 years). For quick context, members of the House serve an average of 4.3 terms, while senators typically serve around 1.9 terms.[2]

No matter the model, term-limit proponents contend that their implementation would accomplish four related objectives. Let's give each one its due.

First, term limits would **eliminate career politicians**. By virtue of their incumbency advantages, politicians already in office have a chokehold on their seats. Limiting their reign would return Congress to the "citizen legislature" envisioned by the Founders and open up service to more diverse candidates who are effectively blocked by, in the words of Senator Cruz, "members of the permanent political class looking to accumulate more and more power at the expense of American taxpayers."[3] This intention is both noble and necessary, as lawmakers in both the House and the Senate have historically been overwhelmingly old (average age of 60), wealthy ($1.8 million median net worth),[4] male (71 percent), and white (72 percent).[5]

Plus, new, diverse members would bring novel, creative solutions to age-old policy problems and congressional processes. As put by term-limit champion Rep. Matt Gaetz (R-FL), "Far too often in Congress we revert to a failed, and often corrupt, muscle memory on how to do things because we have a lot of people who have been doing them for 10, 20 years, sometimes longer. People who are not beholden to the Washington way of thinking will naturally have a more dynamic manner in which to come up with fresh ideas."[6]

Second, term-limit fans expect they would **decrease lawmakers' reliance on lobbyists, special interest groups, and big-money donors**, since lawmakers who are terming out won't need that cash to run campaign ads. This would ensure lawmakers aren't "bought and paid for" by lobbying shops and funders and make them more willing to challenge benefactors by speaking out and voting against special interest groups. "When one feels liberated to speak the truth, to say the quiet part out loud, to vote the way that their conscience dictates, that might be in the best interests of the country, not for a re-election," says Rep. Dean Phillips (D-MN).[7]

Third, advocates predict that adopting term limits would **reduce the historic levels of partisan polarization and conflict in Congress**. With strict time horizons on their service, legislators wouldn't be socialized in tit-for-tat political gamesmanship. Instead, they'd be less indebted to their party for political and campaign favors and more willing to seek bipartisan compromises on legislation.

Finally, term-limit champions believe they would greatly **improve representation for citizens.** Knowing that their years in office are capped, lawmakers would spend less time campaigning and fundraising, untether themselves from their party and donors, and focus more on getting things done for their constituents.

In other words: swamp, drained.

What about the smattering of good folks still trying to paddle around in that bog? While many Americans think all members of Congress are irredeemably untrustworthy and self-interested, most agree that there are at least some good, honest, principled elected lawmakers. In truth, the good-bad divide exists more on a continuum. Yes, there are members who are only in Congress because they enjoy wearing a special member's pin. (Realizing the power of the pin, Rep. Thomas Massie [R-KY] often jokingly refers to it as "My Precious.") Yes, there are members who serve only because they are deeply partisan people interested in having a staff, taking expensive PAC trips on their campaign's dime, and voting with their party. But there are also people who get up every morning and try to change one policy—lawmakers like Rep. Jim McGovern (D-MA), who is deeply invested in making sure that no kid in America goes to bed hungry, or Rep. Dan Crenshaw (R-TX), who truly believes the national debt is an existential threat that needs to be addressed immediately.

"Yeah, yeah, yeah," you may think, "there may be some good apples in the bunch, but not near enough." And if you're sure even the rare pure legislators will inevitably "go Washington" and start to drown in the swamp, term limits make a lot of sense. In fact, because the system is so corrupt, term limits look like the best, and perhaps only, inoculation for the diseases infecting our elected officials. Sure, their adoption would automatically kick out the good, popular, and effective lawmakers, but they would also guarantee that the corrupt, uninterested, and self-absorbed go with them.

At least that's the logic.

Term Limits in Real Life

To understand where this logic falls apart, it's helpful to put yourself in a new lawmaker's shoes.

Imagine that just a few months ago you took the oath as a freshman representative. You were assigned an office based on the results of the House office lottery (and made more enemies than you could have expected from the luck of the draw). Within your first few weeks, you hired about a dozen key staffers for your office, were assigned your committee seats—unfortunately, not the ones you hoped for—and even introduced your first piece of legislation, which, much to your dismay, went nowhere.

Today, like all days, you wake up at 5 a.m. There are 346 new emails in your inbox, most of which have some version of "urgent" in the subject line. You get up off the air mattress in your bare studio apartment, pull on your suit, and grab a can of prefab coffee out of the fridge, leaving only a bottle of ketchup inside. As you chug the caffeine, you rewatch the grainy footage of your kid's T-ball game that you missed.

On your sunrise walk to the Capitol, your chief of staff calls. "It's the Natural Resources Defense Council," she says. "They're pushing for a meeting this afternoon about a pollution mitigation plan in our district that would strengthen penalties on toxic dumping law violators." You tell your chief to wake up your environmental staffer, Christine. The new rule will likely require a change in the formula the EPA uses to measure acceptable levels of air and water contaminants.

"Already did," your chief retorts. "One more thing. I know this sounds like a good bill, and maybe it is. But this new regulation will significantly increase costs for a few of our major employers. If it passes, a few thousand jobs will likely disappear in the next few years, all in our district."

Also on today's agenda are votes on 14 different bills—from a new NASA program to a change in eligibility requirements for student loans. And you're already late for your 7 a.m. meeting with party colleagues. Leadership has a new communications plan they want to roll out for the next election. "The next election? I just got here . . ."

Now, with that in mind, imagine what happens when you take a job so complex and lay off all the people with experience just when they're starting to figure it out.

Fortunately (or unfortunately), we have a testing ground for the real-life effects of term limits to help answer that question. Actually, we have 22 of them—that's how many states have, at one time or another, implemented term limits on their lawmakers. And from California to Florida, term limits in state legislatures have proven time and again to exacerbate the very problems the reform was intended to solve. The lesson is that term limits would not only not work; they would make our politics worse. Much worse.

The trend started when California, Colorado, and Oklahoma became the first states to adopt limits for their legislatures in 1990 (though the laws didn't go into effect, or prevent people from running again, until 1996, 1998, and 2014, respectively). As of November 2022, 22 states had instituted term limits, and more than 3,000 state legislators had been forced out of office after maxing out their terms. Yet in a sign that states have been less than thrilled with the consequences, six of those states have repealed or struck the laws down.

Why the reversals? With decades of data available, researchers have been able to compare the outcomes of term-limited legislatures with nonlimited ones. They've looked at differences in how lawmakers spend their time, how often they compromise, and how much influence outside actors like lobbyists and party leaders exert. They've also compared processes and performance in legislatures before and after term limits within the same state.

The data—backed by countless firsthand accounts—all tell the same story: Term limits don't work, and more often than not, they leave the legislature less functional than it was prior to their adoption. It's like trying to fix that leaky faucet based on a YouTube tutorial and ending up with a flooded basement.

NO SUCH THING AS A CITIZEN LEGISLATURE

If term limits make so much sense, how could they possibly produce a bigger mess than the one we're trying to clean up? Let's tackle the myths, starting with the first one: the idea that term limits would bring back a "citizen legislature" made up of regular, civic-minded people who temporarily leave their everyman jobs, go to Washington, represent their constituents honestly, and then happily return home.

It's a seductive, romantic ideal. But there are two real-life problems with it. First, it's not true and never was. And second, even if it could be true, it would be a disaster for government.

The truth is that the proverbial farm that our first legislators left behind was probably a plantation, and today's lawmakers are more likely to come to Congress from boardrooms than barnyards. Ever since our founding, our political leaders have always been disproportionately from a professional and political class. Of the 55 men who attended the Constitutional Convention in 1787, for example, 43—78 percent—were lawyers or merchants.[8] Dozens of the Framers—including James Madison, principal author of the Constitution—had already served in elected offices at the local, state, and federal levels. Of those Founders whose principal income came from running farms, George Washington chief among them, they almost uniformly oversaw extensive plantations made up of thousands of acres run on the unpaid labor of hundreds of slaves. These leaders were not a true cross section of society—plumbers, teachers, craftsmen. Most were from the richest, most powerful, connected echelons of their societies.

What was true in 1787 remains true in 2024. More than 70 percent of today's members of Congress were lawyers, businesspeople, or medical professionals before their election.[9] And 80 percent of the House of Representatives—and 82 percent of senators—in the latest Congress served in government at the local, state, or federal level before their congressional service.[10]

All of which is to say: A "citizen legislature" has never existed. The reality is that the job attracts a certain type of person. Whether it's a policy change that only a position of power can make possible or the personal validation of winning an election—likely a combination of both—the prize appeals only to some. And like any career, you climb a ladder to get to the top. Politicians typically start in local positions, gain experience, bank accomplishments, and run for higher office.

Do you have what it takes to throw yourself into the political ring? The reality is that very few of us are built to withstand the ceaseless partisan polarization, relentless media scrutiny, million-dollar political campaigns, and forfeiture of any semblance of privacy, all for just a chance—not a guarantee—to actualize our goals.

So let's put the myth of the citizen legislature to bed. With that fantasy retired, we can turn to understanding why term limits will also do nothing to discourage career politicians or improve the diversity of those who represent us. Those myths rest on the assumption that once members of Congress term out, they will happily return home and resume a career outside of politics—thereby leaving Washington free of inside operators.

Spoiler: They won't.

Just as very few members begin their time in politics with a stint in Congress, very few will end their time with one. Instead, the data show that termed-out members simply go get one of the dozens of other jobs connected to politics. Forty-four of the 100 current senators previously served in the House, and 20 percent of current governors—including Florida's Ron DeSantis and Colorado's Jared Polis—previously served in Congress.[11] Numerous former members of Congress have even taken a demotion, electing to run for their state legislatures, to stay in politics. If you'd spent 10 years developing skills and knowledge and a powerful network for influencing public policy, would you be keen to abandon it all and head back to your desk job?

Former members of Congress can also keep their careers and serve as appointed officials in one of the hundreds of state or federal agencies, like former Arizona Rep. and Sen. and current ambassador to Turkey Jeff Flake. Still others stay connected to politics by becoming talking heads on cable news, as former Representatives Jason Chaffetz (UT) and Trey Gowdy (SC) have done with Fox. But perhaps of greatest concern, term-capped lawmakers will walk through the revolving door between Congress and special interest organizations where, as lobbyists or consultants, they will use their clout, expertise, and connections to affect political outcomes from outside the chambers. Members turning into policy influencers is already a major problem in politics without federal term limits—468 former members of Congress (more than the number of lawmakers in the entire House of Representatives) currently work as registered lobbyists or advisors to companies and organizations.[12] Lobbying shops roll out the red carpet for former members of the House and Senate—complete with a fat paycheck that makes their old public salary look like tip money. Former Speaker John Boehner, for example, landed as an advisor at the prestigious law firm of Squire Patton Boggs. He later joined the board of cannabis company Acreage Holdings despite years of public statements against loosening marijuana laws.[13] Scores of former congressional leaders and committee chairs have done the same.

So if you're hoping term limits will clear out the political insiders, you'll find they just make the revolving door spin faster than Buddy the Elf on a sugar rush. And more lobbying firms will have more former members on staff able to advance their special interests by leveraging their relationships and understanding of the ways of the Hill.

The notion that term limits would automatically diversify lawmakers is, unfortunately, also a fantasy. In legislatures across term-limited and non-term-limited states, the numbers show no meaningful differences among members by occupation, income, age, race, ethnicity, or religion.[14] The lack of diversity is likely to be even worse at the federal level. Here's why: The costs—both literal and personal—associated with campaigning and holding a congressional seat are far higher than for state-level seats.

In California, which boasts the most expensive state races in the country, it costs, on average, $1.1 million to win a state senate election and $837,000 to win an assembly seat.[15] By comparison, the average cost of a successful US Senate campaign is $26 million and nearly $3 million to be sworn into the US House.[16] Plus, candidates seeking federal office need to campaign full time for a year or more, with no income. You probably can't do that, and I know for certain I can't. It's especially out of reach for minority and younger citizens who aren't independently loaded. Then, if you win, you have to maintain a second residence in Washington, one of the most expensive housing markets in the country. Rep. Maxwell Frost (D-FL), the first millennial elected to Congress in 2022, was denied a DC apartment by several landlords because of his poor credit score and inability to put down a month's rent for a deposit after a year of campaigning on no income.

Term limits could push this obstacle even higher because they eliminate the potential for making a career in Congress. That means citizens who may be interested in civic duty won't see a commensurate return on their investment in running and serving. Who would reasonably invest in a position for which there literally is no future? The answer is only those with the time, freedom, and resources to do so knowing they'll never get fully paid back. Or as put by one prominent political scientist, term limits would reserve congressional seats, even more than they already are, exclusively for "the old, the rich, and the bought."[17]

EMPOWERING LOBBYISTS, NOT LEGISLATORS

OK, time for term-limit argument number two: the idea that lawmakers on short timetables would be less susceptible to swampy outside influences like lobbyists and special interests.

The opposite, yet again, is true. Studies consistently show that once states adopt term limits, a host of outside actors (like lobbyists, bureaucrats, governors, and even long-serving legislative staff) are more than willing to fill the power vacuum—and lawmakers become more likely to defer to them.

Why? Policymaking is an incredibly hard job. There are very few easy, clear-cut answers, and choices are often fraught with unintended consequences that appear long after initial votes. In federal politics, even the "easy" votes can come with ruinous consequences.

Don't believe me? Consider the government's response to the disastrous 2010 earthquake in Haiti. The 7.0 magnitude quake killed more than 200,000 people, injured 300,000 more, and left 1.5 million Haitians homeless and without food. The US government did what global superpowers are supposed to do: It provided billions of dollars of aid—medical, housing, water. And led by José Andrés, the world-famous chef and humanitarian, the United States coordinated the largest global emergency food distribution in history.[18] "In Haiti in 2010," Andrés said, "the American government and international community had a beautiful response. It's something I commended and I applauded and I was so proud of as an American."[19] No brainer, right?

Not so fast.

"In the process of donating a lot of food, certain unintended consequences happened," Andrés reflects. "We put certain farmers out of work because we were sending so much food for free."[20] And nearly

15 years later, when media cameras filmed a Republican press conference showing surges at the Mexican-American border, "we saw 14,000 Haitians in Texas under a bridge. More than 4,000 of them were those farmers we put out of work through our aid."[21]

What's more, legislators are responsible for resolving not just a handful but an endless catalog of pressing problems and sifting through myriad legislative options for each. Remember your dilemma as a freshman congressman about whether to reduce pollution or preserve jobs in your district? To that you can add vexing questions about asylum claims, lead pipe replacement, and prescription drug price negotiations. And that's just in your eighth week on the job.

Because they are pulled in so many different directions, lawmakers—and their staff—don't have the capacity to maintain expertise on all the proposals on which they'll vote.[22] If you served in Congress, you would get better at all this with time. As with lawyers, surgeons, and pilots, politicians' experience and effectiveness are correlated—a relationship that scholars have labeled the "competency effect."[23] In Congress, there is an unbelievably steep learning curve through the labyrinth of procedures, rules, and precedents. (If you think reading Shakespeare is hard, try learning legislative procedures.) With term limits, just when you'd start to get the job down, it would be time for you to start looking for another one.

This expertise problem is real for Congress now, and it will grow exponentially worse if term limits guarantee a constant slate of new, inexperienced members. Plus, short-timers won't have much incentive to develop deep policy expertise because any accrued knowledge will be effectively worthless once they term out. Without that drive, most will invest only enough time on the issues to speak in talking points and get through votes.

The net effect will be a tremendous brain drain on legislatures, rendering them incapable of fulfilling their most basic responsibilities. Which is exactly what experience has shown. States with term limits conduct less effective oversight of the executive,[24] accept governor initiatives with less pushback, and less frequently construct complex policy solutions.[25] "Long-term issues get ignored, and legislation is smaller and crappier" because of term limits, a long-term California Senate staffer admitted.[26] Or, as an assembly staffer put it, "The Legislature is like the Board of Directors for a company that doesn't know anything about the company."[27]

Who steps in to supply the needed expertise? Well, like most people at the car shop or in a doctor's office, it's only natural to trust those who are more experienced with the work. The same is true in lawmaking. So legislators turn to trusted providers of information, such as well-resourced lobbying shops and government agencies with long-serving staff who hold the expertise lacking in congressional offices (see Quadricos Driskell's lobbying chapter in this book for a deep dive into the real influence of lobbyists).

As one California lobbyist told me about his role in a term-limited state, "There are so many green lawmakers here I have to literally show them where the bathroom is. They don't know up from down. They beg me to brief them on issues so they can speak intelligently about it to their voters and sound semi-informed in front of their colleagues. When they don't know any better, they take what I say as gospel. Do you have any idea how influential that makes me?"

FAST-TRACKING POLARIZATION

Now let's test term-limit supporters' third claim: that their adoption would free up lawmakers to be more bipartisan, thereby reducing historic levels of political polarization in Congress. Reality: Wrong. Congressional term limits would actually quicken and exacerbate polarization. Here's why.

Hastening lawmakers' departure from office will also speed up the need to replace them. Because fewer than 10 percent of congressional elections are competitive and candidate selection is done in primaries where the most ideologically extreme voters show up, these voters would often select more extreme and uncompromising candidates to serve in Congress (read Representative Pascrell's chapter for more on this). Plus, some lawmakers—such as Senators Sherrod Brown (D-OH) and Joe Manchin (D-WV)—have earned enough of a trusted reputation that they continue to be reelected in states that consistently vote overwhelmingly for the opposite party. The minute these more moderate lawmakers term out, they would be replaced by more extreme members of the opposite party who won their campaigns on partisan promises to be uncompromising.

Similarly, the constant need to replace departing members leads interest groups, donors, and political parties to play a more active role in candidate recruitment, training, and promotion. Such political organizations don't spend their limited resources on just any candidates, though; they will target and support those they know will vote in lockstep with their preferred agendas.[28] In states with term-limited lawmakers, these organizations have been found to deliberately recruit candidates with minimal legislative and fundraising experience on purpose because novice candidates will be more dependent on them once in office.[29] It makes sense—anytime you've been new on the job, you've probably leaned on teammates and outside experts to show you what to do. And the data prove this right: Compared to lawmakers in states without limits, term-capped legislators vote with their party significantly more often, engage in less bipartisan collaboration, and are more ideologically extreme in their voting behaviors.[30] The net effect is more extreme partisans voting a hard party line more of the time.

THE SENIORITIS EFFECT IN CONGRESS

Lastly, in the minds of advocates, term limits would allow legislators to forget about reelection and focus exclusively on delivering for their constituents. Politicians would care less about how politically unpopular votes might affect their reputations or fear how a compromise could play in a competitor's attack ad. They'd be free to do the right thing, no matter the political fallout, and the everyday constituent would benefit. Survey says? Wrong again.

What actually holds lawmakers accountable to constituents' preferences is . . . drumroll . . . elections. When their job depends on keeping voters happy, politicians will work to keep (enough) constituents satisfied. Once the electoral connection is severed, lawmakers become less motivated to keep the needs and wants of their constituents at the forefront of their decision-making, instead pursuing their personal policy positions first.

Real-life experience bears this out. Researchers have shown that term limits diminish the need for lawmakers to establish and maintain personal connections within their districts.[31] Term-limited offices respond to constituent mail and contacts at a noticeably slower pace, and time-capped legislators secure far fewer legislative accomplishments while in office.[32] "There is absolutely less interest in the long-term, non-sexy issues. You don't have members pushing legislation that will show its fruits ten years from now; it's of little value to them," says one state committee observer.[33] In fact, compared to their non-term-limited colleagues, legislators facing term limits are significantly more likely to abstain from votes or miss them altogether.[34] It's like lawmaking senioritis—when they don't fear the principal (voters), they ditch. Younger classmen, however, still show up to avoid getting in trouble.

Term-limited officials also tend to play looser with taxpayer dollars, increasing spending and borrowing because they won't be punished by voters for doing so.[35] In Colorado, for example, term-limited state legislators disproportionately voted for tax cuts and higher spending—both popular with voters in the short term—but weren't around years later when the bill came due. California and Ohio faced the same problem twice in each state.[36]

So if you're a freshman congressman, you can imagine that by now it's 4 p.m., and you've consumed nothing but a protein bar, a handful of almonds, and enough caffeine to power a small village. Both the builders association and the dairy farmers—huge employers in your district—have delivered you policy briefs calling for tax breaks on imported lumber and some breed of cow you've never heard of (Isn't milk just milk?). An intern in your office reports that over 400 calls flooded the phones, and her face tells you that the vast majority of them weren't congratulatory messages. More than a few constituents on your must-respond-to list are pleading for help with their visa applications and missing Social Security benefits. As you prep for the three radio interviews and three pop-up fundraisers scheduled for tonight, you can't attend to those right now.

But hey—if you're term limited, you don't have to. Those constituents won't have the chance to vote for you in the next election, anyway.

What About POTUS?

Anytime I have a convo with someone about term limits (which happens way more than you might imagine), I inevitably hear the big fish of term-limit arguments: "What about POTUS? The president of the United States can only serve two terms. If the president needs term limits, don't members of Congress need them too?" It's a perfectly reasonable question, especially as nearly all term-limit opponents support the 22nd Amendment—adopted in 1951 to limit the president to two terms following FDR's 12 years in the White House.

The simple answer (which, I promise you, is hard to sell at a cocktail party) is that the two are fundamentally different offices with fundamentally different powers. Presidents are commanders in chief, the literal head of the most powerful military in the history of the world, and the only person in the country who can order the launch of nuclear weapons. They are also the boss of the entire executive branch, can nominate judges to fill the nearly 2,000 federal bench seats, and serve as the country's chief diplomat. Only the president can sign executive orders or issue presidential pardons. When the president speaks (or tweets), the whole world listens. The financial markets, to say nothing of global stability, rise and fall on his statements. He—and so far it's only been a he—is rightfully considered the most powerful person on the planet. And if you suddenly found yourself with that much power, you might concede that it should be limited, too.

Members of Congress have nothing close to the same level of authority. No matter their personal clout, they are members of collective institutions, unable to process business unless they get a majority of their colleagues to agree with them. They are but 1 of 435 members in the House; 1 of 100 in the Senate. There's very little they can do, beyond drawing attention to an issue through public statements, by themselves to change policy. Of course, a small number of legislators can drastically slow down legislative business or champion a particular issue. But they are in constant battles with their colleagues and the world around them for attention. They can demand and promise results but can't guarantee either. They work in a system infiltrated with veto points and players, where producing consensus is difficult by design. As put to me by one of my Congress nerd friends, "Being a member of Congress is the worst bullshit-to-power ratio we have in America."

Given the power asymmetry between occupants of the two branches of government, it makes sense that the office with numerous unilateral powers at their fingertips has a check against lifetime service. Members of Congress, by contrast, need practically an entire presidential term just to find their place—literally and figuratively—amid the complex workings of the Capitol. Let alone to start being effective.

Big Problems, Targeted Solutions

Citizens have every right to be frustrated with Congress. It's mired in gridlock on nearly all of our most pressing problems, and we can't go a week without seeing more headlines of political gamesmanship or sleaziness in DC. But as much as we wish for it, there is no panacea cure for our ailing Congress—term limits included. Appealing as they look, term limits are tantamount to trying to fix a stubbed toe by cutting off the foot—a draconian measure that would further hobble an already struggling institution. Americans would be better served by pursuing more targeted fixes to the varied problems vexing Congress.

If we agree that Congress isn't made up of the nation's best and brightest and is severely lacking in diversity, we can take steps to make service in Congress more accessible to those who are currently shut out. This can mean local and state parties recruiting and training candidates from underrepresented groups long before their congressional run. Allowing candidates to draw a salary from their campaigns, or at least have campaigns cover their health insurance, would help lessen the financial burdens. To appeal to a new generation of leaders, particularly those with school-aged children, Congress could update its own rules and schedules to allow more remote work and more extended periods at home in the district (though there are obvious trade-offs when elected officials don't regularly work in the same building).

And most controversially, Congress could pay its members more. Their annual salary of $174,000 is clearly nothing to sneeze at. But members of Congress haven't had a pay raise since 2008, which puts their salary just over $115,000 in 2024 dollars. Though a solid number on paper, the cost of maintaining residences in two different cities, particularly for those raising a family, simply isn't feasible on that salary. This means that many highly qualified would-be candidates view service in Congress as unaffordable. And it's also why a lot of solid, effectual incumbents, like former Sen. Ben Sasse (R-NE), voluntarily exit for better paying—and potentially more impactful—gigs.

Everyone who doesn't immediately profit from the chaos also wants to markedly decrease political polarization in Congress. To achieve that, we must concentrate on reforms to an elections process that rewards partisan candidates. This starts with increasing the competitiveness in congressional elections. This goal can be accomplished in a variety of ways, from incremental changes to the primary system at the state level—like allowing the top two candidates to face off in the general election regardless of parties—to flipping the entire system on its head by adopting multimember districts or a proportional representation system.

Term-limit fans believe a constitutional amendment is doable. If they're right, we should pursue one that targets the true underlying bugs in our system that term limits will only make worse. For instance, we can finally outlaw the indefensible practice of gerrymandering congressional districts by adopting an amendment that requires independent commissions or unemotional algorithms to draw fair boundaries. Or, to the delight of the entire nation grown weary of campaign commercials, we could adopt an amendment that puts limits on campaign donations and spending. Such overhauls are incredibly unlikely, but no less popular or unlikely than the term-limit constitutional amendment that would do more harm than good.

More broadly, we need a fundamental countrywide reframe of what makes a good, effective lawmaker and US Congress. What once could have been considered a part-time civic duty—the first Congress met about half of the year, after all—can no longer be thought of as such. Its members are right to think about political service as a career rather than a temporary endeavor. We should, too. The demands of the job and sheer volume and depth of the issues that need attention require a more professional, full-time political servant. Modern lawmakers must be read up on complex bills covering immigration, agriculture, climate, health care, cybersecurity, foreign aid, and everything in between, all in the same week. Their decisions affect trillions of dollars and billions of lives. It isn't a part-time hobby and shouldn't be thought of as one.

In no other profession do we force the best employees into retirement with no consideration as to their abilities or effectiveness. If the lawmaker proves ineffective while in office, voters have every right to find someone else. But if you're a freshman congressman and you make it through that crazy day, then another, then another; if you hold on to your values as those days add up to weeks and months and years; if you build relationships and skills and knowledge along the way, to the point that you can effectively work with your colleagues to craft and pass laws that make an impact; and if your constituents in your district like your performance—then it only makes sense that you be allowed to keep your job.

"Bipartisanship Is Dead"

Dr. James M. Curry and Dr. Frances E. Lee

Cue the funeral march. Ink the epitaph. Bipartisanship is dead—or at least dying. It has been said more times than anyone can count . . .

"Why Bipartisanship in the Senate Is Dying"—ABC News, 2021
"Someone Please Tell Joe Biden That Bipartisanship Is Dead"—The New Republic, 2019
"[John] McCain's Death Marks the Near-Extinction of Bipartisanship"—NPR, 2018
"Democrats, Republicans Will Agree: Bipartisanship Is Dead"—CBS News, 2009

This is the conventional wisdom: Democrats and Republicans do not and cannot work together in Washington. The patriotic bipartisanship of past eras is gone, we say, replaced by political parties that prefer to engage in bad-faith negotiations and zero-sum political warfare. Voters clamor for compromise, but bipartisanship is rare—if not impossible. The only way for either side to get anything done is to try to go it alone, win more seats, and gain more power.

We're here to tell you this is a myth. Reports of bipartisanship's death are greatly exaggerated. Compromise, as it has been throughout history, remains the name of the game in Washington.

Let us be clear: You are right to perceive Congress as much more partisan and contentious than it used to be. It is. There are many issues on which Democrats and Republicans simply cannot find agreement, and the halls of the Capitol are no lovefest. But what lawmakers say about one another on TV is very different from what actual governing requires them to do at the negotiating table. And despite the public posturing, behind closed doors, there is often more cooperation and compromise than we would ever guess.

The truth is that lawmaking in Washington is a necessarily bipartisan exercise. This is not because Democrats and Republicans in Congress enjoy collaborating. Most don't, and many lawmakers can lose their jobs if they are too friendly with the other side. No, the parties work together to make laws in Washington because they have to. The structure and processes of the American policymaking system demand it.

If that sounds like fiction, maybe some real-life evidence can help convince you. Despite the widespread belief that Congress is hopelessly unproductive, the numbers show that recent congresses have actually passed more legislation than those in the 1960s, '70s, or '80s. People often focus on the number of individual laws passed, and those have indeed become fewer. But Congress today passes laws that are much, much longer and include many more individual policies—and that's a better measure of productivity.

Think of it this way—when you were five years old, you likely measured your birthday loot simply on the *number* of gifts you received; a wrapped-up paper clip counted as one gift the same way as a remote-controlled car. But what if all those gifts, plus five more, were stuffed into one big box (what Congress nerds call "omnibus bills")? The five-year-old you would be upset that you only received one gift, when in reality your haul would be much bigger. The same is true within Congress and the way it now legislates—fewer laws passed, more policies on the books.

The net effect is that the overall amount of policy enacted per Congress has not declined at all—it has increased. In the 1960s and 1970s, for instance, each two-year Congress passed an average of 3,244 pages of new law. Between 2001 and 2022, that average more than *doubled*, to 6,914. In fact, by this measure, the 116th (2019–2020) and 117th (2021–2022) Congresses were the most productive in history.

Congress has enacted a truly colossal amount of important legislation in recent years. Congress's response to the Covid-19 pandemic was massive. The total amount spent to combat the virus and its effects was more than twice as much as was spent during the entirety of the New Deal, adjusted for inflation. And despite 30 million Americans losing their jobs, Congress's laws actually *reduced* poverty in the United States while simultaneously underwriting the fastest vaccine rollout in world history. No big deal. Oh, and all but one of the eight Covid-19 relief laws passed with overwhelming bipartisan support despite constant public bickering between the parties about the right governmental response to the pandemic.

Congress has done a lot more than crisis-response Covid aid lately, too. In the last few years, it has taken bipartisan action on various hot-button issues, including gay marriage (the Respect for Marriage Act, 2022), gun control (the Bipartisan Safer Communities Act, 2022), sexual assault (the Speak Out Act, 2022), medical marijuana (the Medical Marijuana and Cannabidiol Research Expansion Act, 2022), federal lands (Great American Outdoors Act, 2020, and the John D. Dingell Jr. Conservation, Management, and Recreation Act, 2019), free trade (United States–Mexico–Canada Agreement, 2019), criminal justice reform (the First Step Act, 2018), and more. None of these laws went far enough in any one direction to completely satisfy either side. But Democrats and Republicans worked through serious disagreements on each of these efforts to find something they could agree on and help the country move forward.

For how often we're told it's dead, bipartisanship is looking awfully lively.

We get it, though. Griping about Congress may have replaced baseball as our national pastime. Our perception of a partisan impasse persists even though the kinds of outcomes outlined previously are exactly what most of us say we want our elected officials to do. We want our leaders to cross the aisle, negotiate, and hash out compromises. So if they are in fact doing that, why does it matter that we feel like they're failing? What's the harm in some dinner-table grousing about Washington gridlock? It matters because the myth that bipartisanship is dead is a big part of what stalls our progress as a nation. If we believe that the parties cannot work together—and if the people elected to Congress believe that the parties cannot and do not work together—then the logical conclusion is that each side must try to go it alone to make policy. Steeped in this belief, we are inclined to support policymakers who tell us they are going to Washington to fight, not work with others. We end up promoting the kinds of elected officials who take fierce, unyielding positions and insist on their way or the highway. But it is precisely those kinds of politicians, and those kinds of one-sided party efforts, that produce the stalemates we all hate. And those stalemates stop our country from solving real problems. Bipartisanship, by contrast, is how most policymaking gets done.

The implications for our collective future are big because our national problems are big—and history has taught us bipartisanship is usually the only way to solve them. Understanding why policymaking requires compromise and how it happens is the first step to understanding what is possible, and what is not, in Washington. Once you know that and have a clearer view of what we can and cannot expect from our lawmakers, you can advocate more effectively to change the policies they're making.

Bipartisanship: Alive and Well

In order to believe that bipartisanship is still kicking, you may need some additional evidence. We don't blame you; you have good reasons for skepticism. The media, advocacy groups—and often politicians themselves—overwhelmingly present Americans with images and stories of Democrats and Republicans fighting with one another. News headlines like those listed previously (and as Matt Fuller's chapter on the media will detail) elevate disagreement and obscure the cooperation and agreement that is not only alive in Washington but surprisingly thriving. Those stories attract more eyeballs and generate more clicks, and the news media is happy to provide consumers with more red meat. Politicians know this and play into it, too, competing to come up with the best one-liners and attacks on their opponents to get more face time on TV and more followers on social media, which can in turn advance their careers. Case in point: Tim Walz's viral comments labeling Republican politicians as "weird" may have helped him secure a position as Kamala Harris's running mate.[1]

But as the old saying goes, you can't believe everything you see on TV (or on the internet for that matter).

Let's start with some simple data showing how many of our lawmakers cast votes in support of the things that become law.

If you've been told that Democrats and Republicans don't work together anymore, these figures might surprise you. They show, first, that most things pass with overwhelming support. This is as true today as it was in the past. In the 1970s and 1980s, on average, 86 percent of House members voted in support of new laws. Since 2009—the start of the Obama administration—it has been 89 percent. The picture is similar in the Senate. In the 1970s and 1980s, 87 percent of senators voted in support of new laws. Since 2009, 80 percent. In those earlier decades, large and bipartisan majorities passed the Clean Air and

Clean Water Acts, the first real campaign finance reforms, a whole bunch of open government laws, a massive overhaul of the tax code, and more. In recent years, bipartisan majorities have backed criminal justice reform, massive investments in health research, historic expansions and protections for public lands, and the codification of same-sex marriages—all while trashing one another on cable news.

Beyond the airwaves, very little has changed.

The numbers also show that it's not just the majority party that supports the laws passed in Washington. The minority party does, too. In the 1970s and 1980s, 78 percent of House minority party members supported new laws. Since 2009, 82 percent have done the same. In the Senate, there's been a small drop between those time periods, from 82 percent to 69 percent of minority party senators. But more than two-thirds of minority party senators still typically vote in support of the laws Congress passes. This is a lot of agreement for people who supposedly never agree!

Sure, you might say, maybe they agree on some stuff. But not the stuff that really matters. Not the things anyone really cares about. Well, it turns out, even if we focus on each party's core legislative agenda, we still see a lot of bipartisanship.

For our book, *The Limits of Party*, we collected every stated policy goal of every majority party in Congress from 1985 to 2022 (the 99th to 116th Congresses). These are the things that the party leaders said they wanted to accomplish when their party held a majority in the House or the Senate. Things like the Democrats' stated goal to pass infrastructure legislation at the start of the Biden administration, or the Republicans' stated goal to reduce federal spending. Using this list of 295 items, we took stock of two things: First, what was the result? Did the party shepherd through a new law achieving *most* or *some* of what it hoped to achieve? Or did it *fail* outright? Then looking at those cases in which a majority party succeeded, did it do so by building support with members of the other party, or did it jam the bill through over their objections?

Figure 2: Support for new laws, 1973–2022

(1) US House of Representatives

—o— % yea   —■— % minority yea

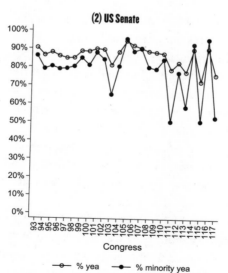

(2) US Senate

—o— % yea   —●— % minority yea

The clear answer was that there wasn't much jamming going on. The results show that the majority party—Democrat or Republican, Obama, Bush, Trump, or Biden—rarely achieves "most" of what it wants to. A clear win like this happens less than 20 percent of the time. About half the time, majority parties simply fail to make any progress on their policy priorities. Something worth underscoring for voters who are promised the world by politicians every campaign cycle: Failure was the most common result in almost every Congress since 1985.

But the second most common outcome—and the one that drives most of the legislative progress our country makes—was for the majority party to pass a law that achieved *only* **some** of what it wanted. Especially over the last decade or so, when the majority does succeed, it does so by compromising. The 2022 gun safety law (the Bipartisan Safer Communities Act) is a good example. Democrats wanted sweeping gun control changes, like an assault weapons ban. But these were things that Republicans were never going to accept. By working with Republicans (rather than only fighting with them), Democrats (and the country) were able to make real progress: expanding background checks, keeping guns out of the hands of domestic abusers, and giving states more funding for school safety and mental health resources. Democrats didn't get everything they wanted, but they ended up with a law that will have a real impact . . . much more slowly than many of us want. And this is frustrating. Really, extremely, deeply frustrating, especially on issues that affect lives. But that is the agreement we all implicitly make as members of a democracy—to bring together an incredibly diverse array of people and priorities and work our way toward progress together. It's messy. But we have collectively concluded that it beats the pants off autocracy.

These policymaking victories—whether achieving most or some of what the majority wanted—are overwhelmingly the result of bipartisan negotiations. In fact, our work found that the majority has the endorsement of at least one of the minority party's top leaders on more

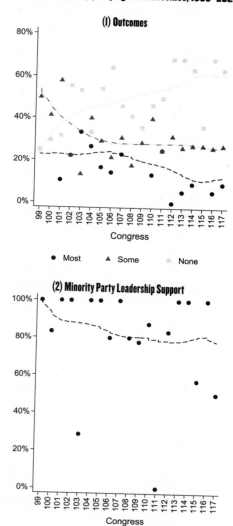

Figure 3: Majority party agenda outcomes, 1985–2022

than 80 percent of the majority-agenda bills that actually pass. What's clear is that *the majority rarely succeeds without the minority's support.* Most times it's either teamwork or stalemate.

Are there exceptions? A few. Across the 295 party agenda items, we found just 13 (4 percent) that ended with one party achieving a clear policy victory over the sustained opposition of the other. These rare, partisan laws loom large in our political consciousness: Obamacare, the Republicans' 2017 tax law, some of the Bush tax cuts. But they are unusual.

This last point is key. It's not that Democrats and Republicans work together all the time. It's that **if a majority party wants to actually come through on its promises, it needs the minority to help do it**.

What this means in practice is that the way most citizens say they want policy to be made—through negotiation and compromise across the aisle—is actually how it still gets done. The efforts of the Biden administration and the Democrats to pass a large-scale infrastructure bill in 2021 offer a good example. Infrastructure was a priority for the Democrats after the 2020 elections. Biden's "Build Back Better" proposal, also termed the "American Jobs Plan," would have encompassed $2.3 trillion of new investments, including over $600 billion in physical infrastructure—highways and roads, bridges, airports, railways, electric vehicles, and charging stations. The American Jobs Plan also included more than $100 billion to upgrade the country's drinking water infrastructure. These were proposals that, in principle, both sides could agree to.

At the same time, much of Biden's Build Back Better agenda had little appeal to Republicans: $100 billion in green energy infrastructure; $200 billion for public housing; over $100 billion for schools, childcare centers, and community colleges; and $400 billion to expand access to care for seniors and people with disabilities, among other things, all to be paid for by raising corporate taxes and eliminating subsidies for fossil fuel companies. Republicans would rather book a camping trip in Chernobyl than support a bill with these provisions in it.

Mitch McConnell (R-KY) called the agenda a "Trojan horse for massive tax hikes and other job-killing left-wing policies."[2] Sen. John Barrasso (R-WY) described it as "trillions and trillions of dollars of reckless spending."[3] The Republican counterproposal was much smaller and much more focused on physical infrastructure. McConnell maintained that the right price tag should not exceed $800 billion.[4]

The parties debated, deliberated, and fought—often very publicly and very harshly—over the bill for months. The contest made for spicy soundbites and provided plenty of meat for partisan pundits. But ultimately, the sides did hammer out an agreement. The Infrastructure Investment and Jobs Act passed with a bipartisan majority in the Senate and strong endorsements from both Biden and McConnell. A diverse array of senators supported the bill, from Trump BFF Lindsay Graham (R-SC) to Mr. Socialism himself, Bernie Sanders (I-VT). More importantly, the substance of the bill focused on something Democrats and Republicans could agree on: physical infrastructure.

Focusing on common ground is how the parties today achieve policy change on many matters. It's not rocket science; it's common sense. In contrast, when one of the major parties tries to shoot for the moon and go it alone, they routinely fail. In fact, one of the things we've noticed is that when a party is unwilling to try to compromise, it usually fails to pass any new policy at all.

Need an example? They are infinite. How about the Democrats' 2021 social policy proposal (the "American Families Plan"), RIP. This ambitious $3.5 trillion bill fell victim to opposition from both Republicans and moderate Democrats, including Joe Manchin (D-WV), who doomed its passage in the Senate. Or how about the Democrats' crown jewel overhaul of voting rights—the John Lewis Voting Rights Act—that they vowed to pass? Nope. Or the Republicans' years-long promise to repeal and replace Obamacare in 2017, which collapsed after a dramatic "thumbs down" from John McCain (R-AZ). President George W. Bush's plan to "privatize" Social Security never even made it to the floor in either the House or Senate. Bill Clinton's much-discussed comprehensive health-care reform plan collapsed under the weight of Republican opposition and internal divisions among liberal and moderate Democrats. We could go on.

The parties today may come to Washington with ambitious agendas and bold policy visions. It's how they get elected. And once they're in the swamp, they may argue and spit venom in one another's direction seemingly every day and about every conceivable topic. But lawmakers quickly find out that if they want to get something done, they simply have to work together.

How Is Bipartisanship Possible?

That last point is really important. Our system for electing lawmak-ers and passing laws makes it too difficult for one party to impose its will. This feature was baked right into the system from the beginning (see Lindsay Chervinksy's chapter about the Founders). But when we believe that cooperation is impossible, we discredit leaders who com-promise for seeming weak and too willing to sacrifice their principles. We also embolden those who gain political clout by rejecting compro-mise and cause still more gridlock.

Why can't a party that holds a congressional majority and the Oval Office just jam its whole agenda through? They promised us they would! The requirement for bipartisan cooperation starts with our political system's famed "checks and balances." In Washington, poli-cymaking power is first divided between the executive and legislative branches of government. Laws must be passed by Congress and signed by the president, or else there must be enough support in Congress to override a veto. Power is then divided again *within* Congress, with a House and Senate that function as two entirely separate legislatures with different rules, norms, and traditions.

It is important to remember that every new law needs support from three very different political bodies, each representing different people and political interests. House members represent their individual districts, with more populous states receiving greater representation. Senators represent each of the 50 states, with each state given an equal voice regardless of its population. Presidents try to represent the country as a whole—or at least the parts that might vote for them. New laws must satisfy at least a majority in each of these institutions. That's hard to do. James Madison and the other Founders saw these checks and balances as necessary to avoid governmental tyranny. It turns out, they also necessitate a broad consensus before anything can get done.

To make policymaking more complicated, our geographic system of representation creates divisions not only between but *within* the parties. We elect our representatives and senators independently, and separately, from one another. So our congresspeople approach lawmaking by considering how new policies or laws will affect residents in the districts or states they represent, not the country as a whole. A Democrat from Sandusky, Ohio, is going to want different things than one from San Francisco, California. A Republican from Long Island, New York, is often going to find they disagree with one from Little Rock, Arkansas. These kinds of considerations can still trump all else, including partisanship. And none of this is new. This combination of separated powers and fractured parties has made policy change difficult throughout American history, and politicians have acknowledged this. Almost 60 years ago, legendary congressman Richard Bolling (D-MO) wrote, "Compromise is the name of the game in the legislative process. Very few bills . . . become laws and still retain more than 50 to 75 percent of what their authors originally envisioned as necessary in the public interest."[5] Almost 100 years earlier, before his time as president,

Woodrow Wilson complained that the constitutional structure made the administration of government too difficult.[6]

Like snarky social media influencers whose jabs we relish until they take a shot at our side, we love this system in principle—that is, until we want a new law that can't get passed. But as frustrating as it is, it's worth remembering that the checks and balances system cuts both ways. When lawmakers from the other party want to jam something through, most of us are pretty happy that they can't. Have you cast a vote for someone you trust to stop the other side from enacting their policies? We bet you have.

Time and again, parties win the majority and get tempted to push through their priorities all on their own. And time and again, they fail. Consider the Democrats' ambitious policy agenda following the 2020 elections. In addition to the massive Build Back Better framework, Democratic leaders hoped to overhaul federal elections, bolster voting rights protections, pass comprehensive immigration reform, revamp the nation's gun laws, reform policing, raise the minimum wage, and more.

In the House, the Democrats tried a go-it-alone approach on every one of these items. After working out disagreements between their moderates and progressives, Democrats pushed through bills on party-line votes covering all three tranches of Biden's Build Back Better agenda. With every Republican voting in opposition, they passed the For the People Act, an ambitious elections reform bill, and the John Lewis Voting Rights Act. They passed comprehensive immigration reform (the American Dream and Promise Act) with just nine Republicans voting in favor. They passed the George Floyd Justice in Policing Act with just one Republican voting in favor. They passed various bills reforming gun laws, expanding background checks, banning assault weapons, and more, each with just a few Republicans voting in favor.

House Democrats bragged about all this passing of bills. But what was missing? Actual laws. Every one of these efforts died in the Senate. Each faced strong Republican opposition, of course. But that wasn't the only problem. As it turns out, House Democrats and Senate Democrats wanted different things because they represent different people and places. House Democrats are elected overwhelmingly from coastal states and urban centers. But to earn a majority in the Senate, Democrats need to win elections in states in the country's interior, too. Democrats' narrow, 50-seat Senate majority in 2021–2022 included senators from Montana, Ohio, Wisconsin, Arizona, Georgia, and West Virginia, among other places. Some of these senators put the brakes on the House's legislation.

Consider the vote taken in March 2021 that would have added a $15 federal minimum wage (a key plank of President Biden's policy platform) to the American Rescue Plan. This $15 mark seemed to have become the party's cause célèbre. Every candidate for the Democratic presidential nomination that year backed it. But when it was brought to the Senate floor, it failed—not just because every Republican opposed it, but because eight Democrats voted no, too. As a result, there wasn't any wage hike at all. By going for $15 or bust, the Democrats ended up with nada. Does anyone doubt millions of workers across the country would have been better off with a compromise at, say, $12? Instead, the federal minimum wage, as of 2024, still sits at $7.25 per hour, which hasn't budged since 2009 and which pencils out to an unlivable $15,000 per year.

Senators from purple and red states were a thorn in the side of the House Democrats' progressive ambitions throughout Biden's first two years in office. Joe Manchin and Kyrsten Sinema, both needing to woo moderate voters in their typically red-leaning states (West Virginia and Arizona), were the thorniest. "I've never been a liberal in any way, shape, or form," clarified an exasperated Manchin as he explained the deadlock between him and much of his party over its policymaking plans in 2021.[7] Both he and Sinema eventually quit the Democratic Party over continued disagreement with its agenda.

Lawmaking has always been this way. Opposition from moderates doomed the Obama administration's efforts to pass a cap-and-trade climate change bill in 2010. Republicans literally lost control of the Senate in 2001 when Sen. Jim Jeffords quit the party over disagreements with its direction on taxes and other issues. Civil rights reform was hampered by divisions among Democrats throughout the 1940s, '50s, and '60s.

Simply put, the US political system makes policymaking hard—by design. So hard, in fact, that it's usually impossible for one party to make policy on its own. That means that if you want to get something done, you have to work across the aisle to do it. If you don't, you're going to get nothing done at all.

The Partisanship Paradox

Bipartisanship may be alive and well, but it's also true that our politics have become more partisan and polarized. More than at any time in recent history, the parties stand for different things, represent different kinds of Americans, and campaign on completely different agendas. Politically speaking, Democrats and Republicans operate in two completely separate universes. Rather than leading to more one-party lawmaking or more stalemate, however, these divisions may only be *increasing* the prospects for bipartisanship.

Let's stop to make sense of this. How can more partisan politics spur more bipartisan agreement? Well, party leaders today are hit with a triple threat of obstacles, and the only way over them is more compromise.

The first obstacle is the impossibility of unilateral lawmaking. Even though their members are probably more unified than at any time in American history, there's still enough disagreement within each party to throw a wrench in most plans. Thus, they need votes from the other side to get anything done.

Second, when they look across the aisle, they don't find many lawmakers who are likely to agree with their plans. Stop us if you've heard this before, but Democrats and Republicans today are deeply polarized. Once upon a time, party leaders could win over enough votes to secure a legislative victory by negotiating with centrists in the other party. This is what Ronald Reagan did. He negotiated with centrist Southern Democrats on issues like taxes and defense spending and was able to put together bipartisan coalitions. But today, fewer centrists exist. When Joe Biden and Mike Johnson and Chuck Schumer look across the aisle, they usually can't find enough centrists to cobble together a winning coalition. So they have to sacrifice some of their preferred policies to make a deal.

This is challenging enough, but there's still one more obstacle to deal with. Neither side has been able to secure anything but the smallest majorities in the House and Senate for some time. No party has held a majority larger than three seats in the Senate since 2016. In the House, neither party has had more than a razor-thin, four-seat House majority since 2021. Even in the years before 2020, congressional majorities were historically small. With fewer votes available on their side, party leaders need even more votes from the other side. It's simple math.

These combined challenges of small majorities, intraparty disagreements, and the decline of centrists leave party leaders with a simple choice: compromise and get a law or try to go it alone and end up with bubkes. But if they choose the compromise route, they have to go directly to the leadership of the other party to do it. When that happens, the deals that get cut are generally going to be those that can earn very broad support from both parties. Either Republican and Democratic leaders find an agreement acceptable to most members of both their respective parties or nothing happens.

These are the challenges that have hampered House Republicans in 2023 and 2024. They are also the exact reasons we have continued to see such high levels of bipartisanship on the things that did become law despite (or because of) all the partisan nastiness and discord.

Take the federal spending fight that consumed much of the 118th Congress (2023–2024), for example. It ended in a compromise, but many House Republicans did not start out wanting it to be one.

After taking control of the House, Speaker Kevin McCarthy (R-CA) signaled that cutting spending was one of his party's top priorities, describing the national debt as "the greatest threat" to the nation's future.[8] Democrats had just wrapped up two years of expanding federal spending. Republicans staked their new position of power on a promise to cut a lot of this away.

But there would be no easy agreement between the parties or even within the GOP. While almost all Republicans wanted spending cuts, they couldn't agree on *what* to cut.[9] What's more, they disagreed on tactics. Some wanted to use the federal debt ceiling to force cuts. Others found this strategy unacceptable.

Disagreements within the party might not have been such a problem if Republicans had a larger majority. But with just a four-seat margin, they had no room for error. Almost any dissension would unravel any plan. With Biden refusing to even negotiate with House Republicans until they passed *something*, Republicans narrowly rallied around the Limit, Save, Grow Act, a watered-down plan that backed away from the party's original ambitions to balance the federal budget or impose deep cuts.[10] Republican hardliners were not pleased, and the bill passed by just two votes. But it got the White House to the negotiating table.

Even then, more problems loomed for Republicans. Democrats still controlled the Senate and the White House, and a month of contentious negotiations ensued. When a deal emerged in late May, it was clear that both sides had made compromises they previously vowed never to accept. Republicans secured a range of policy concessions from the White House, including new work requirements for SNAP (food stamp) recipients. But they could not secure the deep spending cuts they promised their base. Discretionary spending would not be reduced at all under the agreement. Its growth would just be limited in future years.[11] And yet the result, the Fiscal Responsibility Act, passed easily, earning over 300 votes in the House and 63 votes in the Senate—despite being opposed by 71 House Republicans.

From there, the fight only got uglier. Congress still needed to pass spending bills that fit within the agreed-upon framework. Hardline Republicans, frustrated with Kevin McCarthy and the Republican leadership, began rebelling against unrelated bills their leaders tried to bring to the House floor.[12] By fall, tensions reached their limit. To avoid a government shutdown, McCarthy finally brought a bill to the floor that would give Congress more time. It passed overwhelmingly, though 90 Republicans opposed it. And just a few days later, McCarthy was booted from the Speakership by his own party. His crime? Compromising with Democrats.

Did compromise die along with McCarthy's leading role? No. Mike Johnson (R-LA) eventually emerged as the new leader, promising to fight for his party's goals. But a change in leadership could not change the underlying dynamics at play. Republicans were still divided and held a narrow majority. The parties were still miles apart on spending policy. There was no way forward except to cut a bipartisan deal.

The final spending package, agreed to in March 2024, largely resembled the deal cut between Kevin McCarthy and the White House in May 2023. The bill passed with overwhelming bipartisan support in both chambers. Conservative Republicans, who would have liked to go it alone, didn't like it. But the American system of government didn't really give them a choice.

A similar pattern has repeated over and over again in recent history. Lawmakers on one side or the other want to do big, bold things to deliver on their campaign promises. They don't want to compromise. But they discover, eventually, that to achieve anything at all—to move the ball forward on any of the issues that are important to Americans—they must.

As citizens, we need to understand this. This knowledge empowers us to identify the genuine possibilities for progress. And it can help us more readily identify when members of both parties are leading us down a futile or dangerous path.

Empower the Compromisers

Seeing this clearly gives you an edge at cutting through the rhetoric spewed by politicians and connecting to reality. You may hear candidates promise huge and fast fixes to entitlements, our deficit, and college tuition if only they are elected. You may hear elected officials call one another names like "Hitler Pig" or "Crooked Joe." But you know that whatever they promise is worlds different from what they can actually deliver. And that when the ink hits the paper, those same public enemies will be sitting at the table together, searching for common ground whether they consider it pleasant or not.

Knowing this is, by itself, incredibly powerful. Being able to spot the huge gaps between what you're promised and what is possible—including how to achieve it—will change your voting calculus for the better. It will help you avoid the candidates who promise you the world and clearly expose the politicians who only seek the fight for the cameras. And ultimately, rewarding the compromisers and demoting the polarizers—who are usually the loudest in the room—will go a long way to changing the incentive structure for lawmakers. If they know they will be rewarded for making some progress rather than punished for not getting everything, more of them will pursue good faith legislating rather than race to throw more gas on the partisan fires.

The conventional wisdom is that gridlock and stalemate generally stem from an inability of Democrats and Republicans to compromise.

The truth is that they result from one party refusing to compromise at the expense of progress.

Most lawmakers know this, deep down. They know that they won't win by holding a hard line or expecting ideological purity in legislation. So why do they do that, at least out loud in public, so often? Well, we citizens and voters are partially to blame. Those of us with strong views on politics, perhaps inadvertently, encourage our representatives to be fighters rather than compromisers. We tend to lionize the fighters—those who give us the partisan red meat we prefer. Those we vote for precisely because they promise to stop the other side. Voters on both sides tend to express greater admiration for those who present themselves as purists. Senators like Elizabeth Warren (D-MA) and Bernie Sanders (I-VT) have high favorability among liberals and Democrats. Sen. Ted Cruz (R-TX) and Rep. Jim Jordan (R-OH) are beloved among Republicans. The many dealmakers on Capitol Hill, by contrast, are either not well known—for example, Sen. Maggie Hassan (D-NH) or Rep. Brian Fitzpatrick (R-PA)—or are viewed with skepticism by voters in their own party—think Joe Manchin or Mitch McConnell.

You see, lawmakers know that taking uncompromising positions helps them politically. They know that hardline stances help them raise millions from passionate small-money donors and win support and admiration from voters on their side of the aisle. But this is exactly why we should be skeptical. It's why when a politician or Washington insider tells us that bipartisanship is dead or that compromise is impossible, we should recognize it for what it is: a trick.

Smashing the myth that one party can do whatever they want also means accepting that big change comes slowly. Maybe too slowly. We recognize this is hard to swallow. It's not easy for a parent living in fear of gun violence at their children's school to hear that big, sweeping change is probably impossible. We have a long and growing list of issues that incremental progress won't fix fast enough. The climate. Immigration. Education. Small fixes feel like Band-Aids. We want big changes.

But we have to recognize it is almost never possible to achieve major change in just one bold stroke. History shows that when one side or the other tries to swing for the fences, they tend to strike out. There are no shortcuts. And trying to take them backfires. While it's undeniably painful to let the biggest versions of our hopes go in the immediate term, we can take comfort in knowing that huge changes have happened throughout history—but they came about after many failures, often over decades.

Take the generation-defining Civil Rights Act as a prime example. We talk about it as a singular breakthrough for a long-overdue injustice. But it wasn't just one act. It was a series of them: the Civil Rights Act of 1957 (voting), the Civil Rights Act of 1960 (equal protection), the Civil Rights Act of 1964 (outlawing discrimination), another Voting Rights Act in 1965 to close the semitruck-sized loopholes of the first, and the Civil Rights Act of 1968 (fair housing). The passage of each made the next more possible, more necessary, and stronger. We forget that passing these acts took over a decade and tend to overlook the decades of civil rights failures that came before. As frustrating as it was and is, we can fight for and celebrate this kind of stepwise progress knowing that steps in the right direction, however small, are better than the alternative—no progress at all.

We can each do our part by recalibrating our expectations. We can ask ourselves: What should we expect from our lawmakers? Should we expect that they can go to Washington and achieve our partisan hopes and dreams? No. We absolutely should expect that they will fight for what they believe in. But we should also expect that they will need to make compromises to actually pass any new laws.

This means we understand that when we—or our lawmakers—hold out to try and get everything we want in Washington, we tend to get nothing at all. Through bipartisanship and compromise, however, we can make things better, a little bit at a time. This is the kind of thing that happens every day on Capitol Hill. It is the kind of progress many of our lawmakers work at, day in and day out. Those constructive, hardworking lawmakers need our backing and our support, and we should give it to them.

"I Wish the Parties Would Work Together"

Rep. Bill Pascrell Jr., with Mark Greenbaum[1]

Congressman Pascrell represented New Jersey in Congress from 1997 to 2024. He served as chairman of the House Ways and Means Subcommittee on Oversight in the 117th Congress. Pascrell was a member of the New Jersey State Assembly from 1988 to 1997 and mayor of Paterson, New Jersey, from 1990 to 1997. Prior to serving in office, Pascrell received his BA and MA from Fordham University. He was a longtime public school teacher and is a veteran of the US Army and US Army Reserves. Congressman Pascrell was a lifelong resident of Paterson. This essay was completed shortly before his passing in late 2024.

On February 4, 2024, a trio of US senators made a momentous announcement. James Lankford (R-OK), Chris Murphy (D-CT), and Kyrsten Sinema (I-AZ) unveiled a legislative deal to address America's southern border crisis and frayed asylum system.[2]

The package was the product of months of painstaking behind-the-scenes negotiation among the senators on one of America's most pressing issues. The effort had been declared dead by reporters and congressional insiders more times than you've accidentally been on mute the past several years. And yet, like Punxsutawney Phil, who emerged just hours earlier on Groundhog Day, the draft bill saw the light of day.

Members of the public and elected officials had been clamoring for this kind of action for literally decades. Daily news reports showed thousands of immigrants walking or swimming over the US border in a desperate attempt to find safety, employment, or freedom. Many of them would wait months or years to have their cases heard by backlogged asylum or immigration courts. Republican governors of border states were busing migrants to Democratic-led northern cities to make a performative point about how tough it was for their states to absorb them. Former President Donald Trump had repeatedly called the porous border an emergency threat to the country, asserting in 2018 that "the only long-term solution to the [border] crisis" was congressional action.[3]

The border deal addressed at least some of these challenges. It would have made it more difficult to apply for asylum, sped up the asylum process, and expanded federal power to stanch border crossings into America, among other things.[4] It also provided funding to hire nearly 6,000 new asylum officers and border agents as well as 100 fresh immigration judges and staff. The agreement represented one of the most conservative overarching reform packages in decades—and the first one with broad Democratic buy-in in just as long.

Democratic support came swiftly. President Biden called for the bill's passage.[5] So did Senate Majority Leader Chuck Schumer, who wanted to begin debate on the bill immediately. House Democratic leaders signaled their support, indicating it probably would have gotten at least a majority of Democratic votes there. As a New Jersey Democratic congressman of nearly three decades, I likely would have been one of them.

Though it was supported by many liberals, the bill was loaded with features conservatives could love. Murphy had called the negotiations "torturous," mostly in reference to the bitter policy pills Democrats were prepared to swallow. Many, like augmented border security, were concessions Republican lawmakers had sought for years.[6] And Senator Lankford, who holds a 97 percent lifetime rating from the American Conservative Union, had negotiated the bill with the blessing of Senate Republican leader Mitch McConnell.

Goodness knows Republican voters wanted action. Fox News spotlighted a daily parade of problems at the border. A Gallup poll at the start of 2024 found an overwhelming majority of Republicans identified immigration as their top priority.[7] Other coverage called it voters' number one issue overall across parties in 2024.[8] McConnell himself told his conference that this deal was Republicans' best chance, maybe ever, to obtain many of their long-standing border demands with Democratic support and without consenting to liberal goals like a pathway to citizenship.[9]

The bill had all the markings of a true conservative win.

And it should have been.

Lankford, Murphy, and Sinema released the details of the deal on a Sunday, but they did not hold a press conference that day. Nor did they jointly meet the press the next day. For three legislators with reputations for press savvy, this may have struck observers as surprising. Politics 101: When you strike a major agreement, you announce it.

Their silence was more than an omen—it was an outright acknowledgment that their compromise bill was dead before it ever had a chance. As early as January 25, McConnell—the same leader who encouraged Lankford to find a deal—warned his colleagues that passage would be difficult, which meant (in Capitol Hill–speak) that the votes weren't there.[10] The same day, Speaker Mike Johnson said the Senate deal would be "dead on arrival" in the House.[11] Johnson's control of the floor made that threat a guarantee.

But Republicans didn't just deny the bill their own party co-negotiated. They dismissed it entirely. Johnson told his Republican colleagues the deal was insufficient and nothing less than a "surrender" to Democrats.[12] Utah Sen. Mike Lee called the text a "disqualifying betrayal."[13] Ted Cruz, whose home state Texas is more directly impacted by the border crisis than any other, proclaimed that "we don't need a border bill."[14] That's right: The senior senator from Texas worked to kill an immigration compromise that would help his own state as it struggles with the influx of immigrants.

Why the seemingly self-defeating (and country-defeating) reversal? The immigration bill bashing had trickled down from the de facto Republican leader. Donald Trump publicly called for killing the bill on January 29, posting online that the Senate bill was "horrific" and that "no legislation is needed."[15]

On paper, the Lankford-negotiated bill was the congressional action that Trump had previously called for. It went a long way to solving what Trump and conservatives had long said was America's most pressing crisis.

Yet Republican Texas Congressman Troy Nehls laid bare the GOP's politics-over-progress strategy when he bluntly told reporters on the Capitol steps, "Why would we do anything right now to help" President Biden, a cigar dangling from his hand and a grin dangling from his lips.[16]

Republicans in Congress fell in line. The bill was not debated or brought up for a vote in the Senate, and it never arrived in the House. "This proposal would have had almost unanimous Republican support if it weren't for Donald Trump," admitted a Republican senator.[17]

The Republicans' top policy issue was killed by Republicans on the legislative runway. Within days, the press largely moved on.

When Compromise Becomes Irrational

The easy conclusion to draw from this episode is that the GOP just wants to play political gotcha instead of governing. In part, that is true. Republicans extinguished a border fix that was the main plank in their own campaign platform because Trump and his strongest supporters in Congress believed solving the immigration crisis—or at least improving it—would give the Democrats a win on the issue most agreed was their biggest political liability. Keeping the crisis a crisis ensured that the issue stayed unsolved, with blame pointing toward President Biden and Democrats heading into an election year.

As GOP Sen. Mitt Romney (R-UT) put it, "[Trump] doesn't want us to solve the border problem because he wants to blame Biden for it."[18] Gridlock was politically preferable to progress.

That conclusion, however, is incomplete. It is a truth hiding inside a much larger, much more important truth—one that seems invisible everywhere outside Washington, DC. And that larger truth is hard to unpack, especially as a member of Congress tasked with solving these big, complicated issues.

The Republican sabotage of the immigration bill appears, on its face, irrational. But the reality is that, electorally speaking, their actions *were* rational. Even strategically smart, if looked at a certain way.

Was their decision good for the country? No one can say yes with a straight face.

But was their decision rational in their minds as a way to win elections? Absolutely.

We all sing the praises of compromise—congressmen, senators, and citizens alike. We warm to the idea of our elected representatives crossing the aisle, rolling up their shirtsleeves, and hammering out a healthy bipartisan bill that solves our country's problems. In principle, it sounds wholesome and patriotic. But the notion that there is a consistent, collective push for compromise is a myth.

Say what we might about compromise in our more reflective moments, winner-take-all politics is what voters prioritize at the ballot box. There is little, if any, room for nuance. And so that is what happens in the halls of Congress. Compromise is how you get progress on policy—as the bipartisanship chapter in this book proves—but for members in today's political climate, compromise can also be one of the fastest ways to lose your seat.

And consequently, political gridlock has tragically become electorally rational. For both parties. While Republicans have mastered this approach, Democrats can use the same calculus, too (though not as effectively or nearly as aggressively, as we'll discuss).

Voters (and I'm a voter as well) elect our leaders to pass laws that solve problems and strengthen our nation, and political candidates run for office promising to do so. But when those candidates are elected, they often do the exact opposite in office: Instead of pursuing positive change, they run from it. Instead of pursuing new roads to progress, they will pick—even seek out—cul-de-sacs and dead ends. Doing so keeps the issues alive, which keeps voters—particularly primary voters—engaged.

It would be easy to blame our elected officials themselves, to call them cynical or dishonest. I can tell you firsthand that some of my colleagues are quite cynical. But by and large, elected officials' behavior directly reflects the will of the voters who send them to office. Politicians want to get elected and then reelected. It's how they get and keep a chance to do good work. That happens by having a happy electorate. Those of us who carry out the electorate's wishes are generally reelected; those who don't are defeated.

The immigration debacle was a perfect embodiment of why American national politics feels broken and a rejection of the idea that the American people, and by extension all their elected representatives, want compromise and results. Very often, the opposite is true. But while these problems seem intractable, the fact that an immigration bill even materialized on paper in hard terms was itself major progress after decades of inaction. We came close. Seeing how we failed shows how close we are to a breakthrough and what we can do to overcome the negative incentives that dominate Capitol Hill. And as far off as the halls of Congress might feel from your home, the fact is that some of the power to drive that change is in your hands as citizens.

Why Stalemate Started Making Sense

It was not always this way. When I first came to Congress in 1997, the opportunities to come together between parties were many. I worked together with my Republican colleagues on matters big and routine. One moment of my tenure is especially illustrative.

I am from Paterson, New Jersey, and have lived there all my life. Our crown jewel is probably the Paterson Great Falls, which helped power the American Revolution and remains one of the most beautiful spots in our nation. For a long time, I worked to have our falls designated a national park. The effort was harder than it may seem. Finally, after many years, it appeared our efforts were on the goal line. Standing on the House floor, I expected the vote to sail through by a mundane voice vote. But at the last minute, a group of hardline conservatives objected, upping the requirement to a two-thirds vote for passage. Not easy.

At first I fumed at this move. But after a few moments, I knew what needed to be done. I strolled right across the floor to the Republican side to my friend Don Young, the late Congressman for all of Alaska and the former dean of the House. He was also the top Republican on the Natural Resources Committee. He told me he would help, and together we started lobbying his fellow Republicans. So many of them were people I dined with, traveled with, even smoked cigars with on our Capitol balconies on cool evenings. One by one, we flipped lots of votes. The bill passed. When the Great Falls National Park was signed into law, it was one of the proudest moments of my career. And I did it through my relationships with members on the other side.

Now the opportunities for those moments and those relationships are scarcer. The gridlock everyone says they hate has become good politics for political parties and elected representatives. Yet by understanding how this came to be, we can see the ways to reverse it.

Princeton political scientist Frances Lee's seminal book *Insecure Majorities* describes the changes we lawmakers saw and made in how we went about our business. As Dr. Lee argues, one word flipped the entire incentive structure for parties and politicians, shifting the focus from cooperation to confrontation.

That word? *Competition*.

These days we have grown accustomed to knock-down, drag-out elections every campaign season, but historically, competitive elections between the parties are more the exception than the rule. In fact, for decades following 1930, Democrats, drummed into power by the Depression, completely dominated congressional elections—regularly winning over 65 percent of seats in the House and Senate—even in elections where Republicans Dwight Eisenhower, Richard Nixon, and Ronald Reagan won massive national victories. No matter if the president was popular, what Republicans accomplished, the state of the economy, or if we were at war or peace, Democrats maintained their stranglehold on congressional power, often with very sizable majorities. Like death and taxes, Democratic control of Congress was a fact of life.

This all began to change in 1980. Thanks to a variety of factors—including conservative Southern voters slowly realigning with the Republican Party, Democratic scandals and interparty squabbles, and the Reagan Revolution—Republicans won a Senate majority for only the third time since FDR's first term. Senate Democrats "were just gobsmacked. They were just as stunned as they could be. It seemed inconceivable that they could lose," recalled one former Senate staffer.[19]

Then in 1994, Republicans did the unthinkable: Led by firebrand Newt Gingrich and his "Contract for America," they captured a majority of the House for the first time in 40 years, ushering in a new era of party competition. Since then, both parties, no matter if they are in the minority or majority, see a path to winning a majority in each chamber after the next election. This simple change in congressional politics—the possibility of gaining majority power every two years where none existed for decades prior—flipped the incentive structure for political compromise on its head.

In Congress, being the majority party is everything. The majority party has control over the floor agenda, deciding what gets voted on and when and, just as importantly, what doesn't get a vote. The majority chair committees decide what hearings are called, receive greater staff resources, and typically maintain fundraising and messaging advantages. As put by one senior Senate aide, "Without the majority, you have nothing."[20]

Once Republicans proved they could win after decades in the wilderness, genuine competition for majority status in Congress emerged. Each election cycle became a fight for control, not just a debate over ideas or policy proposals. And as any political operative will tell you, the best way to win is to give busy voters reasons to choose your party over your opponent's party. The goal for members and leaders, then, is to draw as stark a contrast as possible between the two parties. We stand for this; they stand for that.

In practice, this meant the two parties began to offer diametrically opposite solutions on many issues. Whereas in the past, party platforms looked more like a Venn diagram with more overlap than you might think. "We committed to fashioning an alternative to every bill or amendment the Democrats proposed," explained former Republican House Majority Leader Tom DeLay (R-TX). "This proved to be an effective strategy. . . . It illustrated to the American people that they had a choice."[21] Similarly, parties began to voice unified party messages about what they stood for and how drastically their position differed from the opposition.

Perhaps most important, parties learned that they could make these distinctions even clearer by making the other side look weak, ineffective, or incapable of governing. One of the best ways to do this was to stop the other party from doing what they promised voters they would do. In other words, one party could gain an advantage not by getting legislative wins but simply by stopping the opposition from accomplishing any of their promises. In this zero-sum game, if one party loses, the opposition wins.

The problem with compromise in this scenario is that it muddies the differences between the two parties and clouds voters' clarity about which party they should reward with support. Lawmakers "don't want to be caught being bipartisan," longtime Rep. Sander Levin (D-MI) once said. "It's going to blur the political message."[22]

In the decades prior to 1980, the need for partisan contrast was less important simply because Republicans didn't have a reasonable shot at winning either chamber. As a result, the parties didn't feel the same incentive to be as conflictual or outright obstructionist. This gave their representatives more room to negotiate and compromise. In many cases, a record of legislative dealmaking was a valuable campaign commodity for lawmakers in both parties to tout come election time. Not anymore.

Even after Republicans tasted victory in 1994, avenues for compromise and joint success remained. My passage of the Great Falls Park was one. Another came after Hurricane Sandy ravaged my state, New Jersey, in late 2012. After the superstorm hit, our communities were in trouble and needed aid. Our delegation came together. I worked side by side with Republicans like South Jersey Rep. Frank LoBiondo for months to make sure our state got a generous federal aid package to begin rebuilding. Our Republican governor at the time was criticized by members of his own party for appearing chummy with President Obama after the storm, but Republicans like Frank did what was necessary for our state. It was an important moment for New Jersey and our Congress that I never forgot.

These days, those of us who want to collaborate have to look harder to find willing collaborators. Not only are there fewer moderate lawmakers within Congress, but members of both political parties have been convinced that voters—despite what they tell pollsters—don't want their side to give an inch to the other side. In fact, following the Gingrich playbook, they've learned that a more confrontational, obstructionist style of politics provides two huge benefits. First, it stops the other side from getting policy outcomes they fundamentally disagreed with. And second, it could help them win back the majority by making the other party appear weak and ineffective. Simply by withholding votes on key legislation, they are well on their way to achieving that perception. This oppose-to-win strategy was vocalized best in 2010 by then-Republican Senate Leader Mitch McConnell when he admitted the Republicans' "single most important thing we want to achieve is for President Obama to be a one-term president." McConnell's primary means to that end was voting no and blocking compromise.

The calculus to avoid compromise becomes even clearer when you factor in that over 90 percent of our congressional elections are uncompetitive. In these contests, the winners are effectively chosen in the primary, where a small segment of Americans—usually less than 20 percent of eligible voters and among the most partisan—select the party's nominee, who is all but certain to prevail in the general election.

Ardent partisans abhor political compromise. They punish it. They view accommodation or concession to the opposition as a sacrifice of principles rather than a necessary feature of politics. As a result, partisan primary voters look to oust lawmakers they view as too compromising and replace them with candidates who promise to fight the opposition rather than work with them—or work toward any other concrete goal.

Just ask former Rep. Liz Cheney (R-WY), once in line to be GOP Speaker and one of the most reliably conservative votes in Congress. She was primaried, crushed in her reelection bid, and kicked out of the Wyoming Republican Party after she denounced Donald Trump for his role in the January 6, 2021, insurrection. A similar story could be told of my close friend former Rep. Joe Crowley (D-NY), a terrific lawmaker who many thought could ascend to be Democratic Speaker but lost a 2018 primary to a more liberal challenger, Alexandria Ocasio-Cortez.

Fearing this fate for themselves, many lawmakers who want to keep their jobs work to stave off primary challenges from the more extreme flank of their party by showing their partisan bona fides while in office.

They do so—as Dr. Lee documents—via a more confrontational style of politics: holding press conferences to publicly trash the other side and their ideas, using the powers of their office to investigate the other party, or introducing bills that send a message but have zero chance of ever becoming law (such as legislation to defund the IRS or the FBI) to force the other party into electorally difficult votes. Such tactics rally their partisan base, create ample opportunities for party messaging and fundraising, and draw the all-important contrasts between the two parties—a perfect trifecta for members and parties aiming to win majorities in Congress.

Primary Motivations

Once compromise becomes irrational, there are big forces that align the parties' priorities behind obstruction rather than bipartisanship. These incentives play out politician by politician, district by district, to push our leaders' positions ever further toward the extremes. And though we hardly notice it when we head to the ballot box, these forces, like the larger ones, ultimately spring from the will of the voters. Certain voters, at least.

Let's be clear about this: You may feel small and powerless, and you may suspect that bigger players' interests count far more than yours, but politicians actually care about your vote. A lot. As an elected official, I filter my choices first and foremost through the prism of whether they will help or hurt my constituents. But for some of my colleagues, their first consideration is whether it will help or hurt their electoral standing. That is not the only factor they weigh, but it's a big one.

Before you consider this mindset craven, consider that elections *should be* a healthy motivator for politicians. It means we work to keep our voters happy. The distortions of our modern electoral map, however, have sent this healthy motivator into toxic territory.

The problem begins in the primaries.

Our election system is designed to secure balance. More partisan voters participate in primary contests held in spring or summer, but in a fall contest, the voter pool grows and becomes less extreme as fewer partisan voters show up to pick the ultimate winner. In a perfect world, a politician may have to lurch to the left or right to win their primary, but then in a general election, where all registered voters can cast a ballot regardless of party, they must appeal to everyone to win.

But not so fast. To paraphrase a line from *Office Space*: What if you didn't have a balanced, two-tier election system? What if one of these elections . . . stopped mattering?

No, general elections have not stopped happening. But by and large, they no longer matter because they are no longer competitive. This is due to a confluence of related factors: voters sorting themselves both geographically and by party; low engagement in primary elections; and yes, the imposition of unfair, gerrymandered maps locking in seats for one party over a long period.

David Wasserman, one of the smartest analysts of congressional elections out there, has shown the decimation of House swing seats. At the start of the congressional term in 2023, there were just 45 seats Wasserman rated as toss-ups (ones where neither party had a clear edge). That's just 10 percent of all House elections, the fewest in history. By way of comparison, in 1997 there were about 170 swing seats.[23]

As for the other 90 percent of House seats, we already know which party is going to win, no matter the candidates, their backgrounds, or their messages. In these races, the real election occurs in the primary, which means candidates often race to the most extreme wings of their parties to prove they are partisan enough to serve.

This matters tremendously for who actually serves in Congress and how they behave once they get there. In Congress in 2024, for example, just 11 Democrats represent Republican-leaning districts.[24] The number of House Republicans representing Democratic-leaning districts in 2024? Ten. Similarly, in the Senate, just three Democrats represent states Donald Trump won in 2020 (with all three seats up in November 2024), and just one Republican represents a state Joe Biden won.

In other words, in the 118th Congress, just 25 sitting members out of 535, less than 5 percent, occupy seats where they have reasonable fear of losing a general election. That leaves 510 members of Congress who are probably more worried about losing a primary than anything else.

The fewer swing seats there are in Congress, the less general elections matter. Primary elections matter more. A member who only caters to primary voters will embrace ideological purity in a constant sprint to prove their partisanship to the only voters likely to determine who represents the district. That person has far less—if any—incentive to work with the other side or pass laws that the other side agrees with.

To trace how this backward logic plays out, let's return to the bipartisan immigration deal Senators Murphy, Lankford, and Sinema constructed. Let's say for the sake of argument that South Dakota Republican Sen. John Thune was considering voting yes, as was reported. Thune represents a deep red state in the Great Plains, but he does not have a reputation for being a bomb-thrower. Had Thune endorsed the deal, he would have gone against the position of his party's titular head, Donald Trump, and been pilloried by the very voters who dominate GOP primaries in South Dakota. It would have created considerable headaches for Thune, and even potentially cost him politically. If primary voters ousted him, his opportunity to pursue policies he cares about for the citizens of South Dakota would be over.

Real talk: Yes, it is antithetical to democracy that lawmakers and parties would deliberately ignore voters of the other party. But I've seen this type of thinking grow more and more common in my decades in Congress.

Sometimes there are exceptions and surprises. The 2010 repeal of Don't Ask, Don't Tell; the 2013 reauthorization of the Violence Against Women Act; opposition to the antiworker Trans-Pacific Partnership Trade Authority; the Bipartisan Safe Communities Act; the CHIPS and Science Act; the 2023 debt ceiling increase; and the Respect for Marriage Act all garnered bipartisan support. Sometimes the totals were paltry, but doing the right thing is never wrong.

Nevertheless, the more typical party-blindness ignores that there is still deep core political diversity across America. Republicans live in blue states, and Democrats live in red states—lots of them! My home state of New Jersey is reliably blue, but in 2020 Donald Trump still received 41 percent of the vote—nearly two million Garden Staters. In that same election, deep blue California had more than six million Trump voters, while red Texas had more than five million Biden voters. But the voting records of those senators don't reflect those minority segments.

This is, again, electorally and politically rational: Why worry about voters who do not control your political destiny?

No, It's Not All Gerrymandering's Fault

The withering of general elections and swing seats occurred gradually over the past few decades as several factors drove the moderate middle to the sidelines—in elections and in our own minds as voters.

First, let's look at one factor that matters—but less than everyone seems to think.

Gerrymandering certainly dials up the distorted incentives against compromise. That said, it is a minimyth that the biased drawing of congressional districts is the main cause of partisanship and gridlock. It is one cause, but it's not the primary one that so many assume.

Gerrymandering is when a state legislature draws district lines around certain neighborhoods to maximize the number of voters of their party in a district while dividing up voters of the other party into such small groups that they lack the numbers to elect anyone. It has existed throughout America's history, which is why it is named for an 18th-century politician, Elbridge Gerry. But it has unquestionably widened and worsened in recent years.

To see gerrymandering's real impact, keep in mind that senators are elected regardless of population, so district maps only matter in the House. And it does matter where unfair maps dominate, particularly in several large states.

In 2023, Florida Gov. Ron DeSantis pushed through a congressional map that heavily favors Republicans, creating a 20–8 split. This means that, unless something extraordinary happens, Florida will send 20 Republicans and 8 Democrats to the House of Representatives every two years until the districts are redrawn in 2032. That's over 70 percent of Florida's House seats, even though former President Trump won the state with just 51.2 percent of the vote in 2020. If we based the House seats on Trump's vote share, a fairer map would give Florida Republicans a much narrower 15–13 advantage in the House.

Ditto the 25–13 Republican map in Texas that does not reflect a politically tightening state. Nor does Ohio's 10–5 map. Gerrymanders in Missouri (6–2), Tennessee (8–1), and Utah (4–0) produce lopsided delegations where incumbents are all but assured a win in the general election.

And while Democrats have not abused the district-drawing process as grossly as Republicans, they have engaged in it, too: The current Illinois congressional delegation of 14–3 is courtesy of a grotesque-looking map, with one district resembling a prone eel stretching from the Indiana to the Missouri and Iowa borders and a spattering of indescribably shaped seats clustered around Chicago. The 7–1 Maryland map has its own collection of modern art forms masquerading as House districts.

Having more lawmakers in one-sided seats creates fewer swing districts and more members beholden to the extreme wings of their parties. That means fewer members willing to straddle the center and put their names—and political futures—next to a legislative compromise. The more comfortable a politician is with their position, the less likely they are to pursue both broad compromises and reforms in general.

Of course, it's easy to blame gerrymandering for a lot of problems. After all, it's one of the most blatant political maneuvers—about as subtle as a sledgehammer in a china shop—so it makes an easy villain. But gerrymandering is only one part of our national gridlock and government dysfunction. The larger part still comes back to—brace yourselves—all of us.

As Wasserman and others have shown, nationwide sorting, with Americans living in communities composed of people who share their political stripes, has exploded. Think about it: How many people of a different political persuasion live in your neighborhood, or even your town? Write down a list of places you'd be willing to move—I'll bet many of those locations share your politics even if you never thought about it explicitly. Gerrymanders have a much easier job to do, and even become useless, when communities are overwhelmingly composed of one party. We're doing the work ourselves.

For example, Tennessee Republicans may have carved up Davidson County after 2021 to keep Nashville from electing a House Democrat, but Democrats in Tennessee would have had a hard time drawing more than one more safe seat around the state capital if they could. The state has become so reliably Republican, with Democrats clustered almost entirely around Nashville and Memphis. The days when Democrats could win exurban and rural seats feel like a relic from another era—practically ancient history at this point. Similarly, even if Republicans on Beacon Hill had the means, they would have a hard time drawing a GOP House seat anywhere in Massachusetts. The Bay State today is not gerrymandered; it is just super blue.

Two of my closest friends in Congress, Jack Murtha and Tim Holden, represented rural enclaves of Pennsylvania for decades. Both men were hugely effective legislators. But Democrats are no longer competitive in Johnstown or Schuylkill County and probably won't be for many years.

Combine self-sorting with the nationalization of America's politics and the slow death of split-ticket voting (voting for candidates from different political parties for different offices on the same ballot), and there you have it: a recipe for rational stalemate.

Before the 2010 Republican landslide, split-ticket voting in federal elections had been relatively common across the country for generations. In many places, it was even a tradition. Voters were proud to support the candidates, not just the parties. In red states, you might see long-standing support for Republicans at the top of the ballot (for president or Senate), but votes for Democrats for lower offices, including US House and state legislatures, were fairly common. And vice versa. This is how Democrats like Bud Cramer, Gene Taylor, Chet

Edwards, and Ike Skelton, among others, could get elected over and over in conservative strongholds like Huntsville, Pascagoula, Waco, and the Ozarks. And it is how senators like Joe Manchin in West Virginia, Jon Tester in Montana, and Sherrod Brown in Ohio could still represent states Donald Trump carried by double digits.

Today, it's rarer than ever. At the start of 2009, approximately 70 Democrats represented Republican-leaning districts in the House. In 2024, that number is fewer than a dozen. After 2010, none of the Southern Democrats named above were returned to Congress, and not one of their seats has been remotely competitive since then. Voters—Democrats and Republicans—are less and less likely to break party ranks.

This is because, in many voters' minds, the battle lines are drawn from Washington, DC, on down. Remember the old adage that "all politics is local"? That used to be somewhat true. Today, it's a nostalgic memory. National politics now defines local politics and everything in between. And that nationalization has been driven heavily by American political media. Matt Fuller's chapter in this book provides a deep explanation of the media's role, but I will offer this snapshot from my experience.

If you are unfortunate enough to watch cable news on a given day, you will see where so much of our political gridlock is nurtured. Hosts tut-tut on Congress's inability to come to solutions, pundits blather on about the day's fight, and a steady stream of elected officials always appears to play the role of perturbed Democrat or Republican, everyone in perpetual aggrievement and outrage.

As New York University professor Jay Rosen puts it, our political media frames its coverage not on the stakes, not on why our political debates matter, but on the odds—that is, who is winning and losing and where the odds will be tomorrow. This spin earns the media eyeballs, and it provides publicity-hungry politicians a national stage on which to display their gamesmanship. A win-win.

In a political reality where obstruction is rational, the national media plays a particular role. It enables politicians and candidates to tout their partisanship and court their primary voters on the national airwaves. Here's an example: Any public hearing we hold on Capitol Hill is available through C-SPAN and on congressional web pages. If you decide to watch a hearing, whether it be the Judiciary Committee, Education, Energy and Commerce, Ways and Means, Homeland Security, or even Veterans Affairs, you will not have to look long for theater.

This past spring, I was sitting in on a Ways and Means markup hearing (where we revise draft bills) when a Republican member introduced a contentious amendment she knew would never become law. When she finished, a Democratic member spoke earnestly about why he opposed the amendment and asked why it was written as it was. While he spoke, the Republican member kibitzed with her neighbor, paying less than zero attention to questions about her own amendment. She never so much as glanced in his direction.

Throughout that hearing and countless others like it, there are few true exchanges—because for many members, the hearings are not an opportunity to question witnesses, debate policy, or assess complex legislation. They are an audition. An audition to catch the eye of a TV booker for Fox or Newsmax (for Republicans), MSNBC (Democrats), or CNN (both). What is more attractive to a booker: a member who asked a witness about the nuts and bolts of Medicare drug negotiation, or a member who screamed at his hearing about Hunter Biden's laptop? The answer is obvious.

The media didn't make our gridlock problem—after all, it plays what people want to watch—but it does amplify the incentive for extremism. The number of slots a TV booker can fill each night is small, and that means that to command attention, each audition must be bigger and louder and wackier than the one before. The leaders who want to make compromises don't end up on TV as much—and the cycle perpetuates itself.

And while this incentive structure affects members of both parties, the elephant in the room is the elephant in the room. Political gridlock in America today at the federal level comes from elements in both of our two main political parties, but one of them decisively owns the larger share of responsibility: the Republican Party. If you doubt that assessment when it comes from a Democrat, you can take it from a few Republicans instead. In defending his strategy to be the "Party of No," former GOP House Majority Leader Eric Cantor warned his fellow Republicans, "We're not here to cut deals and get crumbs and stay in the minority for another 40 years. We're here to fight these guys."[25] (Appropriately, Cantor would be ousted from office by a far-right political outsider in one of the biggest primary upsets in modern US political history.) And even after taking back the majority, the GOP often bypassed compromise in favor of take-it-or-leave-it conservative policy overhauls. My Republican colleague Rep. Tom Cole (OK) put it this way when his fellow GOP members started insisting on impossible, even dangerous, outcomes like defaulting on the government's debt: "The second we got the majority back, people started making unrealistic demands. . . . It was like putting a gun to your own head and saying: Do what I say or I'll shoot!"[26]

Donald Trump's demand that congressional Republicans reject any immigration compromise, obeyed by his members, may strike a casual observer as extreme. But it fits a years, even decades-long pattern of embracing gridlock and rebuffing substantive compromise for political gains. In 2020, Democrats passed three Covid relief packages even though they could have helped Trump electorally because the country was in desperate need of aid. Conversely, after President Biden took over, a total of zero congressional Republicans voted for the American Rescue Plan in 2021, a bill that provided significant relief to both liberal and conservative voters.

Additionally, the last five government shutdowns were precipitated by Republican member intransigence. Republicans even brought

America to the verge of defaulting on our debt, an unthinkable line that would have obliterated the country but nonetheless led to credit downgrades for the nation and brought lingering pain to the economy. In the 117th Congress (2021–2022), 99 percent of Republicans voted against an assault weapons ban, and 96 percent opposed protections for birth control, measures supported by the majority of Americans. Perhaps most revealing, hours after the January 6 insurrection was quelled, 68 percent voted to throw out the election votes in two states, a symbolic act signaling support for overturning the results of the national election on the flimsiest of pretexts.

These are not the actions of a political party interested in meeting anywhere near the middle. These are the actions of lawmakers who know their job depends on keeping their partisan primary voters happy. Paraphrasing my friend former Speaker Nancy Pelosi, America needs a strong, functioning GOP, and what we have today is not that.

I can imagine my conservative readers are likely thinking "Democrats have their extreme members, too." That is fair. A handful of Democrats opposed the landmark 2021 roads and bridges law. Numerous members of my party routinely vote against the annual National Defense Authorization Act to fund America's military. At other times, some Democrats will speak against strongly funding our law enforcement agencies. These are funding streams vital to our communities, and opposing them, often to make a political statement, is not helpful.

As former Speaker Sam Rayburn said, any jackass can get down a barn, but it takes a carpenter to build one.

The dysfunction in Congress doesn't just affect our legislative productivity; it also influences who even wants to sign up for the job in the first place. We hold fewer hearings, vote on fewer amendments, and introduce fewer bills. Our time in session is shrinking, as are genuine floor debates and committee hearings, and members of Congress spend less time engaging with one another, especially across the aisle. We haven't passed all our spending bills on time since the Macarena topped the charts (in 1996, for those who don't remember—and trust me, you don't want to look it up).

At the same time, staffers—often idealistic individuals who come to DC with dreams of making a difference—are increasingly opting out, seeking better pay, more impact, and work-life balance in the private sector after only a few short years. The same is true for members, too; more and more lawmakers are choosing to exit Congress, disillusioned by the lack of meaningful policy impact and the growing threat of violence. Their replacements, by and large, are politicians who have no experience in any other political environment. All they know is the dysfunction of now, and they are opting into it.

These are all glaring indicators that the incentive structure on Capitol Hill is fundamentally broken. If we want to break this cycle of dysfunction, we need to change the incentives that drive it. And that begins with the solutions we're about to explore.

Unjamming the System

On February 11, 2024, just one week after the immigration deal briefly lived and immediately died, a poll revealed how Americans interpreted the failure. By a double-digit split, Americans unsurprisingly blamed one major party leader over the other.[27]

Only the assignment of blame was the surprise: 49 percent of Americans blamed President Biden for the collapse of the immigration deal he supported, and just 39 percent blamed Donald Trump, whose loud public demands led to the bill's demise.

And this, dear reader, is the engine at the center of the various incentives for gridlock. Yes, insecure majorities in Congress create a constant tug-of-war for party power. Yes, the dominance of primary elections over solid-red and solid-blue seats pushes candidates to the extremes, helped along by a little gerrymandering. And yes, the nationalization of politics, amped up by national TV news, nudges voters to harden the party lines in our minds. But fundamentally, political parties choose obstruction because it works—because people vote for it.

The immigration bill poll laid bare the challenges of making government work to solve problems in this environment. Informed, clear-eyed, farsighted voters are the basis of any functioning democracy. If voters cannot spot and reward the fruits of good governance or the leaders who pursue it, then change is hopeless.

But what may seem like hard news is actually good news, because it shows that some of the levers of change are within our grasp as citizens. Here are a few avenues to consider.

First, since primaries distort the incentive structure for collaboration, reforming our primary election system is essential to breaking the cycle of obstruction and gridlock. We've got a lot of options. One possible approach is reevaluating the first-past-the-post, winner-take-all system we have now with proportional representation (PR). In a PR system, the number of seats a party wins in the legislature matches the percentage of votes that party's candidates receive—so if Republicans win 52 percent of votes in Florida, they will get 52 percent of the state's seats in the House. This system, common in many European democracies like the United Kingdom, could lead to a more accurate representation of state vote shares. It could also motivate voters to turn out even in places where one party dominates. This significant change is unlikely, however, because each state controls its own election laws.

Another model worth studying is ranked choice voting (RCV), where voters rank their preferred candidates in order regardless of party affiliation. If no candidate receives a majority of first-place votes, the candidate with the fewest is eliminated, and their votes are redistributed to voters' second choices. This process continues until one candidate achieves a majority. RCV has been implemented in local elections in New York and in congressional elections in Maine and

Alaska. Critics argue that RCV is confusing for voters, but it could offer a way to ensure that winners have broader support.

Additionally, smaller changes like jungle primaries—where all candidates, regardless of party, compete in a single primary, with the top two vote-getters advancing to the general election—are gaining traction. States like Louisiana, Washington, and California have adopted this model, with others considering it for future elections. These reforms seek to create more competitive elections where partisan primary voters do not effectively choose the general election winner in most districts.

A second strategy, and one sized just right for everyday citizens, is to spot the polarizers in action. Voters should be wary of performative leaders who seem more interested in espousing slogans and booking television appearances than, you know, doing things. If you see the same lawmakers' faces popping up regularly on cable news, that's a pretty good signal that they are prioritizing media hits over the hard work of legislating.

At the same time, simply pledging bipartisanship as if it were a magic solution can be a red flag. While the intentions behind these promises are often good, they can sometimes be a cover for achieving very little. Lawmakers know that compromise on many tough issues is unlikely, so they can then easily blame the other side for not doing their part.

Third, if you value bipartisanship, vote for it. This means you can't demand that your lawmakers give no ground to the other party. It also means you can't expect to get every letter of every policy you want signed into law. Compromise in Congress requires compromise by voters, too. But if more of us do this, we will get genuine progress, which is a lot better than what we're getting now.

What we really need are leaders with clear, concrete, and direct priorities and the freedom and trust (derived from us) to pursue the best passable policy. If legislators feel confident they won't be punished—likely in the primary—for compromising, they will be more willing to pursue it.

And *if* we can return to a world where we reward compromise, watch how fast lawmakers will update their incentive structures to seek it. That's the powerful silver lining of having leaders who want to stay in power: They will go where the votes are. If being a dealmaker nets more votes than being a flamethrower, we'll see a sudden surge in lawmakers who fancy themselves the next great compromiser.

Fourth, demand the end of gerrymandering, and hold leaders to it. And because states are largely responsible for their own election laws, this means your best bang for your gerrymandering buck is to vote in state legislature races (and their primaries). This, at least, is a problem with a straightforward solution: Gerrymandering should be outlawed.

While the House of Representatives voted to ban gerrymandering in 2021, the bill ultimately died in the Senate. However, some progress has been made elsewhere. Recent decisions by state supreme courts in swing states like Michigan and Pennsylvania have resulted in much fairer electoral maps. Additionally, the US Supreme Court's 2024 rulings against gerrymanders in Alabama and Louisiana will add one Democratic seat in each state (shifting the Alabama map from 6–1 to 5–2 and the Louisiana map from 5–1 to 4–2), helping to create greater balance. While ending gerrymandering won't solve all our problems, it would be a significant step forward.

Without real compromise or institutional reforms, there is only one other way past our stalemate. It is not a coincidence that the most productive congresses in American history—the 37th at the start of the Civil War, the 73rd in 1933, the 88th and 89th that enshrined the Great Society, and even the 117th in 2021—were unified, one-party governments. If you want your party to achieve FDR-sized policy wins, you better hope for FDR-sized congressional majorities.

But the reality is that in today's world, such majorities will be fleeting, if they come at all. The true solution is to fix the broken incentives that reward obstruction—and these begin at the ballot box.

Imagine a Congress where the stars were the serious lawmakers, dealmakers who sweated out tough negotiations and struck real compromises to make progress (not perfection) for the American people. Leaders, in some respects, like James Lankford, Chris Murphy, and Kyrsten Sinema. Imagine that, every election cycle, candidates competed to look more like them during the immigration debate, because they knew that's what voters wanted and would reward.

Change comes down to the people we elect. If you send in clowns, you cannot be mad when they spray you with seltzer and hit you with a banana cream pie. America's officials need to take their jobs more seriously, and it's up to all of us to demand that they do so.

We, as voters, have the power to elect real leaders committed to real progress.

Voting together, we can bring what's rational into line with what's right.

Elected officials are ultimately vessels of the voters' will. If they see greater value in propagating outrage than governing, progress halts. If we demand—through purposeful, engaged action—something better, they will follow.

"The Filibuster Forces Compromise"

Adam Jentleson

Every once in a while, there's an issue that garners such widespread agreement that it's easy even for our polarized lawmakers to act on. Or at least, you would think so.

On June 24, 2022, the Supreme Court overturned *Roe v. Wade* and turned back the clock to 1973, when a woman's right to an abortion was not protected. The many legal scholars and court watchers who had expected a more limited ruling in the *Dobbs v. Jackson* decision were shocked. This was a wholesale rejection of *Roe*'s 50 years of precedent rather than the anticipated recalibration. Even conservatives were taken aback. Chief Justice John Roberts reportedly lobbied against the decision, but his efforts were undercut when a draft of the opinion was leaked to the media, freezing it in place.[1]

What was particularly startling was that the *Dobbs* decision overruled the views of a broad cross section of the American public: According to Gallup, 69 percent of Americans believed that abortion should be legal in the first three months of pregnancy.[2] Yet the justices who made up the conservative majority were confirmed by senators who garnered only around 40 percent of the total votes cast for the Senate.[3] By these measures and many more, this was a monumental change in public policy foisted upon an unwilling nation.

This was one of those times when we'd expect a well-functioning democracy to be able to course correct—to use the legislative process to bring the policies of government into line with the popular will, ideally through bipartisan compromise. Indeed, our system used to be able to do this. But today, it cannot, or more accurately, it won't. This is not because of polarization, gerrymandering, or the flood of corporate money in politics. Instead, our democracy is hamstrung for one simple reason: the modern, mutated version of the Senate's famous filibuster.

A few decades ago, the filibuster actually did work a bit the way you've seen in the movies. A senator would stand on the Senate floor, preventing the chamber from moving ahead with a piece of legislation by delivering endless speeches or just talking nonsense—reading from the phone book or, in one case, reciting recipes for salad dressing and oysters. It was, in essence, a chance for senators to talk for a long time, after which bills would be voted up or down on a simple majority. The myth formed by this rarely used but theatrical tactic was that it forced senators to pause and take time to consider issues more carefully, and ultimately reach bipartisan compromise. No more.

In recent decades, the filibuster has gradually transformed into something completely different and far less democratic—namely, a de facto requirement that every bill in the Senate must have 60 votes to pass, without senators having to talk at all. And far from promoting compromise, this mutated filibuster guts bipartisan cooperation and frequently stops Senate action altogether.

The fight over abortion rights is hardly the only matter where the filibuster has failed the needs of the moment and foiled our chances for a broad-based bipartisan compromise. Gun control. Immigration reform. Campaign finance. Stricter ethics requirements for Supreme Court justices. On every one of these policies, Senate polls indicate that there are more than 50 senators ready to vote yes. But the mere hint of a filibuster means they never even get a vote. They are dead even before arrival.

Abortion rights have met the same fate. Today, a bipartisan majority of senators (49 Democratic senators and at least 2 Republicans, Senators Susan Collins of Maine and Lisa Murkowski of Alaska, as of this writing) would vote for a compromise bill to protect abortion rights nationwide.[4] The nearly 7-in-10 Americans who support that policy would probably thank them for doing it. Yet such a compromise exists in the Senate's version of the Bermuda Triangle: It can secure a bipartisan majority of 51 votes to pass, but not the supermajority of 60 votes for the bill to hit the Senate floor.

This supermajority requirement is a relatively new bar to clear. For most of the Senate's existence, bills passed or failed based on whether they could secure a simple majority (the size of the Senate has grown with the number of states, so today a simple majority is 51 out of 100 members, or 50 plus the vice president's tie-breaking vote). When the Framers created the Senate, they debated the idea of imposing a supermajority requirement but roundly rejected it, correctly surmising that it would create an irresistible temptation for the minority to manufacture gridlock. And true to their design, the Senate was a majority-rule institution from our nation's founding up until about 30 years ago. In the majority-rule Senate, big measures passed with bipartisan support. In 1994, for example, an assault weapons ban passed with 56 votes.[5] As recently as 2006, Justice Samuel Alito was confirmed with 58 votes.[6]

To say that compromise abounded during this 200-year period is an understatement. Pick almost any accomplishment the Senate produced between its founding and, roughly, the 1990s, and it is safe to assume that it passed without having to clear a 60-vote threshold. And most of these bills involved bipartisan compromise—no filibuster needed. That's because (as explained in the bipartisanship chapter in this book) the need to get to 50 votes among a diverse set of senators forced Democrats and Republicans of all stripes to seek common ground to get laws passed—which they did, on everything from creating Medicare to setting tax policy to passing the GI Bill.

During this two-century span, filibusters were rare but dramatic, and they were usually used to delay but not ultimately block legislation. They involved holding the floor, like Jimmy Stewart in *Mr. Smith Goes to Washington*, and constituted major political events that commanded the attention of the press and the public, often spurring a national debate over whatever issue was at stake. Yet with rare exceptions—most importantly on civil rights—filibusters eventually failed, at which point the bill at hand would come up for a simple majority vote. Then almost always, it passed.

Today, the filibuster is about as different from that as a paper airplane is from a 747. It has morphed from a rare but dramatic tool for stalling bills on their path to eventual passage into the inverse: a constant, unremarkable tool for blocking bills altogether. What the filibuster has lost in dramatics it has gained in potency. It is now a powerful procedural weapon that allows senators to raise the threshold for passage on *every single bill* from a simple majority of 51 votes to a supermajority of 60. And senators in the minority party wield that weapon to force almost every bill to win the support of 60 senators not just to pass but simply to be brought to a vote. Unlike in the past, imposing this bar today requires no speeches and no dramatic moments on the floor—in fact, it requires little effort at all. Yet despite requiring less of those who employ it, this new, silent filibuster is more powerful than ever. It has turned the supposedly statesmanlike Senate, which the Framers reportedly envisioned as a saucer to cool the tea of the hotheaded House, into a deep freezer.

To make matters worse, the filibuster's evolution has moved this dysfunction behind the scenes. Instead of senators making their case on the Senate floor, in full public view, the modern filibuster allows them to obstruct via email. Instead of transparency and accountability, the process is shrouded in mystery. As the public decries legislative inaction, critical issues never even reach the Senate floor.

The problem with the myth that the filibuster forces compromise is that it shrouds obstruction in a veil of tradition, fraudulently portraying naked political gamesmanship as something loftier. Breaking down the myth allows us to see what is really going on: politicians rendering our great nation ungovernable to serve their narrow political interests. In the basest terms, the minority party uses the filibuster to stop the party in power from getting things done for the sole purpose of making them look bad, improving the chances that the out-party will retake power in the next election.

Once we see the filibuster for what it really is, we can demand that politicians stop using it as an excuse to grind things to a halt, and instead focus on solving problems for the American people. Together, we can push for a system that cuts through the gridlock, fosters genuine collaboration, and yes, even brings back the lost art of compromise.

Framers Against Supermajorities

To understand how we got here, it helps to know how the filibuster came to be in the first place. The myth of the filibuster rests on the Framers' genuine commitment to checking what John Adams called the "tyranny of the majority."[7] That is, the risk that a simple majority could do whatever they want without ever having to consider the views of anyone else. Their concern was that if the majority could impose its will without constraints, it might do so in ways that were unjust or harmful to those who did not belong to the majority group. With that in mind, the Senate was envisioned as the place in the lawmaking process where cooler heads prevail and extreme ideas unravel. The filibuster, in theory, leverages that role. And on the face of it, a 60-vote requirement does appear to guarantee that senators of both parties have to work together, especially in an era in which neither party is likely to control 60 or more Senate seats for the foreseeable future.

The problem is, almost none of this is true.

Contrary to popular belief, the filibuster is not in the Constitution. In fact, the term did not come into existence for more than a half-century after the Senate was created, and the idea of giving a prolonged speech to delay proceedings was considered unseemly in the Senate's early decades (more on that later). But more to the point, the Framers roundly rejected the idea of a supermajority threshold when they created the Senate. The Constitution's authors were already intimately familiar with the problems of working under a supermajority threshold because they had tried it themselves—and failed. The Articles of Confederation, which imposed a supermajority vote for most major laws in the Continental Congress, governed the land during the Revolutionary War years and presented huge roadblocks to compromise. The supermajority requirement was a principal reason for the failure of our nation's first attempt at self-governance, as the system created by the Articles stonewalled itself into collapse.

Burned by that experience, the Framers rejected the idea that supermajority systems are more conducive to compromise than majority ones. Madison explained that requiring "more than a majority" to pass laws would mean that, "In all cases where justice or the general good might require new laws to be passed, or active measures to be pursued, the fundamental principle of free government would be reversed. It would no longer be the majority that would rule: the power would be transferred to the minority." Alexander Hamilton agreed. He wrote that a supermajority threshold's "real operation is to embarrass the administration, to destroy the energy of the government, and to substitute the pleasure, caprice, or artifices of an insignificant, turbulent, or corrupt junto, to the regular deliberations and decisions of a respectable majority." To counter the argument that a supermajority threshold promotes compromise, Hamilton wrote, "what at first sight may seem a remedy, is, in reality, a poison."[8]

The original design of the Senate reflected this decisive preference for majority rule. The Framers singled out treaties, impeachment proceedings, and constitutional amendments as the only cases for supermajority treatment in the Constitution. All other votes were to be a simple majority. The Framers also made clear that debate should unfold without obstruction, and they inked multiple methods to ensure this. Obstruction was seen as unbecoming of a senator. On the rare occasions when this norm needed to be enforced—when a senator was rambling on and preventing the chamber from moving on with its business—senators would simply talk over their colleague until the loquacious one got the message and sat down, or the presiding officer would instruct them to do so, or the clerks would open and close the chamber doors as a signal to wrap it up.

What's clear from this history is that even leaders as preoccupied as the Framers were with checking majority tyranny believed that a supermajority threshold went too far. They believed that giving the minority veto power would lead to gridlock and that all the other steps to a law's passage—having to secure a majority in a country as big and diverse as the United States (even when it was just 13 states) in both chambers of Congress, securing the president's signature, and withstanding scrutiny by the courts—were sufficient guarantees of moderation and compromise.

And yet, somewhere along the way, the filibuster came about. How? Actually, partly by accident.

The filibuster was never consciously created, but it evolved slowly over several decades. In 1806, acting on the advice of Vice President Aaron Burr—yes, the same guy who shot Hamilton—the Senate streamlined its rules and got rid of a little procedure called the "previous question" motion, which had allowed a majority to vote to end debate and proceed to a vote. This was not a conscious choice to allow unlimited debate but rather an attempt to discard unnecessary rules. Why force the entire chamber to take a cumbersome recorded vote to stop debate when senators knew when to shut their mouths anyway?[9] Senators' confidence in their collective ability to police debate led them to unwittingly create a loophole through which the filibuster would eventually emerge.

For decades after the 1806 rule change, the norms preventing obstruction held sway. What historian H. W. Brands has called the golden age of the Senate, running through the first half of the 19th century, was a majority-rule institution where the filibuster did not exist. This period was marked by monumental achievements and compromise, such as the Louisiana Purchase, the Compromise of 1850 attempting to stave off civil war, and the Missouri Compromise preventing the expansion of slavery in new states north of Missouri—which, notably, eked by on a margin of two votes. Had there been a supermajority requirement at the time, it would have failed.

What we would describe today as the "talking filibuster" began to emerge around the middle of the 19th century. This is what almost everyone who has heard of the filibuster pictures when they hear the word: senators droning on for hours, perhaps reading from the phonebook or Dr. Seuss, to stall legislation. Yet even this classic form of the filibuster was not created or sanctioned by any Senate rule. Rather, it emerged over several decades after the previous question rule was tossed out.

The filibuster's intellectual godfather was Sen. John C. Calhoun of South Carolina, who envisioned a numerical minority empowered to counter the dominance of an unsympathetic majority. Whereas Madison wanted the minority to have a platform to air their views and delay the legislative process to make themselves heard, Calhoun believed the minority was entitled to a veto. Importantly, Calhoun had a specific minority in mind: slaveholders, for whom he was the nation's leading advocate. Calhoun's ideas entered circulation in the 1830s, shortly after he himself helped undermine one of the most powerful tools for policing obstruction: the power of the presiding officer (who oversees the Senate) to cut off debate.[10] With the weakening of this and other mechanisms to end debate, the norms against obstruction eroded, and senators increasingly began to employ delay tactics.

The groundwork thus laid, the talking filibuster emerged in the middle of the 19th century—and senators who cared deeply about the institution immediately saw it as detrimental to the institutional health of the Senate. Far from embracing it as a force for compromise, outraged observers derided the filibuster as soon as it appeared on the scene. The term *filibuster* itself was meant as a pejorative, derived from the lexicon of piracy. Sen. Henry Clay of Kentucky, known as the Great Compromiser, was so alarmed at the rise in obstruction that he tried to restore the previous question rule, but Calhoun blocked him. As Clay and other filibuster critics foresaw, over the succeeding decades, obstruction steadily increased and the reputation of the Senate declined.

Then in 1917, public frustration with the filibuster came to a head. In January, Germany formally notified the United States of its intention to resume unrestricted submarine warfare. With the winds of war swirling, President Woodrow Wilson called on Congress to give him the power to arm American ships against German attacks. The House acted quickly, passing the ship-arming measure on March 1. Then it went to the Senate, which was set to adjourn on March 3—an immovable deadline set by the Constitution that would dissolve the body and scuttle the measure.[11] Headcounts at the time indicated that an overwhelming majority of senators stood ready to approve the bill. But the antiwar Sen. Robert "Fighting Bob" LaFollette of Wisconsin, in tandem with a dozen colleagues, filibustered for a day and a half until the Senate adjourned—at one point hurling a brass spittoon at the presiding officer when they tried to cut him off (this power having been weakened by Calhoun nearly a century earlier)—and successfully killed the bill.[12] Fighting Bob's filibuster triggered a massive public uproar against the Senate—as Wilson described them, a "little group of willful men"—and widespread calls for the chamber to reform its rules.[13]

For a moment, it looked like the end of the filibuster. The Senate quickly reconvened and formed a committee to rein it in. The committee's main recommendation was, effectively, to reinstate the "previous question" rule that had given the majority the ability to cut off debate. But the committee made one change that would prove enormously—and unintentionally—consequential. Instead of setting the threshold for cutting off debate at a majority, as in the original rule, they recommended setting it at a supermajority. (The threshold at the time was set at two-thirds but later lowered to three-fifths, or 60 votes in today's Senate.) The result was Senate Rule 22, otherwise known as the "cloture" rule. (A clunky term, *cloture* simply means to impose closure on debate; if invoked, all senators must "cloture" their mouths and stop talking.)

Today, Rule 22 is what sets the de facto threshold for passage at 60 votes, but it was never intended to do so. The senators who created it assumed that it would be rarely used. They expected that if and when it did become necessary to cut off a filibuster, a supermajority would be easy to secure, as it would have been against LaFollette. The committee that wrote Rule 22 left no doubt about its intent, describing it as a tool to "terminate successful filibustering."[14] And this interpretation survived for several decades.[15]

For half a century after Rule 22, filibusters remained rare. From its inception in 1917 until 1970, the Senate averaged less than one cloture vote per year.[16] During this time, those looking to stall a bill would talk for as long as they wished, and the majority would let them. But then—and this is the key part—once the minority ran out of words, they stopped talking. They voiced their opposition, and then they yielded the floor for the bill to actually be voted on. Senators understood that the filibuster (and its accompanying cloture rule) were not meant to be wielded as a minority veto. Rather, the minority would get to have its say but would ultimately stand down, and the Senate would vote—by a simple majority. This is how America's business got done well into the 20th century—and this is what it looked like to have a Senate that balanced the views of the minority with the will of the majority and forged compromises to respond to the needs of the nation, as the Framers intended.

Civil Rights and Everything Else

Things might have continued this way indefinitely if not for an issue that enough senators were willing to break all norms and precedents to stall: civil rights. Just as the Senate never proactively decided to create or allow the filibuster, it never proactively decided to become a supermajority institution. The decades-long quest for civil rights legislation lit the spark of obstruction.

The transition hinges on the unintended consequences and abuse of the cloture rule. Technically, Senate rules have always stated that debate must end before a vote can be held on a bill—but for most of the Senate's existence, it did not need to *vote* to end debate. Debate simply ended, either in a timely fashion or when filibustering senators tired out. Then starting in the late 20th century and accelerating in the early 2000s, things began to change. Today, the Senate *always* has to vote to end debate—and thus, clear cloture, with its 60-vote threshold.

The reason the Senate always has to impose cloture today is that unlike in the past, when few bills were filibustered, today *all bills* are filibustered. Seriously.

So why don't you see senators on CNN constantly commanding the chamber with a dry reading of *Green Eggs and Ham* to block the latest bill? Because modern-day filibusters are not Mr. Smith–style. Today's filibusters are assumed, not acted out. They are waged silently, mostly over email, usually by staff instead of by senators themselves. Today, a senator simply needs to register their *intent* to filibuster a bill by way of an email to the Senate majority leader, and this counts the same as *actually* filibustering it. This happens so routinely that it is assumed there will be an objection to every bill that comes to the floor.

And here's the kicker: Under the peculiar evolution of Senate rules, the fact that filibusters are invisible, passive, and silent does not change the fact that they need to be cut off. Flip on C-SPAN 2 (the Senate's channel) and you're highly unlikely to see a senator performing a talking filibuster on the floor, even though there is a 99 percent chance that a silent filibuster—or 10—is in progress. Only if and when this phantom "debate" (the staff email) is "ended" by a cloture vote can a bill move to a final vote—which, ironically, is still set at a majority but is unreachable unless the bill can get 60 votes to clear cloture. This is why you haven't seen the Senate even so much as debate a proposal on a huge number of issues that may be deeply important to you, such as abortion protections, prison overhauls, gun control, student loans, or immigration reform. Because somewhere in the background, someone is silently filibustering every one of them.

If this seems like a backward, byzantine, and downright bizarre way to upend 200 years of Senate tradition as a majority-rule institution, it is. But to understand how to move forward, it is important to understand how we got here.

The shift to supermajority rule has its origins in the civil rights battles of the early to mid-20th century. While filibusters were rare during this period, the glaring exception was civil rights. For more than half a century, Southern senators used Rule 22 to impose a de facto supermajority threshold on civil rights bills—and only civil rights bills. Since non–civil rights bills did not tend to face filibusters, they continued to pass or fail on majority votes. Yet civil rights bills didn't just face regular filibusters; they faced endless ones. Working together and united by their shared determination to protect segregation laws, Southern senators were able to tag team and prolong filibusters indefinitely. One senator would speak for as long as he could and then yield the floor to a fellow anti–civil rights colleague to continue the delay until he wore out and passed the baton to another. On and on it went, effectively holding the Senate hostage every time a civil rights bill came to the floor.

The only way to move a civil rights bill to a final passage vote was to invoke cloture—that is, end the filibuster—with 60 votes. The (accurate) assumption that civil rights bills would always be filibustered effectively raised the threshold for their passage to a supermajority. Civil rights bills enjoyed majority support in the Senate as early as the 1930s—as well as overwhelming public support, according to early Gallup polls—and would have passed decades earlier than they did on a simple majority vote. But the supermajority threshold stopped them, at enormous human cost.

Thus, the prototype for the modern filibuster was born.

Meanwhile, every other issue of that era was decided by majority rule. There, compromises abounded as senators handled the nation's business in a reasonably timely and bipartisan fashion. The creation of Social Security, the GI Bill, the creation of NASA—the accomplishments of the first half of the 20th century are too numerous to name. In 1965, the Senate passed the law creating Medicare without ever having to clear cloture. The issue was hard-fought until it was clear that proponents had secured a majority. At that point, opponents knew their fight was lost. Faced with the binary choice of supporting Medicare or opposing it, many senators who had been holding out for further changes to the program crossed over to support it on final passage. When the final vote was called, the bill passed with 70 votes, a bipartisan mix of 57 Democrats and 13 Republicans.[17] That is what a healthy legislative process looks like, at least for bills other than those concerning civil rights.

THE TWO-TRACK TRAP

It wasn't until 1964 that civil rights proponents broke a Southern filibuster by securing the supermajority needed to impose cloture. Quietly and unnoticed at the time, this huge breakthrough also marked the beginning of the end of the talking filibuster and the birth of the silent one.

When the filibuster against the 1964 Civil Rights Act was finally broken, many observers assumed the filibuster would simply fade away, since its primary purpose had been to block civil rights and Southern senators had finally lost that battle. Instead, the opposite happened. Like a brand-name drug whose patent has expired, the filibuster became generic, and senators who would not have touched it due to its association with racial segregation began to experiment with it for their own purposes.

The entrance of the generic filibuster into the market coincided with procedural changes that made it easier to use. By the 1970s, the dramatic expansion of the federal government ushered in by the New Deal and Great Society eras created more business for the Senate—more budget bills to pass, more nominees to process, and more agencies to oversee, all of which meant more scheduling challenges for Senate leaders.

Up until that point, the Senate floor had operated as a single legislative track: When a bill was on the floor, no other legislation could move until the pending business concluded. Having only one track meant that if a filibuster delayed a bill, most other business ground to a halt. Crafty senators identified this as a point of leverage. Filibustering a bill, or even threatening to, could jam all the Senate's business. Typically, the majority leader would be willing to grant concessions to keep the trains moving—unless he knew he had the votes to impose cloture.

Yet the process of marshaling cloture votes became more burdensome as filibusters grew more frequent. In the Senate session that ran from 1964 to 1965, leaders had to halt filibusters by filing cloture motions just 3 times. That more than doubled to 7 in the 1965–1966 session and rose to 20 by the 1971–1972 session.[18] So Senate leaders eager to ungum the works got creative: They created a second track for legislative business. If a bill got blocked by a filibuster on the main track, leaders could move bills along on the other track. Essentially, the Senate created new rules and procedures that allowed it to multitask.

This shift set us up for the senatorial stagnation we suffer today, in several ways.

First, it moved filibusters off the floor. If Track 1 was blocked by a filibuster, the Senate diverted to whatever bill could be moved along Track 2, pushing the bill that was being filibustered out of the spotlight. The opening of this second track meant that senators no longer had to hold the floor in order to filibuster—they merely had to threaten a filibuster to move the bill off the floor for negotiation. Over time, it became customary that once a senator had registered their intent to filibuster, it was honored unless and until they dropped their objection—or until the bill's proponents could muster the supermajority necessary to impose cloture and move to a vote.

Second, this series of changes eased the downside risk of filibustering while preserving the upside potential to gain leverage. Under the single-track system, filibustering required a heavy investment of time and energy—literally standing on the floor for hours and hours—as well as a thick skin to withstand public pressure from opponents. Under the new system, a filibustering senator didn't need to show up at all! There was little public pressure to relent because the public didn't even see the filibuster. And there was less peer pressure because the filibuster wasn't blocking everyone else's business. Filibustering senators enjoyed all the leverage a filibuster could apply without paying any of the costs.

Third—and this is where the modern filibuster system becomes strangest—these new rules and norms led to the creation of an early warning system known as a "hotline." Here, leaders poll their party's senators for threats of filibusters before bringing a bill to the floor. One hotlined objection—one senator—kicks the bill onto the filibustered track. Today, Senate leaders employ their staff to reach out to every office on every bill the leader is considering bringing to the floor to ask if there are any objections. In the past, this happened through phone calls and in-person meetings. Today it happens through blast emails with "HOTLINE" in the subject line. If the senator you work for has an objection, all you need to do is reply to that email, and voilà, the bill at stake is now being filibustered. Now the majority leader has to invoke cloture and secure 60 votes to bring that bill to a vote. Or more likely, the bill is stuffed in the proverbial drawer.

This two-track system and its associated changes made sense in a Senate where only a small handful of bills would face filibusters. But over time, more and more bills—from a bill to abolish the Electoral College to an increase in the minimum wage to a bill to expand background checks on gun purchases—began facing the new silent and passive filibusters. The treatment that had once been reserved for civil rights bills began to extend to all bills. Instead of most Senate business proceeding along the majority-rule track, more and more Senate business required supermajority support to even reach a vote.

Just how pervasive is this impediment? Since there is no direct method of tracking filibusters, they are most commonly measured by the number of times a leader has to file cloture to cut one off, just as an airbag deploying is a reasonably accurate indication that a collision occurred. In the 1990s, these numbers began to rise sharply. After averaging around 20 a year in the 1970s, the number of cloture motions rose to 48 in the 1991–1992 session and to 61 by the close of the

2001–2002 session. Even then, many bills and nominations still passed with a simple majority, without having to clear cloture.

But there would still be one more leap in the filibuster's evolution, one that stretched its power even beyond John C. Calhoun's imagination. This change came in the early 2000s, when minority leaders realized they could use the filibuster threat not only to stop certain objectionable bills but to manufacture gridlock. Just wait.

Supermajority Rules

The real explosion in the use of the filibuster, though, came after Democrats won the Senate majority in the 2006 midterms. In the previous session, from 2005 to 2006, the majority leader (Republican Bill Frist) filed cloture to cut off filibusters 68 times. In the next session, from 2007 to 2008, when Democrats took over the majority, the majority leader (then-Democrat Harry Reid) filed cloture 139 times, setting a new high-water mark by a wide margin. The numbers increased year over year, and even routine business began to be the target of filibusters. From 2019 to 2020, the Senate leader (Republican Mitch McConnell) filed cloture 298 times. And just consider how many times they didn't have the 60 votes to invoke cloture—or, to use our airbag analogy, think about how many accidents happen without the airbag deploying. A whole lot.

These counts are the Framers' fears coming true. Hamilton had warned that a supermajority threshold would create an irresistible temptation for the minority to block the majority—to eschew compromise and productivity and instead seek "to embarrass the administration."[19] That is exactly what happened. What's worse, this dynamic is supercharged in a polarized era dominated by what Princeton political scientist Frances Lee calls "insecure majorities."[20] At a time when neither party tends to enjoy more than a slim majority, there's even more incentive to obstruct the party in power so that your side can call it a failure and win back the majority in the next election.

The senators who led the way toward today's supermajority Senate didn't even try to hide their intent to exploit the minority veto for political gain. At a closed-door retreat among Senate Republicans around the time of President Obama's inauguration, Senate Minority Leader Mitch McConnell explained to his colleagues that his strategy was to oppose every major initiative Obama proposed, regardless of the merits, in order to manufacture gridlock. Sen. George Voinovich of Ohio, who attended the retreat, described McConnell's message thus: "If he [Obama] was for it, we had to be against it."[21] Obama's failures—produced by Republicans—would be their gains.

Later that year, the Obama administration worked with lawmakers to develop the Affordable Care Act. Though "Obamacare" bore a Democrat's name, it did not swing hard left. The bill skirted the left-wing push for a single-payer system and instead was modeled after Massachusetts's "Romneycare," itself based on a proposal by the conservative Heritage Foundation. Yet McConnell worked to prevent any Republicans from working with Obama. Senators like Olympia Snowe, Susan Collins, and Chuck Grassley had made health care a centerpiece of their careers and appeared inclined to collaborate with Democrats on the Affordable Care Act. Yet to deny Obama the political benefits of bipartisanship, McConnell made sure they did not. "It was absolutely critical that everybody be together because if the proponents of the bill were able to say it was bipartisan, it tended to convey to the public that this is O.K.," he told *The New York Times* in 2010.[22] There could be no exceptions. "Just one Republican choosing to support it," McConnell explained in his memoir, "threatened to bring others along, and allowed the other side to then label the measure bipartisan."[23] Bipartisanship wasn't the goal; it was the prize to deny to the other side.

McConnell's strategy reset the conventional wisdom by demonstrating that obstruction would be rewarded and compromise should be avoided. In the early days of the Obama administration, many political analysts believed that voters would punish senators who refused to work with the popular new president. Instead, Republicans reaped historic gains in the 2010 midterms. McConnell's strategic insight—that voters would blame the party in power for gridlock and not penalize the minority for obstruction—crystallized a new set of perverse incentives. New senators like Ted Cruz demonstrated that obstruction could do more than simply defy the majority—it could be a springboard to national prominence and fundraising hauls previously unimaginable for a freshman senator. By leading a rearguard action among a group of rogue senators to shut down the government in 2013, Cruz vaulted himself from a backbencher to a leading national figure, finishing second in the 2016 Republican presidential primary.

Rather than encourage compromise, the new filibuster strategy endowed obstruction with purpose and tangible electoral benefits. In a majority-rule institution, the incentive to obstruct is lower. Had the majority-rule norm prevailed in 2009, senators in the minority still could have banded together and sat on the sidelines of the health-care debate, but to what end? Senators naturally want to work with their colleagues, especially on big-ticket legislative packages on policy areas they care about. But because the need for a supermajority created an opportunity for gridlock, the incentives to obstruct overcame senators' impulses to cooperate. Without the fulcrum of the supermajority, McConnell's case for Republicans to band together would have been far weaker. As it was, he contended that creating gridlock would advance Senate Republicans' political fortunes, which it did, and it put Democrats in a position where losing a single vote could tank the whole health-care effort. It nearly worked.

For their part, Democrats did not shy away from using the filibuster. When Democrats lost the Senate majority in 2014, the number of filibusters initially fell from 252 in 2013–2014 to 128 in 2015–2016, but after President Trump was elected, the number shot up to 201 and increased from there.[24] The filibuster is like the proverbial Chekhov's gun: If it's there, it will be used. Just as the Framers feared, the temptation for the minority to obstruct will inevitably overcome the pull to govern responsibly in the public interest. Among the many other reasons outlined in this chapter, the voters will demand it: In our polarized age, as long as the option to obstruct the other side exists, voters want their side to use it. The filibuster is a user-friendly weapon of mass obstruction readily available to any senator who spies an advantage in using it. In almost every case, at least one senator will, be they Democrat or Republican.

The Filibuster Stress Test

Before we declare the "filibuster leads to compromise" myth completely dead, it's worth putting these ideas through a stress test. In other words, if the supermajority requirement supercharges gridlock, it's still worth asking if it has any positive effects. Does the filibuster foster compromise at all? The answer appears to be sometimes, but only a little, and not enough to outweigh the downsides.

It's a tricky question to address because there is an inherent chicken-and-egg problem: When 60 votes are required and both parties control fewer than 60 votes, bills must be bipartisan to pass. So you could argue that the 60-vote requirement promotes compromise because it quite literally requires it. The problem, of course, is the cost—the critical legislation blocked and the gridlock manufactured because the minority party can effectively stop anything from getting a vote.

This leads to the reverse question: If the filibuster disappeared and laws could clear the Senate with a simple majority, would compromise still happen? The evidence suggests that the answer is yes. There are three reasons why. First, history. During the 200 years before the hotline filibuster reared its head, compromise abounded. Second, lawmakers favor compromise even when they aren't required to find it. Any majority is going to include centrists who have much in common with the moderates of the other party. These lawmakers tend to build bipartisan bridges both by inclination and because (without a filibuster) it benefits them politically. Third, in a Senate free from the filibuster, there would be more opportunities for compromise because more bills would be moving and more senators would be empowered to seek out bipartisan partners and build new coalitions. Put simply, if senators see that their work could actually result in passed laws rather than guaranteed gridlock, there would be far more motivation to do the work. The geriatric Senate of today would have new life.

Filibuster fans argue that, in highly polarized eras (hello, 2025), a majority-rule Senate would lean more extreme than it did in the more balanced past. Imagine a ping-pong match of hard-right and hard-left bills, passed every time the Senate majority switches and then repealed again a couple of years later. That claim is also worth testing, and the first term of the Biden administration offers a real-life opportunity.

Intentionally or not, the Biden administration reestablished the two-track process that existed in the first half of the 20th century. Biden did so by making aggressive use of something called the budget reconciliation process, which is a legislative track created in the 1970s to exempt budget-related matters from the supermajority requirement and decide them on a simple majority. This track is guarded by strict rules: Only policies that are primarily budgetary in nature, as judged by the Senate Parliamentarian, are allowed to pass along it. But the Biden administration designed the lion's share of its domestic policy to pass along this track so that it could avoid the filibuster—first the Covid-response American Recovery and Reinvestment Act (ARRA) and later the Build Back Better plan, which became the Inflation

Reduction Act (IRA). Meanwhile, other policies were left to face the supermajority threshold. This included major domestic issues such as child care, gun control, voting rights, labor policy, and of course, abortion. With Democrats holding a bare 50-vote majority, the legislation that moved along the supermajority track was, by definition, bipartisan, while the bills that moved on the majority-rule track were party line. And there's our test: If the majority-rule threshold paved the way for extremist policies, we would see the evidence of that in the early Biden years.

This is not what happened. The policies in the ARRA and IRA, both of which passed by majority rule, were generally quite moderate and enjoyed broad, bipartisan public support. Those policies include Medicare prescription drug negotiation, increasing Affordable Care Act subsidies to lower health-care premiums, cracking down on white-collar tax evasion and corporate stock buybacks, temporarily expanding the child tax credit, and spurring domestic energy production and energy security. Critics railed that high inflation followed these acts, but inflation was a global phenomenon that also hit countries like England, where conservatives ruled. In fact, inflation in the United States proved lower than in peer countries, and its recovery proved more robust.

Who accrued the benefits of these policies? Essentially, everyone. Many of the benefits of IRA investments in green manufacturing flowed to red states. Domestic energy production, typically coded as a conservative priority, has skyrocketed, with the United States now producing more oil than any country ever. The states that saw the largest year-over-year increases in health-care enrollment were mostly red.[25]

Meanwhile, it's hard to spot any outcomes from that time that reasonably count as extremist. Democrats did not use the majority-rule track to defund the police or pass a Green New Deal. That's because, frankly, relatively few of those 50 Democratic senators were extremists—with the same being true on the other side of the aisle, too. The fact that 50 Democrats represent a wide range of perspectives, paired with the need to get both the House and the president to sign off on every Senate law, protected us against majority tyranny. Just as the Framers predicted.

FREEDOM FROM (MINORITY) TYRANNY

The impact of the mutated filibuster is enormous. It dominates and gridlocks our legislative process. A misguided attempt to require compromise, any potential for positive impact is overwhelmed by its unintended consequence of offering the minority an irresistible opportunity to obstruct. But the Senate's transformation into a supermajority institution does not just affect the Senate. It changes the rules for our entire system of governance. If 40 senators can veto any bill before it ever reaches a vote, then they can effectively veto anything that the House or the president (elected by a majority of voters nationwide) might propose, too.

So here is where you, the reader, come in. Never forget that, with enough agreement, senators can change their rules at any time. In fact, only senators can. When you hear a presidential candidate promising to get rid of or reform the filibuster, understand that they have as much power over the Senate rules as your eighth-grade substitute PE teacher had over the class. But if enough senators decide to do things differently, they can.

And if enough people demand a new approach, they will.

This is the power of myth-spotting. You, as a citizen, have the power to call out the truth whenever you see a politician promoting the filibuster myth and arguing that it promotes compromise instead of gridlock. In the era of social media, that power is amplified. Conventional wisdom exerts a powerful pull on decision-makers, including politicians. If the conventional wisdom holds that the filibuster protects democracy, politicians will defend it. If the conventional wisdom shifts, and it becomes widely accepted that the current iteration of the filibuster promotes gridlock, the path to change will be blazed. By simply calling out the myth when you see it, you can help make that shift happen.

Beyond just calling out the myth, though, remember the power of your vote. *Who* we elect has a direct impact on *how* they act when in office. Search the records of your incumbents: Have they supported *any* bills introduced by the opposition, or are they against everything? If the latter, that's a pretty good indicator that finding common ground isn't their priority. Rewarding obstructionists with reelection is the exact opposite message we want to send when we have the very real problems we do.

If we agree the current application of the filibuster is untenable, the question then becomes, what should reform look like? Rather than delve into the weeds of procedural nerdom, I think it's more useful to establish a set of guiding principles to shape any filibuster reform.

The first and most important principle is that reform should return the Senate to Madison's vision of a free-flowing institution that promotes compromise across party lines. That simply cannot happen when the bar is set at a supermajority, since, as we have seen, the incentives compelling the minority to obstruct are just too strong. The Framers recognized this truth in their time, and we should recognize it in ours. In practical terms, that means any reform must restore the majority rule that prevailed in the Senate for more than 200 years.

Any efforts at reform should also put the burden back on the senator doing the filibustering. In short, restore the talking filibuster and do away with the silent filibuster. The Senate should always be a platform for senators in the minority to be heard—but only if they actually show up and talk. Social media plays an important role here. Long gone are the days when the audience for a senator's floor speech was limited to C-SPAN viewers. If a senator is outnumbered on a given vote, they can still get their idea into circulation with a compelling speech. They might lose the vote—such is the nature of the legislative process. But over time, their idea could win the day. That takes energy, and it should. The current version of the filibuster, however, requires no energy to stall broadly supported legislation. That's exactly backward.

Lastly, a little inside baseball to restore dynamism to the Senate floor: We should return to a system where any senator can call a vote on any proposal. In the past, any senator—majority, minority, junior, senior—used to be able to go to the Senate floor and call up any bill for a vote. Today, largely due to the filibuster, the process for scheduling a vote takes nearly a week and in practice is only done by Senate leaders. This stifles lawmaking and forces senators to run all their ideas through Senate leaders. It's as if you had to ask the CEO every time you wanted to add an item to your team's weekly meeting agenda. Innovation and creativity essentially freeze. This shift would inject a healthy degree of unpredictability into the Senate and allow senators who have spent time formulating new laws to call them up for a vote. Plus, it would give them some skin in the game: To assemble a majority, senators need to put in the work of developing serious policy and assembling a broad coalition of supporters. If a senator calls up a bill and it fails overwhelmingly, they look unserious. But if they call up a bill and it passes because they have put in the work, they not only get their bill passed, but they also receive due credit as a serious legislator responding effectively to their constituents' needs. As a bonus, senators who know they will soon need support from the opposition on one of their bills will be far less likely to throw partisan flames across the aisle. Bridges would be built, not burned.

No one thrives when they're micromanaged—and neither does the product they create. So as a broad rule, reform should aim to do less, not more. Much of the crippling underbrush of Senate rules has sprouted up as attempts to fix specific problems only to result in unintended consequences. Reform should clear away this underbrush by keeping it simple: A majority-rule body, with power decentralized to individual senators, restores the Senate floor to its dynamic glory.

Ironically, the Senate's highest role, as envisioned by the Framers, is to promote compromise. Taken together, these kinds of reforms will bring that purpose back. To solve what ails our nation, we need a Senate where senators are free to roam across party lines, explore new coalitions, and test out their ideas by bringing their bills up for votes. These conditions foster compromise and, ultimately, progress. And we ourselves can drive this change by spotting and calling out myths, voting for leaders bold enough to compromise, and showing obstructionists the exit.

This is the Senate we need—the Senate that America deserves.

"The Media Wants to Polarize Us"

Matt Fuller

I've spent 15 years covering Capitol Hill, and in that time, I've seen a lot of interesting things: Thousands of bills passed, about a dozen State of the Unions, and even a Capitol riot from the House chamber. But these days, the most interesting part of my month is often the 15 minutes of questions I get from people who know next to nothing about what it means to be a congressional reporter.

You see, I frequently lecture at a program for government workers receiving a crash course in Congress, and at the end of the talk, there's a Q&A.

The bulk of my lecture—on the relationship between Congress and the media—is predictable enough. I guide them through the basics of being a congressional reporter: how we formulate our stories, how we refine our questions by talking to dozens of lawmakers, and the best places in the Capitol to catch a Republican for a quote. At this point, I've basically memorized it.

But the Q&A is always different. And a recent question from Trey—a well-intentioned man from Mississippi—is one I won't soon forget.

"When do they put the bias in?" Trey asked, earnestly wondering about the order of operations in the bias process. "Is that something the reporter does? Is that the editor? How does that all work?"

I admit, I took some offense to the implication that our work's purpose is to dupe people. And as a result, I was a little harsher on Trey than I should have been. But I paid him the respect of telling him the truth.

"In my experience," I said, "no one is sitting around thinking about how we influence people—one way or another. No one is intentionally putting in a dash of bias. No one is cooking up the fake news."

I told him what I know to be true: that the politicians convincing him that we're biased think of him as a "bumpkin." And I used that word because I can recall a specific conversation with a specific member of Congress—an influential Republican—where he used that exact word to describe "the base" and their belief that journalists are "fake news." It was his word for Trey, not mine.

But who should we blame for the belief that the media is so self-evidently biased that we're sitting around ginning up fake news to influence people? Those promoting that myth have plenty of evidence on their side. Just turn on the TV or scroll through your newsfeed. You're bombarded with headlines designed to trigger a reaction: "Biden's America: Crime Soars, Cities Burn," or "Trump's Latest Lies: A Threat to Democracy." Every day, it seems like the media is feeding us a heaping pile of outrage, fear, and division. The stories often spotlight dysfunction, corruption, and the horse race of elections. It's near-constant conflict and chaos, and it's easy to feel like the media is less about informing and more about provoking.

When every headline sounds like a smoke alarm going off, it's no wonder people start questioning why we're stoking the fire.

But the notion that the media wants to polarize us is, in fact, not just one myth—it's two. It's a double punch to the public's understanding of reality.

One myth is the phrase "the media" itself. It sounds whole and cohesive that way, a single unit like "the mall" or "the universe." But what people call "the media" actually exists on a spectrum as broad as the menu options at The Cheesecake Factory, encompassing everything from Alex Jones's Infowars to overlit cable TV commentators to a college student with a Substack playing pundit. It also includes TV "news" shows and online "news" pages that serve up news and opinion in a proverbial mixing bowl, mingled together and dressed almost the same.

Somewhere in the middle of all that mess sit the actual journalists—people like me working for serious news organizations with strict standards of accuracy, professionals who literally spend our days confirming that our information is correct and who would get fired if we screwed it up.

To be clear, when I reference "the media" in the remainder of this chapter, I am talking about journalists. Not bloggers or bloviators or political operators peddling propaganda in the guise of news. And I will explain what the difference is.

The second myth is the word "wants."

As I told Trey, the reality for most journalists is that we want to write tough, compelling stories that inform the public of things that would otherwise be kept in the shadows. The Capitol Hill press corps is full of well-intentioned, underpaid nerds who believe in journalism and are fascinated by Congress. Most of us stick around far longer than we should, making far less than we could, because we believe in truth and accountability. We like what we do. We're excited to tell you about the unexpected and the unacceptable, the messy dramas and the major fuck-ups.

We want to write about the stuff that's, in a word, bad. And I want to convince you why that's, in another word, good.

Because you, as consumers and citizens, need to know about these things, and our democracy needs you to know about them. Because you have the power to demand change if you want it. (For a long time, journalists were called and thought of as "watchdogs" because our role was to pay closer attention than most readers or viewers could to the stewards of public money and power.)

In order to understand the press and your role in it though, we have to get past the pervasive assumption that the media wants to drive Americans apart, that we work up stories for the sole purpose of polarizing the nation. It's just not part of the calculus. At least not in my experience.

Without a doubt, the press certainly plays a role in our polarization (and the pseudojournalistic outlets and mediums we conflate with news sources play an even bigger one). But the hard truth is that "We, the People"—by what we consume and how we consume it—drive the media to drive us apart. Blaming the media for these problems is like blaming the bartender for your hangover. It's a subtle but critical difference.

I'm here to give you the straight talk that I gave Trey, to show you how we journalists actually work and why blaming the media conveniently removes your agency and power in shaping the information landscape. It absolves all of us of responsibility for the choices we make as consumers, for the echo chambers we construct around ourselves, and for the demand we create for the kind of content that deepens the divide.

I'm going to try to bring you behind the scenes of a newsroom, give you a peek inside the Slack conversations and conference rooms where so many people assume we're twirling our mustaches and ginning up the news. The truth is far more benign but maybe more interesting.

As someone who has sat in on the meetings about how to increase web traffic, I can promise you this: You hold the ultimate power. And to wield it effectively, you need to understand the media from the other side of the screen.

Inside the Bureau

There may be no wider gap between how cool and influential people assume a newsroom is and the reality of the situation. I say that as someone who still thinks this is the best job in the world—even if it's a bunch of political reporters in ill-fitting clothes that desperately need to be dry-cleaned.

The movie version of a newsroom is a buzzing hub of fast-talking reporters, phones affixed to their ears, notepads at the ready, a pen hanging from their mouths. Maybe someone is punching out copy on a typewriter. Maybe there's a giant press churning out newspapers somewhere in the back.

But today's newsrooms look more like *Office Space* than *All the President's Men*. In fact, a lot of reporters work from home in their sweatpants. (I've always believed a newsroom is the people inside of it, not some overpriced real estate.)

At the Capitol, reporters are jammed into a few spaces—many windowless—with fluorescent lights that would make you sick and office chairs that'd make your back hurt. I've almost always worked out of the House Daily Press Gallery, just off the House Gallery, which is one of the nicer areas. But even there, it's basically a drab office space with cheap furniture and the usual office smells. (Think burnt coffee.)

It's in these cramped spaces where reporters barely have enough room to spread their elbows that folks like Trey assume we are whipping up the fake news.

But before I start shooting down these accusations of a biased media, let's get this out of the way: The media is biased—at least in certain ways. It's just that it's hardly in the ways that people assume. As reporters, we bring our own individual biases to the job. We are humans who see the world through our own human eyes. We're schooled to be disinterested, but our own individual human tendencies still influence which issues we think are important, what context we include, who we interview, what we ask, and what quotes we use. It's important to acknowledge how this kind of implicit bias affects reporting. "Editors at serious places understand that their reporters bring these biases to the work," says former *Washington Post* and *Wall Street Journal* editor Marcus Brauchli. "It's their job to strip that bias out and give people the most accurate version of events they can."

In real journalism, however, "bias" so rarely means trying to influence voters toward a certain electoral outcome.

There are, of course, outlets that do that. Some are not focused on journalism at all but pretend to be. Others are journalism-ish but are heavily slanted, abandoning their impartiality on purpose and blurring the lines between reporting and opinion. (I won't name names only because I'm afraid of a lawsuit, but you can probably guess who I'm talking about.)

Then there are the traditional journalism outfits, which belong in a separate category. Some of these, to be fair, have their own political predilection, which shows up in their story selection, headlines, and opinion pieces. The *Washington Examiner* is a conservative outlet; MSNBC has a liberal slant. *The New Yorker* leans a little left; the *New York Post* sways to the right. That doesn't mean these outlets are equally distant from the middle or have the same standards. But even for outlets with a slant, the requirements for accurate journalism are rigorous and absolute.

Real journalists have real standards. When I hear about a possible congressional mistake or misdeed, I investigate. I pore over documents and call up people who might know something. I don't just talk to one person and run with it; I seek out people who will contradict my story. When the information I find implicates a particular person or organization, I give them as much chance as possible to respond. I use on-the-record sources whenever possible and only resort to background sources when truly required. If a member of Congress tells me their latest bill is going to cure cancer, I will call experts and confirm the truth before I print a word of it. Only after we've applied these rigorous and meticulous standards to a tough story will you see it in print.

This is not just how it works in my newsroom—this is the definition of "journalism." The job is essentially one big process of fact-checking: gathering, assessing, and presenting factual information. The job description is the same at every serious news outlet practicing actual journalism, from CNN to Reuters to NPR to *The Wall Street Journal* to *The New York Times.*

That doesn't mean we always get it right. Sometimes an interviewer doesn't push back hard enough against a blatant falsehood. Maybe they missed the chance to ask the tough question or they let a politician dodge the point. Or, in an effort to preempt accusations of bias, a journalist will fall into the trap of "both sides," presenting the perspectives of Republicans and Democrats as equally valid, even when one side may be distorting facts or evading the truth. These are all valid concerns. And trust me, I've got my own list of gripes every time I watch the news or read a story. Just ask the reporters I edit.

But the full force of the journalism profession—all its standards and practices for training, hiring, firing, editing, and doing the grunt work of putting out a written product every day—drives toward accuracy. When I'm hiring a reporter, I don't ask about their political allegiance. In fact, if they mention it, that'd be a huge, potentially disqualifying, red flag. I do ensure, however, that, whatever their political preferences, it comes way below their allegiance to journalism, to getting the story right in the most responsible and ethical way.

Our standards for accuracy take us down to the level of each and every word. When I was at Congressional Quarterly (CQ), we were instructed to never put the word "only" in front of a statistic—for example, *only 1 percent of the population practices witchcraft.* The point was that to say "only" revealed a certain bias that the number should perhaps be more. (I have no idea how many people practice witchcraft, and I have no strongly held beliefs on whether the number should be higher or lower.)

Many of these aren't just journalistic standards; they're legal standards, too. Our profession has been under attack by a number of states (read: Florida) that have tried to make it easier to sue reporters and newspapers. When you read a story that makes claims that could damage someone's reputation, it's usually been reviewed by a lawyer and interrogated by multiple editors. When there's a key anonymous source, that source has often agreed to go on the record if we're sued. Legal libel standards ensure that we could be sued, and financially devastated, if we don't live up to the high standards of journalism that we, as a profession, have set for ourselves.

Legitimate news organizations also keep news and opinion stories completely separate. The two operations maintain entirely different staffs of writers and editors. In a proper outlet, any opinion piece should appear under the blaring header OPINION.

I am decidedly not including here news outlets and social media personalities that do, well, basically, the opposite of all that. Anonymous posts—especially those from accounts with random numbers in their handles—shouldn't be trusted even if they report what you firmly believe is true. Reports that don't clearly cite sources or provide dates or full quotes should set off alarm bells. And perhaps the most misleading are political opinions, particularly in prime-time cable news slots, that pretend to be investigative news. This is true of—and maybe especially for—the most viewed cable news channel in the United States: Fox News. The network admitted as much in court when it argued that "no reasonable viewer" would take Tucker Carlson, the network's main star during the 2020 election, seriously.[1] It's entertainment, they admitted, not news. (Maybe they should change the name?)

I don't necessarily have a problem with advocacy journalism, as long as it doesn't masquerade as the same journalism that I and most other reporters are doing. But unfortunately for all of us, including the consumer, truly biased "news" doesn't typically come with a warning label.

Through all the safeguards and best practices built into the journalism profession, however, and on top of all the belief in accountability that runs deep in journalists' veins, there is a universal bias across news organizations that greatly impacts the news you see on a daily basis, and you should know about it. It's the need to make money.

THE BUSINESS OF THE NEWS BUSINESS

If I tell someone my profession while I'm at, say, a golf course—and I'll be honest, it's usually at a golf course—I'm bound to get some pointed questions. Why is the news always so negative? Why are you guys so obsessed with drama? How come you never write anything nice about Trump?

Here is my answer.

I regret to inform you that the news business has always been just that—a business. Like most businesses, it has to make money. And as long as there are financial incentives, news organizations will naturally gravitate toward content that provides value to readers. Whether it's CQ delivering granular coverage of Capitol Hill or Bloomberg covering corporate takeovers with the expertise that moves markets. We have to deliver content people want to survive. This isn't some sinister plot; it's simply how the industry functions, and arguably, to a certain extent, that's how it should function. After all, if no one's reading it, what's the point of writing it?

The battle for attention—whether it's ratings, shares, or clicks—drives revenue. And without that revenue, news organizations simply can't exist. This has always been the case, but the stakes are higher now than ever before. We're living in an era of unprecedented fragmentation and competition in the media landscape while simultaneously living in an era of misinformation and distrust—when seeing something with your own eyes may not make it true. Once, newspapers and a few TV stations were the primary sources of news, consumed in the morning paper or on the evening broadcast, and were accepted as truth by the vast majority of the population.

Now we're competing not just with other news outlets but with social media platforms, blogs, YouTube channels, podcasts, and even TikTok videos. Anyone with a cell phone and Wi-Fi can call themselves a "content creator," regardless of journalistic standards. Adding to the challenge, content aggregation sites and AI tools are sucking up the media's work without payment or credit, further eroding the revenue streams that traditional news organizations rely on. These forces are not just competitors; they're siphoning off the very resources needed to keep journalism alive and are accountable to basically no one as they do it.

And perhaps trickiest of all, we're competing with the idea of truth itself.

Add to this the rise of the 24/7 cable news market, where the demand for constant content has only intensified the focus on sensationalism. News is now accessible at any time, from anywhere, and the competition for attention has never been fiercer.

In the midst of this information tornado, it seems that every week another news organization announces another round of layoffs, a stark reminder of the financial decline and desperation gripping the press as advertising dollars (the historic foundation of news operations) have moved elsewhere. Over my 15 years in journalism, newspapers have lost over \$35 billion in ad revenue and nearly half (47 percent) of their newsroom staff.[2] More than 2,900 newspapers have shuttered or merged in the last 20 years, leaving millions of Americans without any local paper at all.[3] In 2023 alone, more than 100 newsrooms closed their doors entirely, putting thousands more journalists out of work. Financial survival is existential for the press—without views, we have no revenue. And without revenue or a benevolent billionaire, we close.

So yes, the news industry does have a hunger for drama. And when people ask me why, one part of the answer is pretty straightforward: Look in the mirror. The modern news industry, like most others, operates in a free market. Supply and demand. To exist, we must supply what consumers demand.

The other part of the answer runs deeper. The idea that we're sitting around our newsroom cubicles cackling, plotting how to stir the societal pot just doesn't track with reality. In fact, we cover what's urgent and troubling because, very often, it matters. We have a bias toward what's new because it's our task to tell you about that (it's literally why it's called "news"). We cover conflict and tension because that's where the story is. Hope, failure, harm, victory, strife, stupidity—these are the elements that make a story worth telling and, more importantly, worth reading.

Of course we want to cover drama! That's actually our job. And I don't apologize for it. We're not in this business to bore people. I want to write smart, truthful, and interesting stories. And in my experience, readers want to read smart, truthful, and interesting stories. It drives me nuts when I see a reporter who's more interested in writing for themselves than for their audience. As one of my bosses has said, "If you're just writing for yourself, you're not doing journalism—you're writing a journal."

Toward the overarching mission of truth and accountability, I may write a story about someone who's unexpectedly effective or surprisingly doing something good or shockingly nice. But usually, I'm not here to tout how a certain lawmaker is doing such a great job. That's public relations, not journalism. Every Capitol Hill office has multiple people assigned to the former task.

So yes, I'm going to cover the drama and the unexpected. I'm going to lean into chaos and conflict because that's compelling and often relevant. It's actually what you want to read, and more to the point, it's actually what you want us to write.

THE MODERN MEDIA INCENTIVE STRUCTURE

We have a little saying in journalism: "We don't cover the planes that land safely."

Once you get over the darkness of it—journalists tend to be a little morbid—you can start to understand the real meaning behind it. The truth is, the stories that captivate people aren't the ones where everything goes according to plan. They're the ones where the train goes off the rails or teeters on the tracks. And as much as we might like to pretend otherwise, drama is what draws people in.

The explosion of content options has turned the modern media environment into an all-you-can-eat buffet—you can find whatever type, format, version, and source of information you're craving. If you want just the facts, man, go ahead and pile your plate with straight-up news. No one's stopping you. But let's be real—most people claim they want to be about that healthy, no-nonsense news diet, and yet the numbers show they're reaching for the deep-fried drama and sugary sensationalism instead.

I've had the chance to see this firsthand in a range of newsrooms, from the most straight-laced, fact-focused environments like CQ and, currently, NOTUS (a nonpartisan, nonprofit start-up), to outlets that dabble more in the tabloid side of things, like *HuffPost* and the Daily Beast. What I can tell you from working in both types of settings is this: People want drama. They crave it. When Marjorie Taylor Greene calls Lauren Boebert a "little bitch" on the House floor, that's the story that gets clicks. It's juicy; it's immediate; it's got all the elements of a good old-fashioned political brawl. Readers are far less interested—and I've got the numbers to prove it—in my 6,000-word story on why Republicans turned on funding a war in Ukraine. (It's a great piece and you should read it!)

The biggest problem with the myth that the media is solely to blame for our polarization is that it allows us to conveniently ignore the uncomfortable truth: We got what we asked for. We are not just passive recipients of biased news. It didn't just pop up on our phones, in our inboxes, or on our screens at random. We asked for it. We are active participants in a feedback loop that thrives on our own preferences, clicks, and engagement. The media may amplify the polarization, but we're the ones who turn up the dial—and then get incensed when the noise becomes deafening.

This is the heart of my argument, so let me spell it out clearly. The media environment we have today is, in large part, our own creation. It reflects our choices, our habits, our desires. People naturally prefer to consume the news that confirms our biases and satisfies our cravings for drama, conflict, and validation. The biased media we claim to despise—though, let's be honest, most of us only hate the bias that opposes our own views—is the logical, capitalistic by-product of these collective demands.

To put this in perspective, in a typical week, eat-your-Wheaties C-SPAN might average around 300,000 viewers during its prime-time news coverage. Meanwhile, a prime-time show on Fox News or CNN can draw millions. Over the last year, *The Rachel Maddow Show* on MSNBC averaged around 1.6 million viewers each night while Fox News's *The Five* averaged about 3 million.[4] And at the same time, *PBS NewsHour* struggles to hit 1 million on a good day.[5]

So what kind of content gets eyeballs? Researchers recently analyzed 51 million tweets centered around current events and discovered the stories that get the most clicks and user engagement have three things: negativity, blame, and threats.[6] Apparently, that's the magic recipe. Headlines like "Government Corruption Exposed: Who's Really to Blame?" or "Your Health at Risk: The Shocking Truth Big Pharma Doesn't Want You to Know" don't just capture attention—they ignite it. These elements tap directly into our deepest fears and frustrations, and they're designed to make it difficult to resist clicking, sharing, and discussing.

Other studies find that negativity is the single most important element in driving clicks and shares. Negative content doesn't just sell better; it holds our attention longer, and we're more likely to share it with others.[7] This is because our brains are naturally wired to focus on threats and potential dangers, which makes negative stories more memorable.[8] In fact, when researchers looked at 105,000 news stories, they found that each additional negative word increased the click-through rate by 2.3 percent.[9]

During my time at *HuffPost*, we made a brief effort to buck the trend by instituting "Good News Sunday." The idea was that too much of our coverage was too negative and that we could potentially combat the creep of negativity by focusing on positive stories—at least for one day of the week.

The gimmick didn't last long. For one, it's really not how news works. We don't get to decide the tone of the news of the day; it's our job to write the story as soon as it happens. But for another, the good-news content bombed. People didn't want to click on these positive stories, even one day a week as a palate cleanser. Before the idea ever really got noticed, the managers discontinued it.

If in-depth policy examinations were what people genuinely wanted to consume, we'd see a lot more of them. But the reality is, it's drama that sells. The old five o'clock news axiom "If it bleeds, it leads" didn't become a mantra by accident. Consumers' drive for drama, combined with the voraciousness of the 24/7 news cycle, incentivizes sensationalism not only by the press but by politicians themselves.

For candidates and officials to break through all that noise and get noticed, they often race to be the loudest, most extreme voice in the room. Unfortunately, this has fostered a culture of "stunt politics," where the goal isn't to govern but to go viral. Whether it's shouting "You lie!" at the State of the Union, showing off a withering whiteboard sketch, or crashing a press conference that turns into a circus, politicians are increasingly chasing that one moment that will be shared, retweeted, and used to fundraise. People often complain that we, the media, are giving these politicians the attention they crave—and honestly, sometimes it's like handing a megaphone to a toddler and expecting them not to scream into it. But the thing is, it's news when a member of Congress throws a temper tantrum. There are real consequences. And people consume that content and share it. Lots of people.

Sadly for our democracy, this pattern disadvantages the elected officials who would rather write laws than rack up likes. For every politician you see grandstanding on cable news, there are at least a dozen avoiding the spotlight for the same reasons.

This fight-for-clicks media environment compels even the best outlets to prioritize traffic over substance, including outlets I've worked at. It's what leads to those dumb, list-type "stories" that might drive clicks but do absolutely nothing to inform citizens. I've seen it first-hand, and I can tell you it's not always easy to push back against the tide of sensationalism when the ownership is warning that we need more viewers for everyone to keep their jobs.

Case in point: My last day at the Daily Beast was the day I pushed back against a new owner who wanted to run a story titled, "Here Are the 5 Fattest Members of Congress." This wasn't journalism; it was dumb clickbait. I told one of our new owners that such a story would only undermine our credibility. I said there was a difference between being "sharp-elbowed" and "mean-spirited," and readers and politicians both tolerate the former but they won't abide the latter.

As it happens, I had already given my two weeks' notice by then, but after that conversation, the new owner decided that one week's notice would suffice.

But fortunately for all of us, a listicle like "The 5 Fattest Members of Congress" wouldn't even do well in the post-Facebook marketplace of news, no matter what that owner thinks. In my 15 years of journalism, I've seen a lot of pivots: pivots to video, pivots to Twitter, pivots to Facebook, pivots to Google. Usually, the trend works for a couple of years, and then someone high-up at one of these companies decides that, on second thought, we should make Facebook less political, and they nuke political news from the algorithm. Almost overnight, a major source of traffic like Facebook is gone. It can hurt in the short term, but in the long term, stories about "The 5 Fattest Members of Congress," thankfully, never go viral.

In our current, post-Facebook world—and I'll be real, this may have already changed by the time this book is printed—the thing that actually works best is real news. High-drama news, yes, but legitimately so. Readers know when you have real news, and they know when you have warmed-over bullshit. If you break real news, the readers will come. And if you don't, I hope you can write a good headline.

I do think it's worth lingering on headlines for a moment, seeing as it's the way most people actually consume the news. There are some tricks to headline writing, though they're not nearly as sinister as they sound. There's definitely a legitimate argument that overhyped headlines are contributing to our polarization in major ways. But as an editor, I've always thought getting you to read a story is part of my job. As former *Post* and *Journal* editor Brauchli says, "You've made a decision to cover a story because you think it has consequences for readers or should be of interest. You then have to write a headline that persuades them of that." There's an art to writing a headline that earns clicks without shouting.

In the simplest terms, a good headline makes you click. But more than that, it's honest, and it doesn't overpromise.

One effective and totally aboveboard trick is to leave a "curiosity gap" between the questions raised by the headline and the answers in the story, as in "The Big Reason Democrats Think Trump Will Fail." It's a little gimmicky, but people are more likely to click on that headline than, say, "Democrats Think Trump Will Fail Because of His Legal Troubles."

Another rule we used at the Daily Beast when I was there was that we don't write "not" headlines, as in "Republicans Won't Vote on National Abortion Ban." That story wouldn't do nearly as well as, say, "GOP Leaders Refuse to Give National Abortion Ban Bill a Floor Vote."

There's a difference between simple tricks like these and the headlines that people see as pumping up our polarization.

But none of this means there aren't positive stories—or, more importantly, good stories. For all the complaints that we don't have any Walter Cronkites anymore, we actually have a lot of them working at newsrooms all over the country, including at mine. It's because of dogged, enterprising reporters that we've broken stories like Clarence Thomas's proclivity for accepting improper gifts from his billionaire friends, Herschel Walker secretly paying for an abortion, and Harvey Weinstein's litany of sex crimes. All these bombshells saw the light because of some damn good reporters (working with some damn brave sources).

If we didn't consume high-drama content at the rate we do, rewarding sensationalism with our clicks, shares, and screen time, the media landscape would be forced to shift. The bottom lines of news organizations would compel them to change course, and they could put more of those fantastic reporters to work on more stories of serious consequence.

The truth is, the power to change the media starts with us—and it always has. If we want a more balanced, less sensationalized media environment, it's up to us to stop rewarding the content that perpetuates division and start demanding something better.

Part of the difficulty is, many of the people in power don't want us to.

The Strategy of Media Distrust

It shouldn't be a shock that the media (writ large) is quickly rising up the ranks of the most hated institutions in America. We've been told by our leaders, especially those on the right, to be suspicious and unforgiving. The media has been labeled "fake news," "dishonest," "scum," "the enemy of the people," and the "primary opponent" that must be defeated. (Donald Trump said all these things while he was president.) Violent attacks on the media, including multiple murders of journalists, are unsurprisingly on the rise.[10]

Despite this recent trend, using the media as a convenient punching bag is nothing new in American politics. Thomas Jefferson complained about his press coverage back when newspapers were the only medium. "Nothing can now be believed which is seen in a newspaper," he told his fellow citizens. "Truth itself becomes suspicious by being put into that polluted vehicle."[11] Fake news, 1807-style.

Throughout history, whenever the message has been uncomfortable or the truth inconvenient, the easiest thing for politicians has been to shoot the messenger. Politicians—left, right, and center—have gone after the press when they've received unwanted or unwarranted criticism. This is human nature; when we're maligned, we challenge the credibility of the messenger to undermine the credibility of the message. Watch any episode of *The Real Housewives* and you'll quickly see what I mean.

Over time, this reflex to point fingers at the media has been weaponized by those in power, who have learned that sowing distrust in the very institutions tasked with holding them accountable can be a powerful strategy.

Just the moniker "the media" is a big part of this story. That monolithic phrase groups together basement bloggers and cable news talking heads with Pulitzer Prize–winning journalists at ProPublica and mars the credibility of those doing legitimate, fact-checked, watchdog work.

And the dominance of this idea is not an accident. We have Richard Nixon to thank.

Nixon's administration actually poll-tested words and phrases— "reporters," "journalists," "the press"—to determine that it was best to attack "the media." He saw that convincing voters that "the media" was biased against Republicans was in the GOP's long-term interests.

Think I'm just being biased? Well, Nixon famously wrote a memo to his chief of staff, H. R. Haldeman, after the 1971 White House Correspondents Dinner saying it was in the administration's interest to treat the press "with considerably more contempt." Nixon wrote that "in the long run," that was a "more productive policy" than trying to cozy up to them.

And it's also worth mentioning that Nixon's vice president, Spiro Agnew, also famously delivered an address in 1969—that the three TV news networks carried live—on the bias of the TV news coverage.

I wouldn't be doing my job if I didn't note that Agnew had to resign as vice president after he pleaded no contest to a felony charge of tax evasion, that Nixon resigned after it was clear he would be impeached over his lies about the Watergate scandal, and that Haldeman served 18 months in jail for his participation in Watergate. All of them, I'm sure, would have preferred that the American public just disregard whatever the dishonest news media had to say about them at the time.

I also wouldn't be doing my job if I didn't note that the contempt for "the media" persists today as a largely partisan phenomenon. Yes, many Democrats hate the media and think we get it wrong too often. Sometimes, those criticisms are fair (go check out "New York Times Pitchbot" on X) and sometimes they're extremely unfair (again, go check out "New York Times Pitchbot" on X). But about 70 percent of Democrats trust the media, while only 14 percent of Republicans say the same.

There are, of course, some biased outlets out there. But painting them all with the same brush is a tried-and-true method to make us distrust them all. Through this conflation, we end up equating (or dismissing) a finding from *The Washington Post* with one tweeted out by @LiberalWarrior84204. They aren't the same.

By encouraging this oversimplification, politicians can more easily dismiss all media when it suits their political ends. Doing so also positions them as the sole source of trusted information and allows them to operate in a fact-free world with less immediate accountability.

In other words, the simple belief that you can disregard what the media says because "the media is biased" is a lie many politicians would like you to believe. In fact, believing it is its own form of ignorance.

I can't tell you how many times I've seen a political operative—Republican or Democrat—calling out a reporter on X (formerly Twitter) for being biased. And I can't tell you how much traction, shockingly, those attacks generate, particularly when you consider that only one person's job in that scenario is to convince you of some partisan end.

If you take away nothing else, take away this: There are a lot of people—including a lot of politicians—who greatly benefit from you not trusting the press. When people distrust the press, politicians can do whatever they want, say whatever they like, and not be burdened by a fact-check. Living in a fact-free world allows parties and politicians to frame their preferred message as the truth, reshape reality to fit their agenda, and avoid the consequences of their actions. It frees them from the accountability that a vigilant and trusted press would otherwise enforce. It creates a world of alternative facts where everyone can find the message they want to believe and no one is quite sure where the unvarnished truth actually lies.

That lecture I give in Washington—the one where Trey asked me about "the bias"—centers around a "normal Tuesday" for a congressional reporter. I give them a play-by-play of my typical workday. And I always end the same way: I tell the class why they should trust the media. The easiest explanation, I think, is my own self-interest.

If I lie, if I make something up, my career is over. I'll never work in journalism again.

If a politician lies, it's just another Tuesday.

Reclaiming the Narrative

Let's face it: We all would like a little sanity in both our news and our politics, and everyone has a role to play there. Journalists can do their part by resisting the urge to frame every story around conflict or reward the most blatantly partisan performances. But large-scale change will only come when consumers demand it. There is actually a lot you can do to help fuel the solution, all without leaving the comfort of your smartphone.

First and easiest: You are now equipped to spot many of the myths about "the media." When you hear a leader blast "the media" as biased and conniving, you know to question what's in it for them and to scrutinize exactly what kind of media they mean.

Next, you can reward the journalists out there doing serious work with your clicks, reads, views, shares—and, please, with your dollars. One of the best things you can do to support balanced journalism and coverage of your local community is to *subscribe* to the serious outlets providing it.

From there, the solutions can—and need to—grow bigger. In a media environment where *actual* fake news is multiplying faster than the Marvel movie franchise, we need to discuss what effective regulation might look like for combating disinformation.

Imagine a world where social media platforms had to publish exactly how their algorithms work, what factors they weigh to promote stories, and how they target you—yes, you—based on your data. Should Congress pass a law that requires media companies to release anonymized data on consumer habits for continued research on the effects of media framing and fake news dissemination? Should we force media conglomerates to break up their entertainment divisions from their news divisions? Or have the cable news shows include an on-screen label indicating that their shows are for entertainment and not news purposes?

I don't have answers to these questions, because these sorts of regulations can bring us down a dystopian path, too. Before you endorse a "fake news" agency, tasked with policing platforms for misinformation, ask yourself the logical follow-ups: How would that work? Who do we want calling the balls and strikes of bias? Do you want the Trump or Harris administration in charge of officially designating "fake news"?

What I do know is that your biggest influence is your own. Take it from someone who has sat in on the coverage meetings: You, the consumer, wield real power. If your demands for a certain type of media change, the supply will soon follow. We've seen this work time and time again in free markets. Bud Light faced huge declines in sales after conservatives boycotted the beer because of its relationship with a transgender influencer.[12] Fox News was forced to fire its cash-cow personality Bill O'Reilly after *The New York Times* reported on the extensive sexual harassment allegations against him (allegations finally revealed because of good journalism, by the way).[13]

But in the meantime, how do you navigate the overwhelming sea of information and misinformation? How do you discern between fake news, substandard journalism, and the real, reliable deal? Here's a set of simple tests you can run on any story you consume:

- **Consider the outlet:** Is the story coming from a reputable news organization with a history of accuracy and integrity? If you're unfamiliar with the outlet, be a little more skeptical. Do a quick search on the organization's background and ownership.

- **Examine the author:** Who wrote the article? Are they a credible journalist with a track record in the field or someone with dubious credentials?

- **Look for citations and evidence:** Does the article cite its sources? Are those sources named and credible, or are they anonymous and vague? Real journalism should provide evidence and transparency.

- **Find out who gave the quotes:** If the story includes quotes, it's crucial to consider who provided them. Is this person actually connected to the point of the story? If a piece is about how House Freedom Caucus members are upset at GOP leadership, and the quotes are from Republicans outside of the Freedom Caucus, how strong is the story?

- **Spot the intent:** Ask yourself why this story was written. Is it to inform, persuade, or provoke? Be wary of stories that seem designed primarily to incite strong emotions (especially negativity and blame) rather than inform.

- **Consider the language:** Is the language neutral, or does it seem designed to provoke an emotional reaction? Be suspicious of stories that use sensationalist or overly dramatic language.

- **Cross-check the information:** Have other reputable news outlets reported on this story? If it's a major event or claim, it's going to be covered by multiple trustworthy sources.

- **Spot the agenda:** Why was this story written? Why is this particular reporter writing the story? Was it fed to them by someone with a personal interest in it? Who might be driving the story?

- **Evaluate the story's completeness:** Is the story leaving out key details, perspectives, or context that would change its interpretation?

This might sound like a lot to ask of a person doomscrolling on the couch at 10:00 p.m. But it's actually a pretty fun game. Believe me, I play it on just about every story I read. (Besides being morbid, journalists are also characteristically cranky and, paradoxically, opinionated.) The more you play this game, the better you'll get. And pretty soon, you'll be the one calling manipulative public officials "bumpkins."

What's true of democracy is true of journalism: It won't work for us citizens just to sit back and complain about the state of the media—we have to actively participate in shaping it. Whether that means calling out (and unsubscribing from) bad practices, supporting quality journalism, or simply being more mindful about what we click on, each of us has the power to influence the future of media.

And maybe, just maybe, we can build a media landscape that genuinely reflects the values we claim to prioritize. Because until we make that effort, blaming the media for our polarized politics is just fake news.

"Keep Your Politics Out of My Sports"

Jane McManus

In fall 2023, the NFL gained a new fan.

Musician Taylor Swift had started dating Kansas City Chiefs tight end Travis Kelce and attending Chiefs games in the enclosed suites of NFL stadiums. Soon, Swift's fans were learning about the merits of the pass versus the run, and network cameras started looking to catch Swift celebrating after Kelce's catches or find them embracing on the field after a game.

There have been few sports storylines that would make for such a great rom-com. This is essentially a prom queen–quarterback matchup, but one where everyone has a six-figure endorsement deal. He was dashing and, as tight ends often are, tall. She was a beloved, platinum-level artist who could sell out a stadium mere seconds after announcing a tour.

Yet almost immediately, the Swift backlash began.

As broadly popular as the couple was, traditional NFL fans and Taylor Swift's Swifties sparked a culture clash on game day. Swift and her fans pulled ratings up and boosted the percentage of women in the audience when she was at a game. Meanwhile, some NFL fans (and almost always men) used social media to grouse about Swift's image diluting the sanctity of an NFL broadcast. An X (formerly Twitter) user called NFL Memes posted a video of Baltimore Ravens quarterback Lamar Jackson with the caption "Only one man can save us from a Taylor Swift Super Bowl."[1]

About the only thing the Swifties and NFL fans had in common: neither could understand what constituted a fair catch in the NFL's rulebook.

Why was Swift a threat to a segment of NFL fans? How could adding the world's most popular person to the country's most popular sport somehow equal anger?

The answer is complicated and requires a bit of context. There is a conviction in our culture that somehow sports are—or at least used to be, and definitely should be—separate from politics. An idea that fans go or watch games purely to see feats of athleticism and mint new heroes to replace the fading ones. A pleasant fiction that team loyalty, and perhaps the success of a well-placed sports bet, are the only rooting interests to be found in an average television audience.

It's a bit of wishful thinking, really. When members of a highly polarized citizenry are prepared to end relationships with siblings and parents over political affiliations, it's nice to think that our games are a place of political neutrality. That the colors red, white, and blue blend with greens, oranges, and yellows to form team colors that require an easier fealty.

But of course, the truth is much more interesting.

Let's return to Travis Kelce and Taylor Swift with that in mind. Football is more than just a game. It is a uniquely American undertaking, with flyovers by fighter jets and field-sized national flags for "The Star-Spangled Banner." Cheerleaders, commercial breaks, and rampant commercialism take up a big chunk of a game where between-the-whistles action may consume just 15 minutes. But the rest of the time is filled with commentary and projection. An NFL game is a pageant of baritone play-by-play announcers lauding men for their toughness and football intelligence. Those broadcasts are songs in praise of American masculinity.

As a woman who covered the game for a decade for ESPN and other outlets, I became used to the unwritten rules. You never talk about a no-hitter in progress in the dugout. You have to mention two teammates and a coach in the postgame presser. No sex the night before a big match.

A lot has changed as more women have become visible fans (the NFL can only command those massive audiences if women are watching as well), but the reaction to Swift shows that a lot hasn't.

There are established roles for women around sports: sideline reporters, cheerleaders, and WAGs, a somewhat dismissive acronym for "wives and girlfriends." There are celebrated exceptions who are referees, owners, broadcast analysts, coaches, and front office executives, but these are still relatively small in number. Swift doesn't really fit, even as a girlfriend. She is a woman worth far more than her NFL boyfriend, a far brighter star in the cultural zeitgeist. Her financial and cultural power is independent of her relationship with one of the most recognizable players on a Super Bowl–winning team. There are videos of Kelce at her concerts, singing her lyrics like a fan.

If an NFL fan tuned into a football broadcast to be comforted by traditional roles, as he could depend on for decades, Swift's prominence might strike a discordant note. As fan complaints escalated, announcers on game day struggled with how to respond when she was shown on camera. Ignore her? Can't do that. Celebrate her and risk pissing off "true fans" back home on the couch?

Either way, the intrusion of a genuinely powerful woman interrupted the well-worn tread of game day. Former All-Pro running back turned commentator Tiki Barber spoke for many when he said, "The obsession is getting annoying."[2]

And veteran broadcaster and former quarterback Boomer Esiason conspicuously avoided any mention of the pair even as the CBS cameras followed the celebration on the field after the Chiefs won the Super Bowl.

OK, boomer.

The debate about whether or not Taylor Swift should appear on camera during an NFL broadcast was—whether we recognized it or not—a political discussion. Who is the broadcast for: NFL purists or the larger audience? Are women, like Swift's fans, voting members of the fan base or allowed only observer status?

Complicating all this, Swift had campaigned for Joe Biden in 2020, which galled many fans of a sport that reinforces so many conservative cultural values. One X user with the handle @ksMaga87 posted, "Every Time the NFL shows Taylor Swift I am donating $25 to the Trump campaign."[3]

In short: Boy meets girl, boy and girl fall in love, and the term *political football* finally reaches its purest form.

The Swift-Kelce saga is one of countless examples over countless decades demonstrating that the myth of politics-free sports is false—always has been, always will be. The truth is that sports and politics are deeply interconnected and constantly in dialogue. We cannot surgically remove sports from the society in which they're played, nor magically extricate political views from athletes and fans. Like it or not, politics and sports live together on the field just as they live in the world around it.

But there's a deeper mistake in the myth, too. It's not just that politics *are* a part of sports, inevitably. It's that they *should be*.

Sports draw people together regardless of politics and identity. Games contain both conservative and progressive values, like self-determination and equity. The very act of sitting in the stands with 80,000 of your closest friends and sharing an experience is something humans have been doing for thousands of years. This literal common ground—one of the few remaining in America—is a place where we should be having these conversations.

In fact, sports have historically played a pivotal role in driving forward the political debate about critical issues, from women's rights to racial equality to international relations. By believing that politics has no place on the playing field, we close ourselves off to not only reality but also the opportunity to explore our differences in one of the most accessible spaces we still have. Sports are our sandbox for testing solutions to societal problems, together with an incredibly diverse array of fellow Americans who all have our hearts in the game. A place to play, compete, and grow, in our ideas as well as our athleticism.

So if we came to play, let's play. And may the best team—and the best ideas—win.

On the Record Books

A little stroll through American sports history turns up a surprising number of pivotal political moments. Tommie Smith and John Carlos, two Black medalists, shocked the Olympic establishment by raising black-gloved fists to signify Black Power and Black unity on the medals podium at the 1968 games in Mexico City. Their peaceful protest on the world's biggest athletic stage sparked a global conversation about both human rights and the limits of freedom of speech for athletes at home and abroad.

Similarly, understanding that only the Olympics could provide a sufficiently embarrassing international rebuke of the USSR's invasion of Afghanistan, President Jimmy Carter boycotted the 1980 Moscow Olympics to unite the world against the Soviets' unprovoked aggression. The USSR retaliated by organizing a boycott of the 1984 summer games in Los Angeles, which sparked a return of the Cold War–like escalation between the two superpowers that citizens in both countries had hoped was behind them.

More recently, WNBA star Brittney Griner's eight-month detention in a Russian prison in 2022 showed that we still are fighting these same battles decades later, with sports standouts used as pawns in a high-profile game of geopolitical chess—because sports matter that much.

The lesson here is that sports—like business, music, and entertainment—are a powerful force; whoever harnesses that power holds a microphone and connection to every level of society.

Politicians often use that force to connect with their voters. Just about the whole country swelled with patriotic pride when President George W. Bush rocketed a fastball right down the pipes at Yankee Stadium after the 9/11 terrorist attacks and as Barack Obama filled out his yearly NCAA bracket live on ESPN from the White House.

It's also a microphone that works both ways, as athletes can incubate entire movements. Think of Colin Kaepernick igniting what would become the Black Lives Matter movement or women's swimmer Riley Gaines galvanizing support to restrict transgender athlete participation in the women's category—sports heroes for people on different sides of the aisle.

In fact, it's important to acknowledge politics in sports because sports often drive politics into important cultural change before the broader society is ready. Some of our most profound societal advancements not only played out against a prosports canvas, but athletes themselves wielded the brushes. Precisely because sports are so powerful in American culture, teams, owners, and leagues have been catalysts for change and societal conversations that would have come more slowly, or not at all, without them.

In 1947, Americans watched Jackie Robinson become the first Black player in Major League Baseball. (There were some Afro-Latinos who played in the early 1900s, but then team owners buckled down on segregation, and the Negro Leagues formed in the 1920s.) Philadelphia Phillies personnel told Robinson to go back to the cotton fields during one of his first MLB games. The backlash against Robinson, and his greatness, appeared on American television sets and in the daily paper as Jim Crow was coming to an end. Baseball made integration a national issue. It was clear that Robinson's skill was more important than his color to a team, and that led to slow but measurable progress in workplaces, communities, and home lending—all segments where Black people had been actively excluded.

Robinson's story is a prominent thread in the American tapestry because his undeniable talent convinced many of the need for profound societal change. And the same is true of Billie Jean King.

Unlike Robinson, King has lived to see her legacy as a champion of equity celebrated. She beat Bobby Riggs in 1973 in a televised tennis match called "The Battle of the Sexes." It was a spectacle, with feathers and a procession, but King's win was wind in the sails of the new Women's Tennis Association as the women's liberation movement upended expectations for women in American life.

Even after the battle, the headwinds against women in sports were strong. In a society that still rejected homosexuality, people feared that girls who played sports would somehow become gay. Some college coaches used this fear in recruiting, claiming an opposing team or coach tolerated lesbians, which likely contributed to more coaching jobs going to men. King herself became a villain to many Americans when she was sued for support by a female former lover. Thus outed, she estimates she lost at least $500,000 in endorsements.

Still, King's victory over Riggs played big. Title IX had passed a year earlier, banning sex discrimination in educational programs that receive federal funding, but at first, it did not apply to sports. It was in the post-battle climate that advocates prevailed to include sports in the equity dictated by the statute. It took many more years of litigation before Title IX became what we now have: an imperfect but important requirement to provide equitable athletic opportunities in schools. Participation in women's sports bloomed, and generations of women since have subsidized their studies through athletic scholarships. There is hardly a more visible example of the union of sports and politics than that.

Countless other sports celebrities have used their prominence to shape our political history. Muhammed Ali, for example, protested the Vietnam War by refusing to be drafted. In 2010, Phoenix Suns owner Robert Sarver used his franchise to protest an immigration bill that the Arizona legislature had recently passed. For a nationally televised playoff game, Sarver had his team's jerseys changed to read "Los Suns" to signal support for the Latin community in Arizona and across the United States.

And if you studied law, there is no doubt that you'd study the way major sports unions have influenced American labor law. Even as the union movement ebbed nationally, litigation in baseball and college sports has rewritten rules around free agency and whether or not college athletes are students or employees. These fights will continue until, and even after, they are decided in the courts and by Congress, both explicitly political institutions.

This history underscores a key point that gets missed amid the chants of "keep politics out of sports." Comfortable as it might feel, opting *not* to talk about the political parts of sports (hiring of coaches of color, balancing player salaries, etc.) is actually a political choice in itself. Avoidance guarantees that the status quo will remain, even if it's untenable. Not contending with politics in sports is like not voting—you are voting by not.

Off the Bench, into the Fray

Yet the idea that sports and politics don't go together is not just a myth, it's a demand—but only for some. When Jets owner Woody Johnson became a vocal ally of Donald Trump in the 2016 election, few complained that he had crossed a line. Ten NFL owners donated significant sums to Trump early on, and no one told them to "stick to sports." Ditto for NBA Hall of Famer turned part owner of the Los Angeles Dodgers Magic Johnson, who threw his money and support behind Joe Biden's campaign.

There are different expectations for owners and players when it comes to political speech. Athletes are told to "stay in their lane" because it's assumed they hold lower political and intellectual status. Their job as athletes is to entertain, not tell us their thoughts. This hierarchy means that those who write the checks are afforded more autonomy than those who cash them. If that sounds familiar, it should.

Sports are, for the most part, a meritocracy, which means people who have been denied voice and power in other areas can earn a platform in sports and, by extension, in society—and that doesn't sit comfortably with everyone. When you hear someone say an athlete should "shut up and dribble," as Fox broadcaster Laura Ingraham famously said of NBA star LeBron James when he voiced a political opinion in 2018, it is *because* sports are such an effective platform from which to change hearts and minds.

Two years later, the women of the WNBA demonstrated that sway—and arguably gave the Democrats a functional majority in the Senate—when they turned against Atlanta Dream co-owner and appointed Georgia Sen. Kelly Loeffler as she ran to win the seat outright in a special election.

In a letter to WNBA Commissioner Cathy Englebert, Loeffler had equated player support of Black Lives Matter with calling for "removal of Jesus from churches and the disruption of the nuclear family structure." Players did not shut up and dribble.

Instead, they launched a campaign to support a little-known candidate named Raphael Warnock. The outcome? Loeffler sold her stake in the Dream and pursued that seat in the US Senate, and Senator Warnock is now serving a full term.

In truth, our games are actually a medium through which our ideas of what it means to be American are playing out. They are a negotiation for space and voice. They are a way to amplify and elicit our patriotism. Why else would the Department of Defense, according to a Senate report, have paid the NFL $6.8 million from 2012 to 2015 for promotional considerations and soldier family reunions? Sports are where we define and display our cultural values and teach our children about cooperation, teamwork, and fair competition.

Advertisers know about this direct connection between sports and values, and they use themes of community and nostalgia to soften up sports fans during commercial breaks. Fans sharing pizza, a father teaching his daughter to play baseball, a bunch of old friends heading for wings, beer, and the Big Game—they know where we live and what we value.

More broadly, when broadcasters laud players for toughness, it is a means of reinforcing our own cultural standards in approaching difficult tasks. When players break the rules, the criticism of betraying one's team is echoed by analysts and sports talk radio callers. This steady drumbeat not only reflects culture, it shapes culture. And therefore we should have and voice opinions about its impact.

After all, the sports networks themselves capitalize on these conversations. ESPN has a number of debate-based shows featuring analysts with a take on issues around sports. One of the best, and most controversial, is Stephen A. Smith, who signed a five-year, $60 million contract extension with ESPN in 2019, according to Bloomberg. His show, *First Take*, has spawned copycats in every format. And in a true crossover for our purposes, Stephen A. has been tapped to give his political takes for CNN. The latter are not quite as well-received; stick to sports, his critics argue.

The beauty of talking about politics via sports, though, is that it's approachable. The conversations are often indirect but with well-known characters. Debating whether or not Aaron Rodgers's ayahuasca use is a wellness breakthrough or a catalyst for conspiratorial thinking isn't quite as personal as debating drug policy. Having a take on whether Caitlin Clark should have stayed the extra year to play basketball at Iowa is easier than arguing with a neighbor about who you are voting for. But both of those conversations are about values: commerce and loyalty and personal liberties.

Sports are a safe place to have these conversations and stay on common ground. Different sports may attract like-minded thinkers (consider the different cultures around surfing and American football), but you don't have to be a Republican to be a Bears fan. There is no political litmus test. And in that way, Americans across ideologies can be in complete agreement about their 2–15 team being assured a better season next year.

That is, psychologically speaking, a starting point. Social scientists have long researched how people can change one another's minds. You'll never *argue* your neighbor into cutting back that hedge. There must be a foundation of agreement somewhere, and among your fellow fans, it is easy to find that. When you see the veteran in your section salute the flag on the field, maybe you stand a little straighter. When you learn how the rookie kicker grew up on the school lunch program, that might shade your opinion on public subsidies.

If we already agree—obviously—that the backup quarterback should be given a start at 0–6, that agreement can be a place to foster discussions on other issues. Or, equally as important in a polarized climate like our present one, maybe we just put down our weapons for the next four quarters.

Stadiums of Influence

When I say that politics belong in sports, I do not mean that bitter differences should disrupt our shared joy at the peak of the game. In fact, the exhilaration of that moment itself packs a kind of political power.

Games instill in fans a deep shared passion that crosses all political lines—the same way they have for literally thousands of years. If you are fortunate enough to have visited the Colosseum in Rome, you know that this isn't just a modern cultural phenomenon. As you walk in, the large arena is immediately recognizable to any sports fan. The seats may be eroded and the marble stripped, but it doesn't take much imagination to hear the roar of those ancient crowds. For two summers, I've cotaught a summer class on sports in Rome. I've seen the look of awe and recognition when students enter for the first time. They know this place; they've practically been here. The corridors and entry, the hierarchy of the seating, the sightlines—very little has changed in the shape of stadiums since Rome built them for each major outpost of its empire. There are remains of more than 230 such amphitheaters across the Roman world.

Why was it so important to have this space? First off, the Colosseum was the definition of mass communication. It was where the emperor could exercise public power by commuting a prisoner's sentence or enforcing it (cue your mental flashback of emperor Joaquin Phoenix reluctantly saving gladiator Russel Crowe's life with a meek thumbs-up at the chanting crowd). The Colosseum, built in AD 72, is located next to the Roman Forum, the center of public life. A recently uncovered ancient inscription says it was built with gold taken from the Jewish Temple in Jerusalem, and a carving in the nearby Arch of Titus depicts the sacking of the city.

Imagine how that must have resonated with the people of the ancient city. The spoils of war and conquest were being lavished on the people of Rome, the empire was converting foreign treasure into a domestic spectacle, and sport was at the very center. On purpose.

The building itself was a way of communicating. You knew your place in society by the section where you sat. The wealthy and important had the best seats, while the higher, hotter seats were farther up. Yet even thus segregated, all the citizens of Roman society were together in one space experiencing the same thing at the same time. This is the same physical and emotional connection that we experience at games and concerts today (though not when watching a high-def television from the couch).

The Colosseum was not a place for dispassionate reason. This was not the cool palazzo where citizens debated Plato's ideas. It was a place of sweat and effort, and your neighbor was so close you might have felt their spit hit the back of your neck when they yelled.

Our modern stadiums are rooted in this epic tradition, and it is entwined with politics and the exercise of power. The rulers of Rome knew the power of a stadium and of harnessing the visceral emotion that lives within those tiered walls. An arena is the cradle of catharsis.

Still today, there are few places in modern life where you can communally experience and express the heights and depths of human emotion with 80,000 people. If you've ever been ringside of a boxing match, you've felt it. The way one fighter's punch can hit every fan in the place.

In this way, sports bring us together even as politics drive us apart. There is simply no questioning whether anyone wearing your team's colors is liberal or conservative; you unite in your support. You exchange hopes and frustrations with a shared goal. You share the immediacy of that emotion, and camaraderie is the result.

Perhaps I've let my imagination run away with me, but I attended many a Knicks game in the mid-1990s, and I feel like I've lived the sports fan's experience of ancient Rome.

Mass communication, mass connection. We watch sports together because there is power in the experience that is hard to get in other parts of our lives. The personal intersects with the communal in precious ways. In a postpandemic world, it's even easier to see why that matters.

And it's precisely this shared, visceral experience that holds the key to bridging our divides. When 80,000 people rise to their feet, not in response to a political speech, but in response to a game-winning touchdown, we're reminded that there's more that connects us than separates us. The roar of the crowd is a collective expression of passion, joy, and even frustration—emotions that transcend political boundaries.

This communion in the stands, where we cheer and groan together, lays the groundwork for finding common ground beyond the arena. It's in these moments, drenched in the sweat of shared excitement, that we remember the power of sports lies not just in the game but in how it brings us together across our differences, reminding us of the common humanity we all share. And in that unity, we find the potential for political common ground, where the energy of the arena can translate into the power to create a more connected and understanding society.

The Historically Uneven Playing Field

Given our modern stories of King and Robinson, you'd think it was an arc of inclusion. But the reality is that sports has not and does not get everything right. Its history and present are littered with errors and injustice. And sports were the medium through which segregation and misogyny were enforced long before Robinson donned a Brooklyn Dodgers jersey.

When the Kentucky Derby was first run in 1875, 13 of the 15 jockeys were Black. In fact, the first 15 derbies were won by Black riders. Those men were former slaves or their children, and many grew up on the farms where those horses were reared. Once the races became popular, jockeys like Isaac Burns Murphy could command serious purses, and once that happened, Black jockeys were systematically excluded from racetracks.

There is a similar story when it comes to Black boxer Jack Johnson, who became the heavyweight champion in 1908 and whose success triggered race riots. He married a white woman in an era of strict segregation and spent a year in prison on charges of transporting a woman across state lines for "immoral purposes."

Around the same time we have the story of Jim Thorpe, the great Native American athlete who won track and field gold in the 1912 Sweden Olympics. He grew up playing for the great college football powerhouse the Carlisle Indians and played professional baseball and football as well. But Thorpe, like Johnson, was censured on trumped-up charges—stripped of his Olympic medals for playing in a summer baseball game and receiving a nominal fee.

One could argue that the amateur system itself, where playing for money is forbidden, was designed to keep players like Thorpe out. Originally a British concept to keep working-class men out of the aristocracy's games, American sports adopted amateurism at the Olympic and college levels. It was rigidly enforced for decades and, even now, revenue-generating college sports are wrestling with how to transition to a fairer model for so many players who aren't sons and daughters of landed gentry.

Segregation was also enforced in baseball and football, too. From 1933 through World War II, there weren't any Black players in the NFL. Washington Redskins owner George Preston Marshall did not hide his opposition to integration. The Washington team, now the Commanders, was the last among a recalcitrant group to add a Black player. When the legendary Jim Brown began his NFL career with the Cleveland Browns in 1957, the Washington roster was still all white.

"Jim Brown, born ineligible to play for the Redskins, integrated their end zone three times yesterday," wrote the great Shirley Povich in the *The Washington Post*.[4] Marshall wanted Povich to stick to sports so badly that he eventually pulled Povich's credentials and sued him. Marshall lost that game, too.

This legacy continues to the present day, where NFL locker rooms may be diverse places, but positions are still often aligned by race. What were called the "thinking positions" of quarterback, center, and middle linebacker have traditionally gone to white players. After a decade of calling out the lack of Black quarterbacks, there has been movement on that. However, Black head coaches are rarer than you'd think given the number who have played in the league.

The idea that professional team owners don't see color (or gender) but only see green is refuted by nearly 100 years of evidence to the contrary. This is particularly true in women's sports, where new rules were sometimes written to reinforce cultural objections to women playing professionally. The film *A League of Their Own* familiarized Americans with the history of women's baseball during WWII, but there was an even bigger soccer league in the United Kingdom during WWI. The Dick, Kerr Ladies (named for the company sponsoring the teams) could draw 50,000 fans to a match. The games became so popular that, after the end of the war, England's Football Association banned members from letting women play on their fields. Those were, not coincidentally, the venues with the stands and quality turf to accommodate games like this. The ban lasted until 1971 and was copied by football associations all over the world.

There are other political stories to be told when it comes to unions or medicine or compensation. You can chart cultural ideas about betting or smoking, or taking money from companies or nations looking to launder an ideology, through sports. Those who think the Saudi Arabia–funded LIV Tour is solely about offering golfers a better option than the dominant PGA Tour are missing its fundamental point:

Saudi Arabia knows that the billions it's investing in paying players hundreds of millions to join the tour is money well spent to distract a sports-obsessed world from its horrendous record of corruption and civil rights abuses.

The ancient Roman emperors understood the same.

There Is No Sticking to Sports

Whether we admit it or not, our politics are written in box scores. As they have for centuries, negotiations will continue about who can and should play, where they should rank, and how much they deserve to be paid. The social groups and subject matter at play change—now transgender players and name/image/likeness debates are the focus—but the vitality of the discussions remains the same. Beyond civil rights, we also see the cultural shift to individual rights appear in sporting arenas, as marijuana testing in the United States has waned and sports betting partnerships are a revenue stream for teams and leagues. The NFL's Raiders even moved to Vegas. This wasn't a coincidence.

Whatever the era, the most foundational political issues of today (and even tomorrow) arise, and are sometimes decided, through sports.

There is no sticking to sports, not really.

This is why we can and should embrace the presence of our deepest debates in sports and even participate in them ourselves. Perhaps not in that exuberant moment when our star point guard sinks a three-pointer or our Olympic gymnast clinches gold (which brought out not a liberal or conservative pride in us, but a distinctly American pride). But in the aftermath, when our hearts are full of fandom and our connection to one another is apparent, absolutely.

So what kinds of myth-pumping should you be ready to spot now? Start with the idea that sports are just a game, free from the political debates that shape our world. When you hear calls to "keep politics out of sports," recognize that this is often an attempt to silence voices that challenge the status quo. Remember that the demand for athletes to "stick to sports" is itself a political statement, one that usually reinforces existing power structures.

Also, watch for the myth that certain issues don't belong in the arena—whether it's debates about race, gender, or identity. The truth is, these issues have always been part of sports, and if they were kept out of the conversation, that was a political statement, too. The next time you hear someone argue that a particular topic shouldn't be mixed with athletics, ask yourself, Who benefits from keeping this conversation out of the public eye?

Finally, consider how you can react better to these myths. Instead of retreating to the comfort of believing that sports are just an escape, engage with the discussions they provoke. Use the shared experience of fandom as a platform for deeper conversations about the values we hold as a society and a world. The next time your team takes the field, see it not just as a competition but as a reflection of the larger social and political currents that affect us all, across borders and cultures. And at the very least, use the connection—unspoken and spoken—you feel with your fellow fans as a model for how we should relate to one another concerning the strength of our one shared team: our larger polity.

The fact is that as much as critics claim they want to keep politics out of sports, that is in part what drives their popularity. Ratings for the Swift Super Bowl, which the Chiefs won for the second straight year in 2024, were up 7.4 percent over the prior year. Over 123 million people tuned in, an outrageously high number in the era of media fragmentation. Call it the Taylor Swift effect.

Sports aren't somehow separate from politics. They are entwined, and we should admit and, yes, embrace it. Even if George Preston Marshall would like you to get off his jock about it.

Epilogue

Now the Real Work Begins

Dr. Casey Burgat

As I write this it's fall 2024, and there's a gnawing uncertainty in the air. The election is looming, and all we know for sure is it's going to be close—too close. Only weeks ago we experienced two "where were you when you heard?" events, with the assassination attempt on former President Trump and the shoving of President Biden from the race by leaders of his own party. History won't take a day off.

Many of us are simultaneously activated and exhausted, the exact wrong combination of somewhat engaged but unwilling to hear anything new. We're trying our best to mentally prep for any outcome, from triumph to disaster.

This sense of uncertainty has seeped into every aspect of our lives. Even the planning of this book had to account for all possible scenarios. I've literally sat on calls with my publishing team where we discussed whether to delay publication if the next administration drowns everything in chaos. Or if no winner can be chosen while the courts weigh challenges to vote totals. We actually asked ourselves: Do we make the tone more serious if, god forbid, we face political violence? Do we update the examples to reflect the latest crazy that's inevitably on the horizon?

These are, unfortunately, completely fair questions.

But let me be clear: This book isn't about one election, one person, or one party. It's much bigger than that. It's about the very fabric of our politics—and how they desperately need to change.

Today, we're hamsters on the political wheel, wasting too much energy chasing the silver-bullet fixes that aren't. It's not that people aren't involved enough—though that's still a problem—but that they're laser-focused on the wrong issues. They're shadowboxing myths while the real problems go unaddressed (oftentimes, as you learned by reading, on purpose).

As my Uzbek driver Pavel asked me on a rundown highway in Tashkent, "How can we have any real change when all we do is argue about the same things over and over and over?"

It's long past time to take that energy and put it to much better use. Right now, much of our political engagement is driven by anger and fear. These emotions only drive us apart—and are, not at all coincidentally, really good emotions to activate when trying to win elections.

We can't make real change that way. And we won't unless we finally change the conversation.

To have any shot at doing so, each and every one of us has to look in the mirror and JFK ourselves: Ask not when our politics will finally get better—ask what we are doing to make it happen.

Yes, some of the changes we need are bigger than ourselves. They're systemic, requiring changes in law or even the Constitution. Many others require action—and a much different focus—from those we've elected. But we, the people, are far from powerless. There are things we can do, right now, at this very moment, to ensure we're doing our part to set the compass in the right direction.

Here is how to begin.

When you look in the mirror, be honest: Do you watch politics for entertainment? To hear your stances vindicated by your cable news channel of choice? Do you love it more than you should—and always click the link—when you see a person on the other side get owned by someone on yours? Have you convinced yourself that doom scrolling is the same as staying informed? If any of these is true, that's not being an engaged citizen. That's having a hobby. Get a healthier one, like sports gambling.

On a more human level, start seeing supporters of the other party as human beings with different perspectives rather than as the enemy who must be stopped. It's OK to disagree—even adamantly; our country thrives on diversity of opinion. But remember that everyone has fears, dreams, and worries, just like you. They want good schools, clean air, and the freedom to pursue their dreams. They have traumas and loved ones who struggle to belong, too. If we start seeing those who disagree with us as dumb, wrong, evil, or unpatriotic, we've already lost. Give grace.

Get out of your bubbles. My basketball coach always used to say, "Do you hear or do you listen?" Hearing means your ears work—you pick up sounds, but that's where the information flow ends. Listening means you internalize, you understand, and hopefully, you empathize. It means you can see at least a small part of where someone else is coming from, even if you've never been there yourself. This connection often comes by asking questions without wanting a specific answer and using fewer sentences that start with "I" or "my." Next time you're in a tough conversation, try counting. I bet you start way more sentences with "I" than you think you do (and I just failed my own test).

When you really listen, the conversation changes. You stumble upon common ground—shared perspectives, fears, hopes—you didn't know was there. Start there.

You may soon discover that the NRA member you think you detest also has a child with autism. Or that the climate change crusader who irks you fought their way out of poverty working overtime as a journeyman plumber. Or the neighbor you'd like to muzzle on the school email chain stays up all night worrying about a parent with dementia. We are far more than our partisan identities, and we miss the best in folks if we judge worth or belonging based on such fleeting labels.

In America's great democratic experiment, judgment and resentment are our quicksand. Shared humanity is our bedrock. And once we stand on that, we can start changing our country for the better.

The operative word here is "we." If you're waiting for a new law, amendment, president, or party to come along and magically fix everything, you're ignoring history. Change doesn't just happen. It comes in fits and starts, after many, many failures. And it comes, in the words of Teddy Roosevelt, from those in the arena—not those shouting criticisms from the cheap seats.

If you don't want to be involved, someone else is more than happy to decide for you.

My family—including our five- and seven-year-olds—repeat our family mantra every morning before we all go our separate ways. It's our simple guide for how to attack life, not just live it.

"Don't talk about it. Be about it."

You can be about it like this: Spot the myths in this book out in the wild, and challenge them when you see them. Expand your political circles outside your curated echo chambers. Ask questions without aiming for your desired answer. Check the impulse to reduce those who disagree with you to being wrong, dumb, or dangerous. Support local journalism. Turn off cable news, and please, for the love of all that is holy, get off social media, at least for your politics. Go to a school board meeting. Join the PTA. Message your local and state representatives—they will be so glad to hear from you. Press your senators and congresspeople to reign in the president, reform the filibuster, and fulfill their constitutional duty to hold the Supreme Court accountable. Celebrate (and vote for!) the brave leaders who cross the aisle to compromise. Get three friends to register to vote. Volunteer. Start a book club (no burning!). Write a petition. Then get signatures in support.

The list goes on and on, but anything that can make a difference requires at least some effort. And it requires the commitment and humility to sustain the effort, celebrate small steps, and collaborate with people who are different from you. Shit ain't free (another family saying we haven't quite introduced to the kids yet).

Don't talk about it. Be about it.

And as a country, let's make an investment that matches the need of our political moment: We must create a wholesale civics education revolution in this country. We need more than history and government classes, though they are essential. Civics is something different. And right now, across the country, there is very little actual civics being taught. That has to change. Yesterday.

Civics is how to be an active citizen in a system that depends on an engaged, informed, government-literate electorate. That means understanding how to build coalitions, relate to and persuade skeptical audiences, stay active between elections, and effectively advocate for changes in party platforms—or better yet, work to get more parties into the mix.

Civic responsibility and engagement aren't innate skills; they're learned. And like any skill, the more you practice, the better you get.

I recently had dinner with a room full of high school social studies teachers, and all of them shook their heads at how little their students knew about the basics of government and politics—including the basic nuts and bolts of our system—by the time they reached their classes as juniors and seniors. They could do advanced calculus (a skill I'm still waiting to apply) but they couldn't pass the citizenship test every immigrant takes.

Like learning a second language, or any skill for that matter, learning civics as an adult is harder. But if you learn it as a kid, it becomes second nature. It informs, without you even realizing it, how you see the world, interpret events, and navigate life.

The minute people turn 18, they can vote, and their vote counts just the same as the president's. This equality of voice is a beautiful and powerful ideal. But without any real semblance of applied civics education, it's like telling adults to build a house with nothing but the Lego sets they played with as kids. Only if they mess up, children won't eat, the elderly won't retire with benefits, and you might never be able to afford a house or health insurance. That's madness.

For those who are past their schooling years, you're not off the hook. Invest in your civics literacy like our country depends on it. If you've found yourself quietly admitting "I should know the answer to that . . ." make a note to find the answer to that. You are seconds away from accessing the information (from a reliable source) without anyone finding out. If you're in need of a refresher on how the government works, find it at USA.gov or my favorite (and it's not just because I worked there) on the Library of Congress website. If you want to understand more than you ever wanted to know about money in politics—including fundraising amounts for every election and the companies that spend the most cash on lobbying—familiarize yourself with OpenSecrets.org. If you want to learn how to effectively engage, check out the bounty of explainer videos, templates, and recommendations found at reputable advocacy associations like the National Civic League or Civic Nation.

And in between these education sections, transfer half of your time—shoot, I'll take 10 percent—spent on social media to reading about what was discussed at your most recent city council meeting. Then show up to the next one. Advocacy gets stronger with practice.

As soon as we speak fluent civics, we see that our job as citizens extends far beyond just showing up to vote (though improving our miserable turnout rates would still be a big win). The truth is that politics and government are mostly what happens between elections.

Reducing our impact to binary choices every two or four years minimizes our power as citizens and ignores the monumental changes that can occur every day. It's like paying attention only to the last play of the last game of the season. The outcome also depends on all the plays before the buzzer-beater is shot.

We all want this country to work, to be better. But it doesn't just happen all on its own; it's not like gravity. Change—democracy—takes time, effort, commitment, and perseverance. We will win and lose along the way. But the point is, in this country, we have the chance to do both. Nearly every human in history would love to say the same, but they can't.

Democracy is hard, never-ending, maddening, and messy. And it's the most important, most empowering form of government ever invented.

That's what we've earned—if we can keep it.

Be about it.

Thank you so much for reading this book and joining me in the work of understanding our democracy better. But let's be real—this is just the beginning.

Want more no-nonsense insights delivered straight to your inbox? Subscribe to *Crash Course with Casey Burgat* on Substack. Every week, I break down how government actually works (and why it often doesn't) through explainers, videos, and interviews with DC power players—designed to help you become a smarter, more confident participant in our democracy, all in three minutes or less.

Get involved now!

Acknowledgments

I think and speak in sports analogies, and I finally have a moment where "Dream Team" fits perfectly. This book would still be just an idea without the incredible lineup of people who made it a reality. From the neighborhood fam, who always asked how the writing was going, to my blood fam, who was ready to click "buy" before I even told them about the idea, I love and appreciate each and every one of you.

To the chapter contributors—nearly all of you had no reason to say yes and even less time to make it happen. Thank you for trusting me and seeing what we're trying to accomplish. I hope I didn't let you down. I owe you forever.

Thank you to my agent, Jeff Silberman. What a journey it's been to get this bad boy out into the world. Your time, energy, and most importantly, the questions you asked helped push this book to where it needed to go. Thank you for walking this path with me. Go Broncos.

Dean Liesl Riddle of George Washington University's College of Professional Studies—your support and enthusiasm for this project from its very inception were essential. The meeting of the minds on campus was exactly what we needed to keep the momentum alive, and it wouldn't have happened without you. Thank you for that much-needed shot in the arm.

Marcus Brauchli, your timely feedback and suggestions, coming from someone as seasoned as you in the media world, were a gift. Your expertise sharpened the final product. Ditto for Dr. Tim LaPira and Trey Billing.

To the dynamo squad at Authors Equity: Madeline McIntosh and Don Weisberg, publishing giants who somehow took a shot on an unknown, even after swearing off political books. Got you, suckers! But truly, thank you for believing in yourselves and in a new way of publishing so you could take a chance on me and this idea. I'm beyond lucky to be associated with you both. A huge thank-you to Carly Gorga for driving everything forward with tireless enthusiasm and to Nina von Moltke, Deb Lewis, and the rest of the Authors Equity team for your creativity, support, and dedication throughout this journey.

To my editor, Grace Rubenstein—I can't even begin to capture your contribution. Your talent, clarity, and storytelling magic shine on every single page. From our very first call to the final rewrite of our rewrites, you pulled the best out of all of us, even when we didn't want to give any more. I grew so reliant on your edits that I'm genuinely afraid to speak without your red pen. I couldn't have done this without you. And I trust this is only the beginning.

Finally, to my wife, Sara. All the clichés. But know that I know this—you understood what this book could be before I did, and you never let me forget it. Thank you for knowing me—for understanding that sleep doesn't have to come in eight-hour chunks, that walks are preludes to breakthroughs, and that shit ain't free. And most of all, thank you for feeling the way you do—not many of us can and even fewer still do. I work too much and too often in abstractions. You pull me back. You remind me every day, silently and through who you are and how you treat people, that each story matters and deserves to be heard. Charlie and Huck don't yet know how lucky they are to have you, but I'm going to spend my lifetime making sure they never take it for granted. Yuv3.

Notes

"The Founders, in Their Infinite Wisdom, . . ."

1 "Benjamin Franklin: Speech in Convention," National Constitution Center, September 17, 1787, https://archive.csac.history.wisc.edu/assessments_64.pdf.

2 George Washington to Benjamin Harrison, September 24, 1787, in *Papers of George Washington*, Confederation Series, ed. W. W. Abbot et al. (University of Virginia Press, 1997), 5:339–340.

3 Brendan Cole, "Lauren Boebert Says 'The Constitution Is Not Evolving'—People Point Out Amendments," *Newsweek*, February 4, 2022, https://www.newsweek.com/lauren-boebert-congress-constitution-amendment-twitter-1676112.

4 "Thomas Jefferson Memorial Inscriptions," National Parks Service, excerpted from a letter to Samuel Kercheva, July 12, 1816, https://www.nps.gov/thje/learn/photosmultimedia/quotations.htm.

5 Washington to Harrison, 5:339–340.

6 Adam Liptak, "When Is an Offense Impeachable? Look to the Framers for the Answer," *New York Times*, August 22, 2018, https://www.nytimes.com/2018/08/22/us/politics/offense-impeachable-constitution.html.

7 Seth Delconte, "Supreme Court Supremacy vs Jefferson and Madison," Tenth Amendment Center, December 9, 2015, https://tenthamendmentcenter.com/2015/12/09/supreme-court-supremacy-vs-jefferson-and-madison/.

8 Gouverneur Morris, "Constitutional Convention Speeches," 1787, National Constitution Center, accessed March 30, 2024, https://constitutioncenter.org/the-constitution/historic-document-library/detail/gouverneur-morris-constitutional-convention-speeches-july-5-and-11-and-august-8-1787.

9 S. Mintz and S. McNeil, "The Constitution and Slavery," Digital History, 2018, http://www.digitalhistory.uh.edu/disp_textbook.cfm?smtid=2&psid=3241.

10 "New York Ratifying Convention. Remarks, [20 June 1788]," in *Papers of Alexander Hamilton*, 5:16–26, cited in Ron Chernow, *Alexander Hamilton* (Penguin Books, 2004), 239.

11 "Patrick Henry's Remarks at the Virginia Ratifying Convention," Monticello Digital Classroom, June 5, 1788, https://billofrightsinstitute.org/essays/the-bill-of-rights.

12 Washington to Harrison, September 24, 1787, 5:339–340.

13 James Madison, "Amendments to the Constitution, [8 June] 1789," in *The Papers of James Madison*, ed. Charles F. Hobson and Robert A. Rutland (University of Virginia Press, 1979), 12:196–210.

14 *Daily Advertiser* (New York, NY), V, no. 1385, July 29, 1789, Readex: America's Historical Newspapers.

15 John Adams to Thomas Jefferson, December 21, 1819, Founders Online, National Archives, accessed September 5, 2024, https://founders.archives.gov/documents/Adams/99-02-02-7287.

"I Vote the Issues, Not the Party"

1 Patrick Healy et al., "Why This Group of Undecided Independent Voters Is Leaning Toward Trump," *New York Times*, February 13, 2024, https://www.nytimes.com/interactive/2024/02/13/opinion/independents-biden-focus-group.html.

2 Morning Joe, "Swing Voters on 'Divisive' Trump," MSNBC, August 8, 2024, https://cdn.jwplayer.com/previews/fkwNoiZc.

3 "Deciders Focus Group Highlights: Unions, Housing Costs and Two Bags of Garbage," NBC News, April 4, 2024, https://www.nbcnews .com/video/deciders-focus-group-highlights-unions-housing-costs -and-two-bags-of-garbage-208338501747.

4 Frank Luntz, "'Antihero' or 'Felon': 11 Undecided Voters Struggle with How to See Trump Post-Verdict," *New York Times*, June 4, 2024, https://www.nytimes.com/interactive/2024/06/04/opinion/trump -verdict-focus-group.html.

5 Ari Shapiro et al., "Four 'American Indicators' Share Their View of the U.S. Economy—and Their Politics," National Public Radio, April 22, 2024, https://www.npr.org/2024/04/22/1245872098/four -american-indicators-share-their-view-of-the-u-s-economy-and-their -politics.

6 Lars Hall et al., "How the Polls Can Be Both Spot On and Dead Wrong: Using Choice Blindness to Shift Political Attitudes and Voter Intentions," *PLOS ONE* 8, no. 4 (2013): e60554, https://doi.org/10.1371/ journal.pone.0060554.

7 Christopher H. Achen and Larry M. Bartels, *Democracy for Realists: Why Elections Do Not Produce Responsive Government* (Princeton University Press, 2016).

8 Diana C. Mutz, *Winners and Losers: The Psychology of Foreign Trade* (Princeton University Press, 2021), 36:67.

9 Mutz, 36:68.

10 Morris P. Fiorina, *Retrospective Voting in American National Elections* (Yale University Press, 1981).

11 Geoffrey L. Cohen, "Party over Policy: The Dominating Impact of Group Influence on Political Beliefs," *Journal of Personality and Social Psychology* 85, no. 5 (2003): 808–822, https://doi.org/10.1037/0022-3514 .85.5.808.

12 Cohen, 810.

13 Cohen, 810.

14 Cohen, 808–822.

15 The two policies were slightly altered to make them less obviously distinct. These changes were minor, however. The generous policy was changed to offer $1,000 over seven years instead of $800 over eight years, and the stringent policy was changed to $400 for three years instead of $250 for one and a half years. The rest of the details remained the same.

16 Charles S. Taber and Milton Lodge, "Motivated Skepticism in the Evaluation of Political Beliefs," *American Journal of Political Science* 50, no. 3 (2006): 755–769; Dan M. Kahan, "Ideology, Motivated Reasoning, and Cognitive Reflection," *Judgment and Decision Making* 8, no. 4 (2013): 407–424; Rune Slothuus and Claes H. De Vreese, "Political Parties, Motivated Reasoning, and Issue Framing Effects," *Journal of Politics* 72, no. 3 (2010): 630–645.

17 James N. Druckman et al., "How Elite Partisan Polarization Affects Public Opinion Formation," *American Political Science Review* 107, no. 1 (2013): 57.

18 Michael Barber and Jeremy C. Pope, "Does Party Trump Ideology? Disentangling Party and Ideology in America," *American Political Science Review* 113, no. 1 (2019): 38–54, https://doi.org/10.1017/S0003055418000795.

19 Eduardo Suarez, "Trump Now Says He Plans to Legalize Some Undocumented Immigrants," Univision, August 20, 2016, https://www.univision.com/univision-news/politics/trump-now-says-he-plans-to-legalize-some-undocumented-immigrants.

20 Joe Goldman et al., "Democracy Hypocrisy: Examining America's Fragile Democratic Convictions," Democracy Fund, January 4, 2024, https://democracyfund.org/idea/democracy-hypocrisy/.

21 Henri Tajfel, *Human Groups and Social Categories: Studies in Social Psychology* (CUP Archive, 1981).

22 Lilliana Mason, *Uncivil Agreement: How Politics Became Our Identity*, 1st ed. (University of Chicago Press, 2018).

23 Landon Paul Schnabel, "When Fringe Goes Mainstream: A Socio-historical Content Analysis of the Christian Coalition's Contract with the American Family and the Republican Party Platform," *Politics, Religion & Ideology* 14, no. 1 (2013): 94–113.

24 Nathan Kalmoe and Lilliana Mason, *Radical American Partisanship: Mapping Violent Hostility, Its Causes, & the Consequences for Democracy* (University of Chicago Press, 2022).

25 Karen Yourish et al., "Inside the Apocalyptic Worldview of 'Tucker Carlson Tonight,'" *New York Times*, April 30, 2022, https://www.nytimes.com/interactive/2022/04/30/us/tucker-carlson-tonight.html.

26 Joel Sawat Selway, "Cross-Cuttingness, Cleavage Structures and Civil War Onset," *British Journal of Political Science* 41, no. 1 (2011): 111–138, https://doi.org/10.1017/S0007123410000311.

27 Tim Hains, "Sanders Battles Clinton: 'There Is a Reason These People Are Putting Huge Amounts of Money into Our Political System,'" RealClearPolitics, February 4, 2016, https://www.realclearpolitics.com/video/2016/02/04/bernie_sanders_vs_hillary_clinton_.html.

28 Jennifer Dresden et al., "The Authoritarian Playbook," Protect Democracy, June 2022, https://protectdemocracy.org/work/the-authoritarian-playbook/#spreading-disinformation.

29 Sewell Chan, "'Last Night in Sweden'? Trump's Remark Baffles a Nation," *New York Times*, February 19, 2017, https://www.nytimes.com/2017/02/19/world/europe/last-night-in-sweden-trumps-remark-baffles-a-nation.html.

30 "Statement by Vice President Kamala Harris Regarding the 60th Anniversary of the March on Washington," White House, August 28, 2023, https://www.whitehouse.gov/briefing-room/statements-releases/2023/08/28/statement-by-vice-president-kamala-harris-regarding-the-60th-anniversary-of-the-march-on-washington/.

31 John Sides et al., "Voter Choice in Presidential Primaries," in *The Making of the Presidential Candidates 2020*, ed. Jonathan Bernstein and Casey B. K. Dominguez (Rowman & Littlefield, 2019), 61–78.

32 Ronald Inglehart and Pippa Norris, "Trump, Brexit, and the Rise of Populism: Economic Have-Nots and Cultural Backlash," SSRN Scholarly Paper ID 2818659 (Social Science Research Network, 2016), https://papers.ssrn.com/abstract=2818659.

33 Jon Roozenbeek and Sander van der Linden, "The Fake News Game: Actively Inoculating Against the Risk of Misinformation," *Journal of Risk Research* 22, no. 5 (2019): 570–580, https://doi.org/10.1080/13669877.2018.1443491.

34 Michael A. Hogg and Janice Adelman, "Uncertainty-Identity Theory: Extreme Groups, Radical Behavior, and Authoritarian Leadership," *Journal of Social Issues* 69, no. 3 (2013): 436–454, https://doi.org/10.1111/josi.12023.

35 Michael A. Hogg, "Subjective Uncertainty Reduction Through Self-Categorization: A Motivational Theory of Social Identity Processes," *European Review of Social Psychology* 11, no. 1 (2000): 223–255, https://doi.org/10.1080/14792772043000040.

36 George E. Marcus et al., *Affective Intelligence and Political Judgment* (University of Chicago Press, 2000).

37 Ted Brader, "Striking a Responsive Chord: How Political Ads Motivate and Persuade Voters by Appealing to Emotions," *American Journal of Political Science* 49, no. 2 (2005): 388–405, https://doi.org/10.1111/j.0092-5853.2005.00130.x.

38 Liliana Mason and Scott Warren, "Understanding Pro-Democracy Conservatives: A Report on Current Levels of Election Trust and Partisan Identity," Johns Hopkins University Stavros Niarchos Foundation Agora Institute, March 2024, https://snfagora.jhu.edu/wp-content/uploads/2023/06/Hopkins-SNF-Agora-Institute-Understanding-ProDem-Conservatives-Mar-2024.pdf.

"The President Should Just . . ."

1 "Trends in United States COVID-19 Deaths, Emergency Department (ED) Visits, and Test Positivity by Geographic Area," Center for Disease Control and Prevention, COVID Data Tracker, September 23, 2024, https://covid.cdc.gov/covid-data-tracker/#trends_weeklydeaths _select_00.

2 Eliza Relman, "Trump Directs Experts to See Whether They Can Bring 'Light Inside the Body' to Kill the Coronavirus, Even as His Own Expert Shuts Him Down," Business Insider, April 23, 2020, https://www.businessinsider.com/trump-wants-bring-light-inside -the-body-to-kill-coronavirus-2020-4?op=1.

3 Relman.

4 Peter Aitken, "States See Spike in Poison Control Calls Following Trump's Comments on Injecting Disinfectant," Fox News, April 25, 2020, https://www.foxnews.com/us/states-spike-poison-control-calls.

5 Caitlin O'Kane, "Lysol Maker Warns Against Injecting Disinfectants After Trump Suggests It as a Possible Coronavirus Treatment," CBS News, April 24, 2020, https://www.cbsnews.com/news/lysol-injecting -trump-disinfectants-coronavirus-treatment/.

6 "Sizing Up the Executive Branch, Fiscal Year 2017," United States Office of Personnel Management, February 2018, https://www.opm .gov/policy-data-oversight/data-analysis-documentation/federal -employment-reports/reports-publications/sizing-up-the-executive -branch-2016.pdf.

7 Ezra Klein, "The Unpersuaded," New Yorker, March 12, 2012, https:// www.newyorker.com/magazine/2012/03/19/the-unpersuaded-2.

8 Mark Landler and David E. Sangar, "Trump Disavows Nuclear Deal, but Doesn't Scrap It," New York Times, October 13, 2017, https://www .nytimes.com/2017/10/13/us/politics/trump-iran-nuclear-deal.html.

9 Carol J. Williams, "Out in the World: What's in Kamala Harris' Foreign Policy," Post Alley Seattle, August 28, 2024, https://www

.postalley.org/2024/08/28/out-in-the-world-whats-in-kamala-harris
-foreign-policy/.

10 Daisy Nguyen and Elliot Spagat, "Judge Blocks Trump from Building
Sections of Border Wall," AP News, May 25, 2019, https://apnews
.com/article/e4aa0370816e467bae9e743beed5da02.

11 Adam Liptak and Glenn Thrush, "Supreme Court Ends Biden's
Eviction Moratorium," *New York Times*, August 26, 2021, https://
www.nytimes.com/2021/08/26/us/eviction-moratorium-ends.html.

12 Congressional Record, vol. 165, no. 46, Senate section, article S1857-3
(March 14, 2019), https://www.congress.gov/congressional-record/
volume-165/issue-46/senate-section/article/S1857-3?q=%7B%22search
%22%3A%22%5C%22executive+overreach%5C%22%22%7D&s=9&r=15.

13 Ted Cruz, "The Imperial Presidency of Barack Obama," Senator Ted
Cruz's official website, January 28, 2014, https://www.cruz.senate.gov/
newsroom/blogs/the-imperial-presidency-of-barack-obama.

14 Ingrid Jacques, "Hey Mr. President, You Can't Rule This Country
with 'a Pen and a Phone,'" USA Today, November 18, 2022, https://
www.yahoo.com/news/hey-mr-president-t-rule-100019367.html.

15 Caitlin Yilek, "Senate Votes to Repeal Iraq War Authorizations 20
Years After U.S. Invasion," CBS News, March 29, 2023, https://www
.cbsnews.com/news/iraq-war-aumf-senate-vote-repeal-authorization
-for-use-of-military-force/.

16 Susan Collins, "Impeachment Trial of President Donald John Trump
Volume IV: Statements of Senators," US Senate, S. Doc. 116-18, 116th
Congress, 2nd Session, p. 2009, https://www.govinfo.gov/content/
pkg/CDOC-116sdoc18/pdf/CDOC-116sdoc18-vol4.pdf.

"Members of Congress Don't Do Anything"

1 Mary Layton Atkinson, *Combative Politics: The Media and Public Perceptions of Lawmaking* (University of Chicago Press, 2017).

"The Supreme Court Has Become Too Political"

1 Jeffrey Jones, "Supreme Court Trust, Job Approval at Historical Lows," Gallup, September 29, 2022, https://news.gallup.com/poll/402044/supreme-court-trust-job-approval-historical-lows.aspx.

2 David B. Rivkin Jr. and James Taranto, "Samuel Alito, the Supreme Court's Plain-Spoken Defender," *Wall Street Journal*, July 28, 2023, https://www.wsj.com/articles/samuel-alito-the-supreme-courts-plain-spoken-defender-precedent-ethics-originalism-5e3e9a7?.

3 Randy DeSoto, "Kavanaugh: 'No One Is Above the Law,' US v. Nixon Was Great Moment in Judicial History," *Western Journal*, September 5, 2018, https://www.westernjournal.com/kavanaugh-no-one-law-us-v-nixon-great-moment-judicial-history/.

4 Rivkin and Taranto, "Samuel Alito."

"Lobbyists Are Evil"

1 "Lobbying Data Summary," OpenSecrets, September 23, 2024, https://www.opensecrets.org/federal-lobbying/summary.

2 Katie-Jay Simmons, "18 Valentine's Day Spending Statistics to Know in 2024," Fit Small Business, January 25, 2024, https://fitsmallbusiness.com/valentines-day-spending-statistics/.

3 Alexander C. Furnas et al., "Gaining Access Without Buying It: Campaign Contributions, Allies, and Lobbying on Capitol Hill,"

Working Paper (2024), https://www.alexanderfurnas.com/working
-papers.

4 T. M. LaPira et al., eds., *Congress Overwhelmed: The Decline in Congressional Capacity and Prospects for Reform* (University of Chicago Press, 2020).

5 Lee Drutman, "How Corporate Lobbyists Conquered American Democracy," *Atlantic*, April 20, 2015, https://www.theatlantic.com/business/archive/2015/04/how-corporate-lobbyists-conquered-american-democracy/390822/.

"Term Limits Will Fix Our Broken Congress"

1 "Congress Less Popular Than Cockroaches, Traffic Jams," Public Policy Polly, January 8, 2013, https://www.publicpolicypolling.com/wp-content/uploads/2017/09/PPP_Release_Natl_010813_.pdf.

2 Jennifer E. Manning, "Membership of the 118th Congress: A Profile," Congressional Research Service, R47470, September 12, 2024, https://crsreports.congress.gov/product/pdf/R/R47470.

3 Ted Cruz, "Sen. Cruz Delivers Opening Remarks as Chairman of Subcommittee on the Constitution in Support of Term Limits for Congress," Senator Ted Cruz's official website, June 18, 2019, https://www.cruz.senate.gov/newsroom/press-releases/sen-cruz-delivers-opening-remarks-as-chairman-of-subcommittee-on-the-constitution-in-support-of-term-limits-for-congress.

4 Manning, "Membership of the 118th Congress."

5 "Net Worth—2018," OpenSecrets, September 23, 2024, https://www.opensecrets.org/personal-finances/top-net-worth?display=S&year=2018.

6 Samantha Chang, "Matt Gaetz Torches Democrat Who Tells Him to Retire During His Speech on Term Limits," *Western Journal*,

September 29, 2023, https://www.westernjournal.com/matt-gaetz
-torches-democrat-tells-retire-speech-term-limits/.

7 Rachel Treisman, "As Congress Gets Older, One Lawmaker Makes
the Case for More 'Generational Diversity,'" NPR's Morning Edi-
tion, September 14, 2023, https://www.npr.org/2023/09/14/1199434381/
congress-old-politicians-age-term-limits.

8 "About the Signers of the Constitution," ConstitutionFacts.com, September 23, 2024, https://www.constitutionfacts.com/us-constitution
-amendments/about-the-signers/.

9 Sahil Chinoy and Jessia Ma, "How Every Member Got to Congress," *New York Times*, January 26, 2019, https://www.nytimes.com/
interactive/2019/01/26/opinion/sunday/paths-to-congress.html.

10 Manning, "Membership of the 118th Congress."

11 Manning.

12 "Revolving Door—Former Members of Congress," OpenSecrets,
September 23, 2024, https://www.opensecrets.org/revolving-door/
former-members-of-congress.

13 Christopher Ingraham and Alex Horton, "John Boehner Was a Longtime Opponent of Marijuana Reform. Here's What Changed His
Mind," *Seattle Times*, April 11, 2018, https://www.seattletimes.com/
nation-world/john-boehner-was-a-longtime-opponent-of-marijuana
-reform-heres-what-changed-his-mind/.

14 J. M. Carey et al., "The Effects of Term Limits on State Legislatures:
A New Survey of the 50 States," *Legislative Studies Quarterly* 31, no. 1
(2006): 105–134.

15 Marisa Lagos, "The Cost of a Seat: California Legislators Raise More
Than $1,000 a Day," KQED, https://www.kqed.org/news/10574253/
the-cost-of-a-seat-california-legislators-raise-more-than-1000-a-day.

16 "Election Trends—Total Cost of Election (1990–2022)," OpenSecrets,
September 23, 2024, https://www.opensecrets.org/elections-overview/
election-trends.

17 Nelson W. Polsby, "Some Arguments Against Congressional Term Limitations," *Harvard Journal of Law and Public Policy* 16 (1993): 101.

18 "Earthquake Overview," US Agency for International Development, September 23, 2024, https://www.usaid.gov/haiti/earthquake-overview.

19 Jose Andrés, "Global Food Institute's Launch Ceremony Full Program," George Washington University, May 23, 2023, https://vimeo.com/830328985/7b9a906f65?share=copy.

20 Andrés.

21 Andrés.

22 J. Lazarus et al., "Who Walks Through the Revolving Door? Examining the Lobbying Activity of Former Members of Congress," *Interest Groups & Advocacy* 5 (2016): 82–100, https://doi.org/10.1057/iga.2015.16.

23 James Alt et al., "Disentangling Accountability and Competence in Elections: Evidence from US Term Limits," *Journal of Politics* 73, no. 1 (2011): 171–186.

24 For example, see David R. Berman, "Effects of Legislative Term Limits in Arizona," National Conference of State Legislatures, 2005; and John Straayer and Jennie Drage Bowser, "Colorado's Legislative Term Limits," National Conference of State Legislatures, 2004.

25 Travis J. Baker and David M. Hedge, "Term Limits and Legislative-Executive Conflict in the American States," *Legislative Studies Quarterly* 38, no. 2 (2013): 237–258.

26 Thad Kousser, "The Limited Impact of Term Limits: Contingent Effects on the Complexity and Breadth of Laws," *State Politics & Policy Quarterly* 6, no. 4 (2006): 410–429.

27 Bruce E. Cain and Thad Kousser, "Adapting to Term Limits: Recent Experiences and New Directions," Public Policy Institute of California, 2024, https://www.ppic.org/wpcontent/uploads/content/pubs/report/R_1104BCR.pdf.

28 S. M. Miller et al., "The Consequences of Legislative Term Limits for Policy Diffusion," *Political Research Quarterly* 71, no. 3 (2018): 573–585.

29 G. Moncrief and J. A. Thompson, "On the Outside Looking in: Lobbyists' Perspectives on the Effects of State Legislative Term Limits," *State Politics & Policy Quarterly* 1, no. 4 (2001): 394.

30 J. Alt et al., "Disentangling Accountability and Competence in Elections: Evidence from US Term Limits," *Journal of Politics* 73, no. 1 (2011): 171–186.

31 Miller et al., "Consequences of Legislative Term Limits," 573–585.

32 Michael P. Olson and Jon C. Rogowski, "Legislative Term Limits and Polarization," *Journal of Politics* 82, no. 2 (2020): 572–586.

33 Cain and Kousser, "Adapting to Term Limits."

34 Alexander Fouirnaies and Andrew B. Hall, "How Do Electoral Incentives Affect Legislator Behavior? Evidence from US State Legislatures," *American Political Science Review* 116, no. 2 (2022): 662–676.

35 H. A. Erler, "Legislative Term Limits and State Spending," *Public Choice* 133, nos. 3–4 (2007): 479–494.

36 Jeff Cummins, "The Effects of Legislative Term Limits on State Fiscal Conditions," *American Politics Research* 41, no. 3 (2013): 417–442.

"Bipartisanship Is Dead"

1 Monica Hesse, "'Weird' Is Democrats' Most Effective Insult. Tim Walz Was the Pioneer," *Washington Post*, July 30, 2024, https://www.washingtonpost.com/style/power/2024/07/30/republicans-weird/.

2 Joey Garrison, "Biden Is Pitching a Big Infrastructure Plan, but Republicans Already Panned It as Going Too Far," *USA Today*, March 30, 2021, https://www.yahoo.com/news/biden-pitching-big-infrastructure-plan-090127195.html.

3 Gabby Birenbaum, "Republicans and Democrats Agree on the Need for an Infrastructure Bill. That's About All They Agree On," *Vox*, May 2, 2021.

4 Jacob Pramuk, "Infrastructure Plan Should Cost up to $800 Billion, McConnell Says Ahead of Biden Meeting," CNBC, May 10, 2021.

5 Richard Bolling, *Power in the House: A History of the Leadership of the House of Representatives* (E. P. Dutton, 1968).

6 Woodrow Wilson, "The Study of Administration," *Political Science Quarterly* 2, no. 2 (June 1887).

7 Brigid Kennedy, "Joe Manchin: I've Never Been a Liberal 'in Any Way, Shape, or Form,'" *The Week*, September 30, 2021.

8 Lindsey McPherson, "McCarthy, House Republicans Reframe Debt Limit Strategy," *Roll Call*, February 6, 2023.

9 Catie Edmondson, "Debt Talks Are Frozen as House Republicans Splinter over a Fiscal Plan," *New York Times*, March 29, 2023, https://www.nytimes.com/2023/03/29/us/politics/house-republicans-debt-limit-budget-biden.html.

10 Catie Edmondson and Carl Hulse, "House G.O.P. Passes Debt Limit Bill, Paving the Way for a Clash with Biden," *New York Times*, April 26, 2023.

11 Jim Tankersley and Alan Rappeport, "New Details in Debt Limit Deal: Where $136 Billion in Cuts Will Come From," *New York Times*, June 2, 2023.

12 Manu Raju et al., "GOP Hardliners Revolt and Derail McCarthy's Agenda in Retaliation over Speaker's Debt Limit Deal," CNN, June 6, 2023.

"I Wish the Parties Would Work Together"

1 Deputy chief of staff, Office of Congressman Bill Pascrell Jr.; JD, Rutgers Law School; BA, Cornell University.

2 Chris Murphy, "Murphy: We Produced a Bipartisan Agreement to Help Fix Our Broken Asylum System," Senator Chris Murphy's official website, February 4, 2024, https://www.murphy.senate

.gov/newsroom/press-releases/murphy-we-produced-a-bipartisan
-agreement-to-help-fix-our-broken-asylum-system.

3 Aaron Blake, "GOP Says No Need for New Immigration Laws. That's Not What It Used to Say," *Washington Post*, January 31, 2024, https://www.washingtonpost.com/politics/2024/01/31/gop-says-no -need-new-immigration-laws-thats-not-what-it-used-say/.

4 "Fact Sheet: Impact of Bipartisan Border Agreement Funding on Border Operations," White House, February 29, 2024, https://www .whitehouse.gov/briefing-room/statements-releases/2024/02/29/fact -sheet-impact-of-bipartisan-border-agreement-funding-on-border -operations/.

5 "Fact Sheet: Biden-Harris Administration Calls on Congress to Immediately Pass the Bipartisan National Security Agreement," White House, February 4, 2024, https://www.whitehouse.gov/ briefing-room/statements-releases/2024/02/04/fact-sheet-biden -harris-administration-calls-on-congress-to-immediately-pass-the -bipartisan-national-security-agreement/.

6 Murphy, "We Produced a Bipartisan Agreement."

7 Jeffrey M. Jones, "Immigration Surges to Top of Most Important Problem List," Gallup, February 27, 2024, https://news.gallup.com/ poll/611135/immigration-surges-top-important-problem-list.aspx.

8 Tarini Parti and Michelle Hackman, "Why Immigration Is Now the No. 1 Issue for Voters," *Wall Street Journal*, April 5, 2024, https://www .wsj.com/politics/elections/election-2024-immigration-issue-voters -84916a17.

9 "McConnell to Senate Republicans: Take the Border Deal," Punchbowl News, January 1, 2024, https://punchbowl.news/article/ border/immigration/mitch-mcconnell-senate-republicans-border -deal/.

10 Jake Sherman and John Bresnahan, "What McConnell's Border Play Means," Punchbowl News, January 25, 2024, https://punchbowl.news/ article/mcconnell-threads-trump-needle-border/.

11 Stef W. Kight, "Mike Johnson Calls Rumored Senate Border Deal 'Dead on Arrival,'" Axios, January 26, 2024, https://www.axios.com/2024/01/26/mike-johnson-senate-border-deal.

12 Emily Brooks, "Speaker Johnson Not Dismissing Border Deal to Help Trump: 'That's Absurd,'" Hill, January 30, 2024, https://thehill.com/homenews/house/4437617-speaker-johnson-border-deal-trump/.

13 Andrew Stanton, "Full List of Senate Republicans Trying to Kill Border Bill," Newsweek, February 5, 2024, https://www.newsweek.com/full-list-senate-republicans-opposing-border-bill-1866890.

14 Alexander Bolton, "McConnell Bedeviled as Trump, GOP Move Goalposts on Border," Hill, January 29, 2024, https://thehill.com/homenews/senate/4432635-mcconnell-bedeviled-as-trump-gop-move-goalposts-on-border/.

15 Donald J. Trump, "A Border Bill is not necessary to stop the millions of people, many from jails and mental institutions located all over the World, that are POURING INTO OUR COUNTRY. It is an INVASION the likes of which no Country has ever had to endure," Truth Social, January 29, 2024, https://truthsocial.com/@realDonaldTrump/posts/111840653005061733.

16 Bryan Metzger, "House Republican Says He Won't Accept a Border Deal Because It May Help Biden Politically," Business Insider, January 4, 2024, https://www.businessinsider.com/troy-nehls-senate-border-security-deal-biden-2024-1?op=1.

17 Manu Raju et al., "GOP Senators Seethe as Trump Blows up Delicate Immigration Compromise," CNN, January 25, 2024, https://www.cnn.com/2024/01/25/politics/gop-senators-angry-trump-immigration-deal/index.html.

18 Raju et al.

19 Frances E. Lee, Insecure Majorities: Congress and the Perpetual Campaign (University of Chicago Press, 2016), 34.

20 Lee, 42.

21 Lee, 45.

22 Lee, 49.

23 David Wasserman, "Introducing the 2021 Cook Political Report Partisan Voter Index," Cook Political Report, April 15, 2021, https://www.cookpolitical.com/cook-pvi/introducing-2021-cook-political-report-partisan-voter-index.

24 "2023 Cook PVI℠: District Map and List (118th Congress)," Cook Political Report, April 5, 2023, https://www.cookpolitical.com/cook-pvi/2023-partisan-voting-index/118-district-map-and-list.

25 Michael Grunwald, "The Victory of 'No,'" *Politico*, December 4, 2016, https://www.politico.com/magazine/story/2016/12/republican-party-obstructionism-victory-trump-214498/.

26 Grunwald.

27 Meredith Deliso, "Overwhelming Majority of Americans Think Biden Is Too Old for Another Term: Poll," ABC News, February 11, 2024, https://abcnews.go.com/Politics/poll-americans-on-biden-age/story?id=107126589.

"The Filibuster Forces Compromise"

1 Joan Biskupic, "The Inside Story of How John Roberts Failed to Save Abortion Rights," CNN, July 26, 2022, https://www.cnn.com/2022/07/26/politics/supreme-court-john-roberts-abortion-dobbs/index.html.

2 Lydia Saad, "Broader Support for Abortion Rights Continues Post-Dobb," June 14, 2023, https://news.gallup.com/poll/506759/broader-support-abortion-rights-continues-post-dobbs.aspx.

3 Kevin J. McMahon, "5 Justices, All Confirmed by Senators Representing a Minority of Voters, Appear Willing to Overturn Roe v. Wade," Conversation, May 10, 2022, https://theconversation.com/5-justices-all-confirmed-by-senators-representing-a-minority-of-voters-appear-willing-to-overturn-roe-v-wade-182582.

4 Alice Miranda Ollstein, "Senate Fails to Pass Abortion Rights Bill—Again," *Politico*, May 11, 2022, https://www.politico.com/news/2022/05/11/senate-doomed-vote-roe-abortion-rights-00031732.

5 "Roll Call Vote 103rd Congress—1st Session: Vote 375," Senate.gov, accessed September 24, 2024, https://www.senate.gov/legislative/LIS/roll_call_votes/vote1031/vote_103_1_00375.htm.

6 "Roll Call Vote 109th Congress—2nd Session: Vote 2," Senate.gov, accessed September 24, 2024, https://www.senate.gov/legislative/LIS/roll_call_votes/vote1092/vote_109_2_00002.htm.

7 Luke Mayville, "Fear of the Few: John Adams and the Power Elite," *Polity* 47, no. 1 (2015): 5–32, http://www.jstor.org/stable/24540274.

8 "The Federalist Papers: Text of the Federalist Papers 21–30," Guides.loc.gov, accessed September 24, 2024, https://guides.loc.gov/federalist-papers/text-21-30.

9 Sarah Binder, "The History of the Filibuster," Brookings Institution, April 22, 2010, https://www.brookings.edu/testimonies/the-history-of-the-filibuster/.

10 Robert Byrd, *Senate, 1789–1989, V. 1: Addresses on the History of the United States Senate* (US Government Printing Office, 1988), 92.

11 In 1933, the 20th Amendment changed the constitutionally mandated date of adjournment from March 3 to January 3. The passage of the amendment was motivated in large part by a desire to end obstruction, but it would not have much effect.

12 Will Englund, *March 1917: On the Brink of War and Revolution* (W. W. Norton, 2017).

13 "Idea of the Senate: The Senate as a Body of Individuals," US Senate, accessed September 24, 2024, https://www.senate.gov/about/origins-foundations/idea-of-the-senate/1907Wilson.htm.

14 *Proposed Amendments to Rule XXII of the Standing Rules of the Senate, Relating to Cloture: Hearings Before a Special Subcommittee on Rules and Administration*, US Senate, 85th Congress, First Session, on S. Res. 17, S. Res. 19, S. Res. 21, S. Res. 28, S. Res. 29, S. Res. 30, S. Res. 32,

S. Res. 171, "Resolutions Proposing Amendments to Rule XXII of the Standing Rules of the Senate," June 17, 24, 25, 28 and July 2, 9, 16, 1957 (US Government Printing Office, 1957), 292.

15 Franklin L. Burdette, *Filibustering in the Senate* (Russell & Russell, 1965), 221.

16 "Cloture Motions," US Senate, accessed September 24, 2024, https://www.senate.gov/legislative/cloture/clotureCounts.htm.

17 "Social Security Amendments of 1965: Summary of Provisions," SSA .gov, accessed September 24, 2024, https://www.ssa.gov/history/tally65.html.

18 "Cloture Motions."

19 "Federalist Papers."

20 Frances E. Lee, *Insecure Majorities: Congress and the Perpetual Campaign* (University of Chicago Press, 2016).

21 Michael Grunwald, *The New New Deal: The Hidden Story of Change in the Obama Era* (Simon & Schuster, 2012), 19.

22 Adam Nagourney and Carl Hulse, "Senate G.O.P. Leader Finds Weapon in Unity," *New York Times*, March 16, 2010, A13.

23 Mitch McConnell, *The Long Game: A Memoir* (Penguin, 2019), 191.

24 "Cloture Motions."

25 Victoria Knight, "Obamacare Continues to Flourish in Republican States," Axios, January 24, 2024, https://www.axios.com/2024/01/24/obamacare-aca-health-insurance-republican-states.

"The Media Wants to Polarize Us"

1 Grace Panetta, "Fox News Won a Lawsuit by Persuasively Arguing That No 'Reasonable Viewer' Takes Tucker Carlson Seriously," Business Insider, September 25, 2020, https://www.businessinsider.com/fox-news-karen-mcdougal-case-tucker-carlson-2020-9?op=1.

2 "Losing the News: The Decimation of Local Journalism and the Search for Solutions," PEN.org, November 20, 2019, https://pen.org/report/local-news/.

3 Daniel Silliman, "The News About the News Is Grim," *Atlantic*, January 19, 2024, https://www.theatlantic.com/ideas/archive/2024/01/media-layoffs-la-times/677285/.

4 Alex Weprin, "Cable News Ratings 2023: Fox News Remains on Top as Overall Viewership Declines," Deadline, December 14, 2023, https://deadline.com/2023/12/cable-news-ratings-2023-1235682966/.

5 "*PBS NewsHour* Viewership," Pew Research Center, accessed September 24, 2024, https://www.pewresearch.org/chart/sotnm-public-media-pbs-newshour-viewership.

6 Maryam Mousavi et al., "Effective Messaging on Social Media: What Makes Online Content Go Viral?," *Proceedings of the ACM Web Conference 2022*, TheWebConf 2022, April 25–29, 2022, Lyon, France, Association for Computing Machinery, http://www-personal.umich.edu/~axe/message-effectiveness-hypothesis-testing.pdf.

7 E. Bakshy et al., "Exposure to Ideologically Diverse News and Opinion on Facebook," *Science* 348 (2015): 1130–1132.

8 M. F. Meffert et al., "The Effects of Negativity and Motivated Information Processing During a Political Campaign," *Journal of Communication* 25 (2006): 27–51.

9 Claire E. Robertson et al., "Negativity Drives Online News Consumption," *Nature Human Behaviour* 7, no. 5 (2023): 812–822.

10 Laura Santhanam, "Experts Say Attacks on Free Speech Are Rising Across the U.S.," *PBS NewsHour*, July 24, 2023, https://www.pbs.org/newshour/politics/experts-say-attacks-on-free-speech-are-rising-across-the-us.

11 "The Founders' Constitution, Volume 5, Amendment I (Speech and Press), Document 29," June 14, 1807, University of Chicago Press, http://press-pubs.uchicago.edu/founders/documents/amendI_speechs29.html.

12 Kate Kelly, "How Bud Light Handled an Uproar over a Promotion with a Transgender Influencer," *New York Times*, June 14, 2023, https://www.nytimes.com/2023/06/14/business/bud-light-lgbtq-backlash.html.

13 "Fox News Ousts Bill O'Reilly in Wake of Harassment Allegations," Newsmax, April 19, 2017, https://www.newsmax.com/Newsfront/fox-oreilly-fired/2017/04/19/id/785262/.

"Keep Your Politics Out of My Sports"

1 NFL Memes, "The Patriots are officially in tank mode for the rest of the season," X (formerly Twitter), September 24, 2024, https://x.com/NFL_Memes/status/1749261800044978291.

2 Natasha Papps, "NFL Legend Warns League's Obsession with Taylor Swift Is a 'Slap in the Face' to Fans After Giants Star's Swipe," *Sun*, September 24, 2024, https://www.the-sun.com/sport/10181853/nfl-obsession-taylor-swift-giants-tiki-barber/.

3 Dan (@ksMaga87), "Unbelievable Finish to the Game!," X (formerly Twitter), September 24, 2024, https://x.com/ksMaga87/status/1751689443197468674.

4 Alex Vejar Hess, "NFL Legend and Activist Jim Brown Dies at 87," *Deseret News*, May 19, 2023, https://www.deseret.com/u-s-world/2023/5/19/23730472/cleveland-running-back-activist-jim-brown-tributes/.

Contributors

DR. CASEY BURGAT is a former congressional staffer turned political science professor at George Washington University's Graduate School of Political Management. Respected across the aisle, Casey is an expert on legislative affairs, particularly the workings of Congress. He is a regular contributor to *Barron's* and provides frequent commentary to outlets including CNN, Fox News, *The Washington Post*, and *Politico*. Casey is also the creator of the Substack newsletter *Crash Course with Casey Burgat* and the host of the popular podcast *Mastering the Room*.

DR. LINDSAY M. CHERVINSKY is the executive director of the George Washington Presidential Library and author of *Making the Presidency* and *The Cabinet: George Washington and the Creation of an American Institution*. Chervinsky regularly contributes to publications including *The Wall Street Journal*, *The Washington Post*, and *Time Magazine*, focusing on presidential and American political history.

DR. JAMES M. CURRY is a professor of political science at the University of Utah, specializing in US Congress and policymaking and the author of *Legislating in the Dark* and coauthor of *The Limits of Party*. His research has appeared in leading political science journals and major media outlets, including *The New York Times*, *The Washington Post*, and *The Atlantic*, and he has provided testimony to the US House of Representatives.

QUARDRICOS DRISKELL is the director of government relations at the Academy Advisors, advising health-care executives on federal policy, and was previously vice president of public policy at the Autoimmune Association. Driskell serves as a reverend and adjunct professor at George Washington University, teaching courses on race, religion, and American politics.

MATT FULLER is the Capitol Hill Bureau Chief for NOTUS. Fuller has covered Congress for 15 years in various roles, from intern and researcher to politics editor and Washington bureau chief for *The Daily Beast*.

MARK GREENBAUM served as deputy chief of staff to Rep. Pascrell and is a longtime Capitol Hill staffer. Greenbaum advocates for strong congressional oversight and government accountability and draws inspiration from influential congressional figures including Wright Patman, Phil Burton, and Nancy Pelosi.

ALYSSA FARAH GRIFFIN is an American political strategist and television personality. Griffin was the White House Director of Strategic Communications under former President Trump and youngest Pentagon press secretary in history and currently cohosts *The View* and serves as a CNN commentator. Griffin previously served as press secretary for former Vice President Pence and at the Department of Defense.

REP. STEVE ISRAEL served in Congress from 2001 to 2017, including as chairman of the Democratic Congressional Campaign Committee (2011–2015). Israel now owns Theodore's Books in Oyster Bay, New York, and directs the nonpartisan Institute of Politics and Global Affairs at the Brooks School of Public Policy at Cornell University. Israel is the author of *The Global War on Morris* and *Big Guns* and has been featured on outlets including CNN and MSNBC, as well as in

The New York Times, The Atlantic, The Washington Post, and *The Wall Street Journal.*

ADAM JENTLESON is former chief of staff to Sen. John Fetterman and deputy chief of staff to Senate Democratic Leader Harry Reid. Jentleson is the author of *Kill Switch* and a regular contributor to publications including *GQ, The New York Times, The Washington Post,* and *Politico.*

REP. DEREK KILMER represented Washington's 6th Congressional District (2013–2025) and chaired the House Select Committee on the Modernization of Congress. Kilmer previously served in the Washington State House of Representatives (2005–2007) and Washington State Senate (2007–2012) and currently serves as senior vice president for U.S. Program & Policy at the Rockefeller Foundation.

DR. FRANCES E. LEE is a professor of politics and public affairs at Princeton, focusing on congressional politics, and the author of influential books including *Insecure Majorities* and *Beyond Ideology,* as well as a coauthor of *Sizing Up the Senate* and the textbook *Congress and Its Members.* Lee's research has appeared in *American Political Science Review, The American Journal of Political Science, Perspectives on Politics, The Journal of Politics, Legislative Studies Quarterly,* and other outlets.

DR. LILLIANA MASON is an SNF Agora Institute Associate Professor at Johns Hopkins University and the coauthor of *Radical American Partisanship* and author of *Uncivil Agreement.* Mason's research focuses on partisan identity, social polarization, and political psychology, and her work frequently appears in *The New York Times* and *The Washington Post* and on CNN and NPR.

JANE MCMANUS is an author and professor at NYU's Preston Robert Tisch Institute for Global Sport. McManus wrote *Fast Track: Inside the*

Surging Business of Women's Sports and spent nearly a decade at ESPN covering the NFL and women's sports.

REP. BILL PASCRELL JR. represented New Jersey in Congress (1997–2024), serving as chairman of the Ways and Means Oversight Subcommittee, and was previously mayor of Paterson, New Jersey (1990–1997), and a state assemblyman (1988–1997). Pascrell was a longtime public school teacher and is a veteran of the US Army and US Army Reserves.

STEPHEN I. VLADECK is a professor at the Georgetown University Law Center and expert in constitutional law and national security. Vladeck previously taught at the University of Miami School of Law, American University Washington College of Law, and the University of Texas School of Law. The author of the bestselling book *The Shadow Docket*, Vladeck has argued over a dozen cases before the US Supreme Court, cohosts the *National Security Law Podcast*, and serves as CNN's Supreme Court analyst.